The Edge of Race

The phrase 'the edge of race' can be used both as a description and as a response to two key concerns. The first of these is that while race is increasingly on the periphery of education policy – with a growing disregard shown for racist inequities, as education systems become dominated by market-driven concerns – it is important that we map the shifting relations of race in neoliberal politics and policies. The second concern is that at this time, within and outside the spaces of the academy, even to mention race equity is to risk condemnation, marginalization, and ridicule.

The authors in this collection use 'the edge of race' as a provocation in order to examine the concepts, methodologies, policies, politics, processes, and practices associated with race and racism in education. The chapters offer empirical examples of the perpetuation and perniciousness of racism that point to the continued salience of research about race. Additionally, the chapters make contributions to conceptual and methodological understandings of race and racism. The contributors illustrate the contingency, productivity, and fragility of race as a concept, and point to how educational research continues to be a contested site in, and from which to study, race and education. This book was originally published as a special issue of *Discourse: Studies in the Cultural Politics of Education*.

Kalervo N. Gulson is an Associate Professor in the Faculty of Arts and Social Sciences at the University of New South Wales, Sydney, Australia. His research contributes to, and draws upon, education policy studies, sociology of education, race/ethnicity, and social and cultural geography. His current research focuses on the relationship between education policy and calculative spaces, and what kind of life is possible within and through these calculative spaces. His recent publications include *Education policy, space and the city: markets and the (in)visibility of race* (2011), and *Policy, geophilosophy, education* (with P.T. Webb, 2015).

Zeus Leonardo is Professor of Education, and Affiliated Faculty of the Critical Theory Designated Emphasis at the University of California, Berkeley, CA, USA. He has published several dozen articles and book chapters on critical educational theory. His articles have appeared in *Educational Researcher*, *Race Ethnicity & Education*, and *Teachers College Record*. His recent books include *Race Frameworks* (2013), *Education and Racism* (with W. Norton Grubb, 2013), and *Handbook of Cultural Politics and Education* (ed. 2010).

David Gillborn is Professor of Critical Race Studies, and Director of the Centre for Research in Race & Education at the University of Birmingham, UK. He is founding editor of the journal *Race Ethnicity and Education*. He is twice winner of the 'Book of the Year' award by the Society for Educational Studies, most recently for *Racism and Education: coincidence or conspiracy* (2008). He received the Derrick Bell Legacy Award from the Critical Race Studies in Education Association, for demonstrating 'personal courage and professional commitment to supporting and advocating race equality in education', and was recently named to the Laureate Chapter of the *Kappa Delta Pi* international honour society.

The Edge of Race

Critical examinations of education and race/racism

Edited by
Kalervo N. Gulson, Zeus Leonardo and David Gillborn

Routledge
Taylor & Francis Group

LONDON AND NEW YORK

First published 2016
by Routledge

2 Park Square, Milton Park, Abingdon, Oxfordshire, OX14 4RN
711 Third Avenue, New York, NY 10017

Routledge is an imprint of the Taylor & Francis Group, an informa business

First issued in paperback 2017

British Library Cataloguing in Publication Data
A catalogue record for this book is available from the British Library

ISBN 13: 978-1-138-18910-2 (hbk)
ISBN 13: 978-1-138-30893-0 (pbk)

Typeset in Times New Roman
by diacriTech, Chennai

Publisher's Note
The publisher accepts responsibility for any inconsistencies that may have arisen
during the conversion of this book from journal articles to book chapters, namely
the possible inclusion of journal terminology.

Disclaimer
Every effort has been made to contact copyright holders for their permission to
reprint material in this book. The publishers would be grateful to hear from any
copyright holder who is not here acknowledged and will undertake to rectify any
errors or omissions in future editions of this book.

Contents

CONTENTS

Citation Information

The chapters in this book were originally published in *Discourse: Studies in the Cultural Politics of Education*, volume 34, issue 4 (October 2013). When citing this material, please use the original page numbering for each article, as follows:

CITATION INFORMATION

For any permission-related enquiries please visit:
http://www.tandfonline.com/page/help/permissions

Notes on Contributors

Sophia L. Angeles is a High School Counselor for Santa Cruz City Schools, California, USA. She recently completed an Ed.S. in school counseling at the University of North Carolina-Greensboro, NC, USA.

Alice Bradbury is a Lecturer in Education at the Institute of Education, University College London, UK. She is interested in the relationship between education policy and inequalities in terms of class, gender and, particularly, 'race'. Her research examines the impact of policy in primary and early years education with a focus on issues of social justice. She is also interested in the use of poststructural theoretical frameworks and Critical Race Theory in examining both individual and structural inequalities in education.

Thandeka K. Chapman is an Associate Professor in the Department of Education Studies at the University of California – San Diego, CA, USA. Her work focuses on schooling outcomes of desegregation policies in urban and suburban districts, and she conducts research with teachers and students in urban and racially diverse settings to examine and resolve the ways in which institutional racism is manifested in school climate, curriculum, adult and student relationships, and school policies. She co-edited *Social Justice Pedagogy: The Practice of Freedom* (2010), and *The History of Multicultural Education* (2008), a six volume book set chronicling the development of multicultural education in the U.S. through influential articles.

Roland Sintos Coloma is a Professor in the Department of Teacher Education in the College of Education, Health and Society at Miami University, Oxford, OH, USA. He mobilizes a historical and cultural studies approach to research on teacher education, curriculum and policy. He documents and analyzes the dynamics of race, gender and sexuality, with a focus on Filipina/os and Asian diaspora in the United States and Canada.

Michael J. Dumas is an Assistant Professor in the Graduate School of Education and the African American Studies Department at the University of California, Berkeley, CA, USA. His research sits at the intersection(s) of the cultural politics of Black education, the cultural political economy of urban education, and the futurity of Black childhood(s). His recent publications have appeared in such journals as *Teachers College Record, Race, Ethnicity and Education*, and *Discourse*, and he was an invited contributor to the *Handbook of Critical Race Theory in Education* (2013) and the *Handbook of Cultural Politics and Education* (2010).

David Gillborn is Professor of Critical Race Studies, and Director of the Centre for Research in Race & Education at the University of Birmingham, UK. He is founding editor of the journal *Race Ethnicity and Education*. He is twice winner of the 'Book of the Year' award by the Society for Educational Studies, most recently for *Racism and Education: coincidence or conspiracy* (2008). He received the Derrick Bell Legacy Award from the Critical Race Studies in Education Association, for demonstrating 'personal courage and professional commitment to supporting and advocating race equality in education', and was recently named to the Laureate Chapter of the *Kappa Delta Pi* international honour society.

Kalervo N. Gulson is an Associate Professor in the Faculty of Arts and Social Sciences at the University of New South Wales, Sydney, Australia. His research contributes to, and draws upon, education policy studies, sociology of education, race/ ethnicity and social and cultural geography. His current research focuses on the relationship between education policy and calculative spaces, and what kind of life is possible within and through these calculative spaces. His recent publications include *Education policy, space and the city: markets and the (in)visibility of race* (2011) and *Policy, geophilosophy, education* (with P.T. Webb, 2015).

Zeus Leonardo is Professor of Education, and Affiliated Faculty of the Critical Theory Designated Emphasis at the University of California, Berkeley, CA, USA. He has published several dozen articles and book chapters on critical educational theory. His articles have appeared in *Educational Researcher*, *Race Ethnicity & Education* and *Teachers College Record*. His recent books include *Race Frameworks* (2013)*, Education and Racism* (with W. Norton Grubb, 2013) and *Handbook of Cultural Politics and Education* (ed. 2010).

Nicola Rollock is Senior Lecturer in the School of Education, and Deputy Director of the Centre for Research in Race & Education at the University of Birmingham, UK. She is especially interested in the ways in which racially minoritised groups survive, strategise and work to create legitimate, meaningful modes of existence, belonging and notions of self within mainly white spaces. Her work therefore engages with the concept of education in its very broadest sense to include both formal and informal sites of learning and social reproduction. She is the author of *The Colour of Class: The educational strategies of the Black middle classes* (with David Gillborn, Carol Vincent, and Stephen J. Ball, Routledge, 2014).

David Stovall is Associate Professor of African American Studies and Educational Policy Studies at the University of Illinois at Chicago, IL, USA. He studies the influence of race in urban education, community development and housing. His work investigates the significance of race in the quality of schools located in communities that are changing both racially and economically. From a practical and theoretical perspective, his research draws from Critical Race Theory, educational policy analysis, sociology, urban planning, political science, community organizing and youth culture. He contributed to the 2006 book *Beyond Resistance!* (ed. Shawn Ginwright, Pedro Noguera and Julio Cammarota).

Sofia A. Villenas is Associate Professor of Anthropology and Education, and Director of the Latina/o Studies Program, at Cornell University, Ithaca, NY, USA. She is passionate about learning how families, educators and youths engage in teaching and learning across home, school and community contexts, and the ways in which culture, race, gender and citizenship are implicated and constituted in these endeavors. She is the co-editor of the *Handbook of Latinos and education: Theory, research and practice* (with Murillo, Galvan, Martinez, Muñoz and Machado-Casas, 2010) and *Chicana/Latina education in everyday life: Feminista perspectives on pedagogy and epistemology* (with Delgado Bernal, Elenes and Godinez, 2006).

P. Taylor Webb is Associate Professor in the Department of Educational Studies at the University of British Columbia, Vancouver, Canada. His work examines and critiques how education rationalizes and produces 'governable subjects' within liberal and neo-liberal normative architectures, and he has analyzed such productions by examining policies of education accountability, school choice and through the recursions of such practices and logics in educator preparation programs (e.g. 'professionals'). His books include *Teacher Assemblage* (2009) and *Policy, geophilosophy and education* (with Kalervo N. Gulson, 2015).

INTRODUCTION

The edge of race: critical examinations of education and race/racism

"The edge of race". The phrase has prompted many illuminating discussions among colleagues, students, and friends. We conceived this special issue in response to two key concerns. The first is that while race is increasingly on the periphery of education policy, with a growing disregard shown for racist inequities as education systems become dominated by market-driven concerns, it is important that we map the changing relations of race in and through neoliberal politics and policies (Gulson, 2011; Lipman, 2011).

The second concern is that at this time, and within and outside the spaces of the academy, even to mention race equity is to risk condemnation, marginalization, and ridicule; when to speak out and about race is to risk "being considered almost mad" (Goldberg, 2009, p. 359). We live at a time when politicians, the media, and practitioners are increasingly confident in their assertion that race no longer matters, is irrelevant in comparison to class, and that white children are the new race victims (Gillborn, 2008).

The authors in this Special Issue were asked to use "the edge of race" as a provocation in order to examine the concepts, methodologies, policies, politics, process, and practices associated with race/racism and education. This is work that is fraught with danger yet replete with possibilities, for it is critical to consider the limits, opportunities, and threats of theories of race. This is not to reify the concept of race over the acts and institutions associated with racism. Rather, it is to indicate that, at times, these authors work in precarious areas that engage the cutting edge of theories and politics of race.

The papers contribute to critical studies of race and education, in two ways. First, the papers offer empirical examples of the perpetuation and perniciousness of racism that point to the continued salience of research about race. These papers include instances of "race talk" in public discourses and the media (Villenas & Angeles); the fraught connections between educational achievement, racialization, and model minorities in the UK, paralleling research on the model minorities in the USA (Bradbury); the continued significance of studying race in color-blind contexts (Chapman); and the ways in which market solutions to education converge with mass media representations in films such as "Waiting for Superman", to occlude difference while reinforcing and reifying deficit readings of race (Dumas).

Second, the papers make contributions to conceptual and methodological understandings of race and racism. The authors illustrate the contingency, productivity, and fragility of race as concept, and point to how educational research continues to be a contested site in and from which to study race and education (Leonardo, 2009). These papers include the generation of new concepts to study race, such as exploring the notion of "interest-convergence" in Critical Race Theory to look at "interest-divergence" (Gillborn); the role of psycho-geographies and "ambient fear" in relation to education and Islamophobia (Gulson & Webb); and extending the reading of the model minority myth to a Canadian context with the idea of "ethno-nationalism" (Coloma). Other papers highlight methodology as an ideologico-racial practice (Leonardo); the politics of racialisation and the researcher in undertaking race research (Rollock); and the paradoxical relationships that are formed when undertaking critical race scholarship and activism (Stovall).

Overall, we believe this special issue makes a compelling case for the continuing centrality of race/racism in understanding educational inequity, and the need for a deep commitment to improving racial justice in and through education. The "edge of race" signals intellectual work that pushes educators' limits in confronting the race problem, extending their ability to speak against racism in new ways, and transgressing conceptual boundaries in order to build a clearer understanding of the relationship between race and education.

References

Gillborn, D. (2008). *Racism and education: Coincidence or conspiracy?* London: Routledge.

Goldberg, D. T. (2009). *The threat of race: Reflections on racial neoliberalism.* Oxford: Wiley-Blackwell.

Gulson, K. N. (2011). *Education policy, space and the city: Markets and the (in)visibility of race.* New York, NY: Routledge.

Leonardo, Z. (2009). *Race, whiteness and education.* New York, NY: Routledge.

Lipman, P. (2011). *The new political economy of urban education: Neoliberalism, race and the right to the city.* New York, NY: Routledge.

Kalervo N. Gulson
University of New South Wales, Sydney, NSW, Australia
Zeus Leonardo
University of California, Berkeley, CA, USA
David Gillborn
University of Birmingham, Birmingham, UK

Interest-divergence and the colour of cutbacks: race, recession and the undeclared war on Black children

David Gillborn

Centre for Research in Race & Education, School of Education, University of Birmingham, Birmingham, UK

Drawing on Critical Race Theory (CRT) and illustrating with examples from the English system, the paper addresses the hidden racist dimension to contemporary education reforms and argues that this is a predictable and recurrent theme at times of economic crisis. Derrick Bell's concept of 'interest-convergence' argues that moments of racial progress are won when White power-holders perceive self-interest in accommodating the demands of minoritised groups; such moments are unusual and often short-lived. Presently, we are witnessing the reverse of this process; a period of pronounced *interest-divergence*, when White power-holders imagine that a direct advantage will accrue from the further exclusion and oppression of Black groups in society. Behind rhetoric that proclaims the need to improve educational standards for all and celebrates a commitment to closing the existing achievement gaps; in reality education reforms are being enacted that systematically disadvantage Black students and demonstrably widen educational inequalities.

Introduction

A woman in her 30s, who was involved in the riots in north London, said: 'I think some people were there for justice for that boy who got killed. And the rest of them because of what's happening: the cuts, the government not doing the right thing. No job, no money. And the young these days need to be heard. It's got to be justice for them. (Newburn, Lewis, Addley, & Taylor, 2011)

For me it is clear that the root cause of this mindless selfishness is the same thing that I've spoken about for years. It is a complete lack of responsibility in parts of our society. People allowed to feel that the world owes them something, that their rights outweigh their responsibilities, and that their actions do not have consequences. Well, they do have consequences. (Cameron, 2011c[1])

In August 2011, major cities in England witnessed prolonged periods of urban unrest variously described as 'uprisings' by activists but dismissed as 'mindless' violence and 'riots' by media and politicians (John, 2011). The events began – as they often have in the past – after police action left a Black man dead in the street. Legitimate and peaceful family led protests were treated with disdain; frustration led to more violent protests and disturbances spread, at first throughout London and, eventually, across England (BBC News, 2011a). Subsequent research with participants confirmed what many argued at the time that the escalation reflected widespread anger and resentment towards authority, not least because of the racist use of stop-and-search police powers and the government's withdrawal of the Educational Maintenance Allowance, a welfare payment that had helped fund disadvantaged students to stay in education beyond the legal minimum (Harrison, 2012; Lewis, Newburn, Taylor, & Ball, 2011; Newburn et al., 2011).

On occasion such extreme events can bring about a pause, even a reversal of policy as policy-makers realise that things have gone too far and that it is in everyone's interest to at least be seen to take some action to curb the extremes of racial injustice. This is what the CRT scholar Derrick Bell (1980a) described as 'interest-convergence'. Such situations are rare. Following the 2011 uprisings, policy-makers *accelerated* their reforms and used the 'riots' as yet more evidence that dramatic (Rightist) change was needed. This paper argues that the situation can be characterised as 'interest-divergence', that is, a period where White power-holders perceived an advantage in even greater race inequity. I further contend that this is a predictable and historically familiar process at times of major economic crisis, such as the global downturn sparked by the market collapse of 2008. The paper explores the nature of interest-divergence in education by examining the English case, where contemporary education reforms are having a direct and demonstrably negative impact on Black students.[2] In the first section, I outline the CRT concepts of interest-convergence and -divergence.

Policy in whose interests?

Traditional mainstream approaches to education policy tend to imagine a series of incremental steps leading towards improved attainments and ever greater degrees of equity and social inclusion. In recent decades, however, critical perspectives have become prominent, placing policy within a wider political context, often as part of a global neoliberal project of late capitalism (Apple, Kenway, & Singh, 2005; Ball, 2006; Rizvi & Lingard, 2009). Critical Race Theory (CRT) takes a complementary approach but, rather than emphasising a dominant role for social class inequities, CRT focuses primarily (though by no means exclusively) on the *racial* dynamics of social inequities and the political process. From its origins in radical US legal scholarship of the 1970s and 1980s, CRT has grown into a cross-disciplinary international movement of scholars united by their focus on understanding and resisting the operation of White supremacy as a global political force (Crenshaw, Gotanda, Peller, & Thomas,1995; Delgado & Stefancic, 2001; Zamudio, Russell, Rios, & Bridgeman, 2011). In this perspective, White supremacy is understood not in terms of the crude and obvious fascistic groups that operate at the fringe of capitalist societies but as a system of taken-for-granted beliefs and practices that saturate the everyday mundane reality of society, supporting and extending the dominant position of White people (Delgado & Stefancic, 1997; Gillborn, 2005; Leonardo, 2009):

> White supremacy is the unnamed political system that has made the modern world what it is today … the most important political system of recent global history – the system of domination by which white people have historically ruled over and, in certain important ways, continue to rule over nonwhite people – is not seen as a political system at all. It is just taken for granted; it is the background against which other systems, which we *are* to see as political, are highlighted. (Mills, 1997, pp. 1–2, original emphasis)

Interest-convergence

One of the most influential concepts in the CRT canon addresses the means by which policy is re/made through a process that balances the interests of White elites against the dangers of pushing minoritised groups to the point of rebellion. Coined by the late

African American legal scholar Derrick Bell, the concept of 'interest-convergence' can be summarised as follows:

> The interests of blacks in achieving racial equality have been accommodated only when they have converged with the interests of powerful whites. (Taylor, 1998, p. 123)

Interest-convergence points to the political and power dimensions involved in bringing about racial justice. Active and organised resistance to White supremacy plays a major role in changing the context within which White power-holders make calculations about how much race inequity is sustainable. However, the concept also highlights the uncertain nature of even the most impressive-looking victories. For example, when reviewing the key civil rights decisions of the US Supreme Court, Bell (1980a) shows how, in retrospect, these famous victories can be seen to have operated in much more complex (and ambivalent) ways than is popularly imagined. Hailed as epochal victories that would change the social landscape forever, Bell argues that their progressive impact was not only uncertain and short-lived but that, in the long run, their consequence may be to further protect the racial status quo. Bell argues (and subsequent examination of the public record supports the view) that the famous *Brown vs Board of Education* legal decision, which was hailed as ending segregated education, served the interests of the White elite by removing the most obvious and crass forms of Apartheid-style public segregation while leaving the fabric of *de facto* economic, residential and educational segregation largely untouched (Bell, 1980a; 1980b, Dudziak, 2000). In this way, the USA could continue to present itself globally as the home of democracy while engaged in a cold war struggle with the Soviet Union to win economic and political allies in Africa.

The interest-convergence principle is probably the most frequently cited concept in CRT, but it is prone to a great deal of misunderstanding. In particular, it is vital to remember that interest-convergence, as set out by Bell, does *not* envisage a rational and balanced negotiation between minoritised groups and White power-holders (where change is achieved through the mere force of reason and logic). History suggests that advances in racial justice must be won through political protest and mobilisation that create a situation where – for White interests – taking *some* action against racism becomes the lesser of two evils because an even greater loss of privilege might be risked by failure to take any action at all. For example, the Brown decision may have served certain White interests, but it is inconceivable that there would have been any such change without the civil rights protests that brought the issue to the top of the international news agenda.

Interest-divergence

It is perhaps surprising that so much attention has focused on interest-convergence (which describes an exceptional set of social and political conditions) rather than its reverse, the much more common position, where racial interests are assumed to diverge. In fact, Bell wrote of the dangers of interest-divergence in the same *Harvard Law Review* article that launched the concept of interest-convergence (Bell, 1980a). It was Lani Guinier (2004), however, who placed interest-divergence at the centre of analysis when she addressed the reasons for the failure of the Brown decision to lead to long-lasting change. Guinier argues that interest-divergence holds the key to understanding 'racism's ever-shifting yet ever-present structure' (p. 100). She views it as a powerful explanatory device in understanding how White supremacy is protected and emboldened (through the creation and manipulation of apparent interest-divergence between racial groups):

> Those most advantaged by the status quo have historically manipulated race to order social, economic, and political relations to their benefit... The racialized hierarchies that result reinforce divergences of interest among and between groups with varying social status and privilege, which the ideology of white supremacy converts into rationales for the status quo. Racism normalizes these racialized hierarchies; it diverts attention from the unequal distribution of resources and power they perpetuate. Using race as a decoy offers short-term psychological advantages to poor and working-class whites, but it also masks how much poor whites have in common with poor blacks and other people of color. (Guinier, 2004, p. 114)

Although the concept has received less attention, the global economic crisis that began in 2008 points to the particular dangers of interest-divergence, by which I mean 'a situation where White people imagine that some benefit will accrue from the further marginalization and oppression of racially minoritised groups'. Just as Bell (1980a) and Guinier (2004) highlight the important psychological benefits that poor Whites draw from their sense of racial superiority (despite their own continued economic marginalisation), so periods of economic downturn make interest-divergence an even greater threat to racial justice. When economic conditions become harder, we can hypothesise that White elites will perceive an even greater need to placate poor Whites by demonstrating the continued benefits of their whiteness (as a means of securing their loyalty to the existing structures of race and class inequality).

This form of interest-divergence is clearly evident on both sides of the Atlantic. In the UK, recent years have witnessed a campaign by politicians and the media to present the true racial victims in education as 'white working-class' children, especially boys (see Gillborn, 2010; Sveinsson, 2009). As a direct result, multicultural education programmes have been cut and special programmes targeted at supporting 'poor' white students have multiplied across the country (Gillborn, 2010). The most obvious example of interest-divergence in the USA concerns recent developments in Arizona; here the state has moved to outlaw a Raza Studies programme that demonstrated significant advances in the educational attainments of Latino/students:

> ... students have outperformed all other students on the state's high stakes graduation exam and have graduated at a higher rate than their Anglo peers. In addition... students have matriculated to college at rate that is 129% greater than the national average for Chicana/o students. (Romero & Arce, 2010, p. 181)

Despite – or possibly *because* – of these outcomes, there was a vociferous campaign against multicultural education in the state. The campaign received national attention, and Raza Studies was demonised as stirring up trouble and resentment against White people:

> ... when an ethnically based education, which is bad enough, transmogrifies into an ethnically based education of grievance and oppression that vilifies the United States and anyone with white skin – well, this is simply untenable. And yet this product is exactly that which goes by the name Raza Studies ... (Julian, 2009)

The banning of all ethnic studies programmes in Arizona, and related moves to increase the surveillance and routine harassment of people of colour (based on the need to demonstrate their legal immigration status), amount to what Richard Delgado (1996, 2007) describes as a new form of colonialism; a policy aimed at securing ever greater control over the Latino population as a means of preventing political control shifting away from Whites as they become a numerical minority in certain states. Legal theorist George Martinez has taken these insights to a further level in the development of his 'state of nature theory' of racial oppression (2010):

> This theory posits that the dominant group tends to relate to racial minorities as if it were in a state of nature – i.e., there is a tendency to act as if there were no legal or moral constraints

on their actions or to move to a situation where there are fewer constraints in contexts in which it deals with racial minorities. (p. 202)

According to Martinez's theory, the actions of White power-holders can be understood – and predicted – on the basis that they will tend to act in relation to their perceived 'self-interest or self-preservation' and to adopt 'an amoral perspective' when deciding on the most advantageous course of action (2012, p. 195). Hence, both interest-convergence and -divergence are wrapped together in a theory that makes sense of policy as a never-ending campaign to secure ever greater control and benefit to White power-holders. In this context, periods of economic decline and hardship represent a particular threat to the interests of racial justice; as White interests are threatened, we can predict that minoritised ethnic groups will be in the firing line. In the next section of this paper, I explore the empirical evidence that indicates the operation of interest-divergence in the past and present.

Race, recession and white supremacy

> The job losses that came with the onset of the current crash hit black and ethnic minorities harder than the national average worker. (Dorling, 2009, p. 1)

> The recession is having a further impact on the BME sector and increasing inequalities. (East of England Black and Minority Ethnic Network, n.d.)

Recessions are bad news for most people, but periods of economic hardship and contraction are especially bad news for minority ethnic groups. A clear pattern has emerged in previous recessions that is being replicated in the post-2008 downturn: historically minoritised groups suffer the negative impacts of recessions earlier, deeper and longer than the White population. This pattern is clear in unemployment data for both the USA and the UK. Black unemployment in the UK, for example, rose by more than *twice* the rate for Whites between 2008 and 2009:

> Members of the Caribbean and African community have seen unemployment levels rise by 6.9 per cent – from 13.2 per cent in the first quarter of 2008, to 20.1 per cent in the third quarter of 2009. This compares with a 2.8 per cent rise in white unemployment, up from 4.8 per cent to 7.6 per cent, over the same period. (Equality & Human Rights Commission, 2009)

These patterns of racialised economic inequalities are especially pronounced in the USA. For example, an analysis of US unemployment during recessions over the last three decades shows that White unemployment at the *worst* of times is rarely as high as Black unemployment at the *best* of times:

> The Applied Research Center analyzed statistics from the Current Population Survey over a 37-year period and found that unemployment for people of color rarely fell below even the highest, recession-level rates of white unemployment. Black unemployment was at least double that of whites for all but five of those years. (ARC, 2009, p. 14)

In one sense, therefore, Black unemployment in the States is permanently at (the equivalent of White) recession levels, and race inequities become even worse at times of widespread economic hardship. These patterns are well known and clearly supporta CRT analysis of White supremacy in general and, in particular, the operation of interest-divergence at times of economic crisis. We might predict, therefore, that a similar set of pressures would be at work in the field of education. The following sections explore this question with reference to the situation in contemporary England.

Interest-divergence and the attack on multiculturalism

> The interests of the white working class are habitually pitched against those of minority ethnic groups and immigrants, while larger social and economic structures are left out of the debate altogether ... Instead, there is a fairly consistent message that the white working class are the losers in the struggle for scarce resources, while minority ethnic groups are the winners – at the *direct expense* of the white working class. (Sveinsson, 2009, p. 5, original emphasis)

The attacks of September 2001 have had a profound effect on virtually every aspect of governmentality in societies such as the USA and the UK. In the USA, for example, Pauline Lipman (2004) has noted the use of accountability measures in education to close down critical debate and enforce a limited understanding of democracy and civic education (see also Delgado, 2003). In the UK, these processes have been given an added impetus by the London bombings of 2005. Subsequent policy has adopted an aggressively majoritarian stance that portrays minority communities as a potentially destructive influence and emphasises the need for minorities to 'integrate' while minimising disruption for the White majority (Gillborn, 2008, pp. 81–86). This shift in policy was already well underway before the 2010 general election which resulted in a Conservative/Liberal Democrat Coalition – the UK's first coalition government since the Second World War. The right-wing Conservative Party has determined the majority of the coalition's policy priorities, and the prime minister made clear his position in a speech to the Munich Security Conference. One section of the speech was widely reported in TV news broadcasts:

> Under the doctrine of state multiculturalism, we have encouraged different cultures to live separate lives, apart from each other and apart from the mainstream ... We've even tolerated these segregated communities behaving in ways that run completely counter to our values. So, when a white person holds objectionable views, racist views for instance, we rightly condemn them. But when equally unacceptable views or practices come from someone who isn't white, we've been too cautious frankly – frankly, even fearful – to stand up to them. (Cameron, 2011b)

This sound-bite neatly combined the image of 'different cultures' living outside the mainstream alongside the idea that White people are somehow the victims of a double-standard that judges them more harshly than minoritised groups. The total inaccuracy of this assertion is exposed by the fact that Cameron made no mention of a demonstration that *same day* by the English Defence League (EDL) – a violently anti-Muslim organisation – which brought the town of Luton (30 miles north of London) to a total standstill. Despite the scale of the disruption and the threatening and offensive nature of the demonstration – which, for example, included placards reading 'Disgusting pedophile (sic) Islamist sex gangs deliberately share, molest and rape our daughters' – a senior government figure dismissed the suggestion that Cameron might have tempered his speech simply 'because some people have chosen to march down a street' (BBC News, 2011b).

Education, economy and the widening of achievement gaps

> This policy is driven, like all our education policy, by our guiding moral purpose – the need to raise attainment for all children and close the gap between the richest and poorest. (Gove, 2010)

I am disgusted by the idea that we should aim for any less for a child from a poor background than a rich one. I have contempt for the notion that we should accept narrower horizons for a black child than a white one. (Cameron, 2011a)

These quotations could not be clearer in stating the government's high aspirations for all and, in particular, their commitment to address existing achievement gaps. Despite this soaring rhetoric, however, the coalition's policies follow a path that *increases* disparities of achievement and, in the case of race inequity, amount to a war on Black children. Beneath a colour-blind rhetoric of high standards for all, the government's reforms pursue strategies that are demonstrably weighted against the interests of Black children. In this section, I will outline two of the key changes, involving reforms of school governance (the expansion of 'Academy' schools) and the assessment system (the introduction of the 'English Baccalaureate').

The academies programme

Alongside a small market in private education, schooling in England has traditionally been delivered to the vast majority of children through schools that are administered by the local authority (which answers to locally elected councillors); education funding mostly comes to authorities as a grant from central government. Successive national governments, however, have reformed educational governance to continually remove powers and funding from local authorities. The most dramatic change has come since the 2010 Conservative/Liberal Democrat Coalition came to power. The coalition has sought to rapidly expand the number of 'academy schools' to a point where they become the dominant form of schooling within the state-funded system.[3]

Academy schools were introduced by a Labour Government in 2000 (Lipsett, 2007). They are funded by a combination of private sponsorship and direct resourcing from central government. Academies have more control over their curriculum, stand entirely outside local democratic control and usually receive greater funding than comparable local schools (because their income is not top-sliced by the Local Authority in order to provide shared services such as provision for students designated as having 'special educational needs'). Originally academies were focused on areas of considerable social and economic disadvantage, but the coalition has made the expansion of academies a priority for existing schools with good inspection reports. This is highly significant because the government's own data suggest that Black students do not draw equitable rewards from attending academy schools; to add insult to injury the data were made public in the 'Equalities Impact Assessment' for the Academies Bill, that is, in the document intended to show that the reforms would *not* have an adverse equalities impact (DfE, 2010a); perhaps predictably, a subsequent reform removed the requirement to conduct such assessments (BBC News, 2012).

Figure 1 compares the achievement in the first 63 academies alongside the national average for students in each of the crude ethnic groups described in official statistics,[4] plus attainment in a specially selected 'comparison group' of schools. The Education Department describes this group of 310 local authority schools as 'in similar circumstances to Academies in that they have pupils with similar levels of prior attainment and are in similar areas of social deprivation' (DfE, 2010a, para. 10).

It is not surprising that students in academies are less likely to attain the benchmark level of achievement than their peers nationally; as already noted, the first academies served areas of higher than average social disadvantage (where achievement is generally

THE EDGE OF RACE

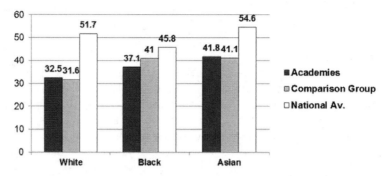

Figure 1.   Achievement by Ethnic Group in Academies, Comparison Schools and Nationally: England, 2009 (percentages).
Source: Adapted from DfE (2010a: Table 2).

lower). Turning to the 'comparison group', Figure 1 shows that White and 'Asian' students were marginally more likely to attain the benchmark in academies (the difference was less than 1% point in both cases). For Black students, however, the academy students were 3.9% points *less* likely to reach the benchmark than their peers in the 'comparison group'. According to a comparison crafted by the Education Department itself, therefore, the best available evidence suggests that for Asian and White students the advantage of attending an academy is negligible, while for Black students there appears to be a clear disadvantage. Despite this shocking finding, the academy reforms went ahead unchanged.

The English Baccalaureate: how changing the assessment widens the gaps

The coalition's first set of education reform proposals, published in November 2010, introduced the 'English Baccalaureate' as a new summary measure of achievement for students at the end of their compulsory schooling. To qualify students need higher grade General Certificate of Secondary Education (GCSE) passes in a specific range of subjects: English, maths, two sciences, a modern or ancient foreign language and a humanity (history or geography).[5] The stated rationale was 'to encourage schools to offer a broad set of academic subjects to age 16, whether or not students then go down an academic or vocational route' (DfE, 2010b, p. 11). The composition of the 'E.Bacc', as it has become known, gives immediate cause for concern because only a minority of students even *enter* the requisite subjects, let alone gain pass grades in them.

According to official statistics (DfE, 2012), only around one student in five (21.6%) sit examinations in all the subjects required to qualify for the E.Bacc. These include high-status subjects (such as separate sciences) which schools often restrict to the students they judge to be 'most able'. Sometimes these judgments reflect genuine differences in achievement, but research (both quantitative and qualitative) has consistently shown that teachers' preconceptions about certain groups also play an important role, especially in relation to ethnic origin (Araujo, 2007; Bradbury, 2011; CRE, 1992; Gillborn, 2008; Gillies & Robinson, 2012; Hallam, 2002; Hallam & Toutounji, 1996; Rollock, 2007; Strand, 2012; Sukhnandan & Lee, 1998; Tikly, Haynes, Caballero, Hill, & Gillborn, 2006). Put simply, teachers' expectations of Black students tend to be systematically lower than warranted by their performance in class. These stereotypes exert a powerful influence on students' opportunities to succeed, making it less likely that they gain access to high-status courses and resulting in their being disproportionately placed in the lowest teaching groups (where they cover less of the curriculum and have a reduced chance of achieving the highest grades). As a result, all children do not have an equal chance of attaining an E.Bacc. Whereas 32.8% of Indians and 21.5% of White British students entered the full range of E.Bacc subjects, this was true of 17.3% of Pakistani and only 13% of Black Caribbean students (DfE, 2012, Table 2a).

The same stereotyping processes that restrict access to high-status courses for some groups, also depress their overall levels of attainment. Consequently, the patterns of differential access are compounded by differences in attainment. The introduction of the E.Bacc, therefore, has immediately widened inequalities of achievement between certain ethnic groups.

Figure 2 shows the different levels of achievement for students measured alternatively by the previous benchmark (five or more higher grade GCSEs including English and maths) and by the E.Bacc. The illustration shows the overall achievements of students in the largest ethnic groups, accounting for around 90% of the student population.[6] Students in every group are much less likely to attain the E.Bacc than the GCSE measure. Considering all students in state-maintained schools in 2011, the proportion of academically successful young people shifts from the previous dominant measure (overall 58.2% achieve the GCSE benchmark) to the new measure (15.4% achieved the E.Bacc). At a stroke, therefore, overall levels of achievement have been slashed from a target achieved by more than half of students to a new level achieved by less than one in six.

As Figure 2 illustrates, the impact of introducing the E.Bacc is not equally harsh on all groups. This can be seen more clearly in Table 1, which calculates the cost of the E. Bacc to each group: what we might think of as an *E.Bacc penalty* (column D). It is clear that the shift to the E.Bacc has a particularly racialised impact: the highest penalties are suffered by Black Caribbean students (where 84.3% of students successful under the old measure are excluded from E.Bacc success), followed by Bangladeshi students (83.4%), dual heritage students with White and Black Caribbean parents (81.2%) and Black African students (80.6%).

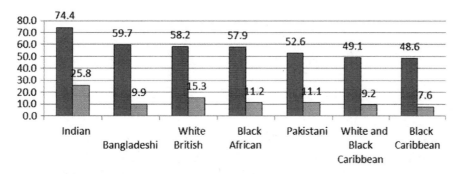

Figure 2. Two measures of pupil achievement compared: England 2011 by Ethnic Origin (percentages), all state-maintained schools.
Source: Adapted from DfE (2012: Table 1).

Table 1. The *E.Bacc Penalty*: England, 2011, by ethnic origin.

Ethnic origin	[A] 5+ A*–C grades inc. English and maths GCSEs (%)	[B] Achieved the English Bacc. (%)	[C] Percentage point difference between GCSE and E.Bacc benchmarks	[D] E.Bacc Penalty ('C' as% of 'A')	[E] odds ratios for GCSE benchmark	[F] Odds ratios for English Bacc. benchmark
White British	58.2	15.3	42.9	73.7	–	–
Indian	74.4	25.8	48.6	65.3	2.09	1.92
Bangladeshi	59.7	9.9	49.8	83.4	1.06	0.61
Black African	57.9	11.2	46.7	80.6	0.99	0.70
Pakistani	52.6	11.1	41.5	78.8	0.80	0.69
Mixed: White and Black Caribbean	49.1	9.2	39.9	81.2	0.69	0.56
Black Caribbean	48.6	7.6	41.0	84.3	0.68	0.46
All pupils	58.2	15.4	42.8	73.5		

Source: Data in columns 'A' and 'B' from DfE (2012: Table 1).
Note: Total for 'all pupils' includes those in ethnic groups that are not shown in the table.

Differences in achievement can also be expressed as an Odds Ratio (OR). This shows the odds of academic success for one group of students relative to the odds for another group. If the figure is *greater* than 1, the first group is *more* likely to succeed, but if the figure is *less* than 1, it indicates how much *less* likely the first group is to succeed. Table 1 details the OR for the GCSE benchmark (column E) and for the E.Bacc (column F) for each minoritised group relative to White British students. The results are clear: in each case the odds of success for minoritised groups get worse in the E.Bacc. Black Caribbean students, for example, are only around half as likely to achieve the E.Bacc as their White British counterparts.

The introduction of the E.Bacc. as an indicator of success, therefore, has a significant regressive impact on race equality in the English educational system. This move dispro-portionately penalises minoritised groups, especially Black Caribbean and Bangladeshi students. The prime minister's 'contempt' for those who 'accept narrower horizons for a black child than a white one' (quoted earlier) obviously does not extend to those who champion policy changes that institutionalise lower achievement for Black children compared to White ones. It could be argued, of course, that the government's 'horizons' (their *aspirations*) for Black children are as high as anyone's despite their *actions* having a clear discriminatory impact on Black youth. But these inconsistencies between policy rhetoric and policy impacts are not new, and they should not surprise us. The present government is by no means the first administration to proclaim a set of goals that are not reflected in the real-world impact of their decision-making, and we need to view this as something more significant than a case of mere hypocrisy or faulty policy-making. The reforms – by increasing the scale of race inequity in education – serve White interests and represent a clear case of interest-divergence in action.

Conclusions

> [The riots of 2011 were] an explosion of anger to police and authority in general who have let them down. Possibly the only way to be heard when they feel no one listens or does anything about their problems. (Community stakeholder, Salford. Quoted in Report for the Cabinet Office, Morrell, Scott, McNeish, & Webster, 2011, p. 33)

> We've had 50 years of carrot... Now it's time for some stick.

> We have had 50 years of the carrot – welfare, rehabilitation, social conscience and rights. It has not worked. It is now time for the stick – law, justice, discipline, individual conscience and responsibilities. (*Mail on Sunday*, 14 August 2011)

One of the most frequently cited concepts in CRT is the notion of interest-convergence, where apparently progressive reforms come about because White power-holders become convinced of a White advantage to some modicum of greater racial equality (Bell, 1980a). In this paper, I have argued for attention to be focused on the CRT concept of interest-divergence, where White power-holders perceive an advantage in pursuing even greater race inequalities in society (Bell, 1980a; Guinier, 2004). I have argued that this concept has wide application in understanding the routine shape of policy-making in societies, like the USA and UK, that are structured in racial domination. The concept has particular relevance at times of perceived threats to the well-being of White people, especially during economic downturns. On both sides of the Atlantic, Black people are known to experience the effects of economic depressions more quickly and deeply than the ethnic majority. I hypothesised that interest-divergence would also be present in education policy-making and have traced evidence of this in recent reforms to the English education system.

The widespread civil unrest in English cities during August 2011 made headline news around the world. Subsequent studies, both independently organised and government funded, undermined the official interpretation of the events as 'criminality, pure and simple' (Cameron, 2011c). But despite growing awareness of the anger and resentment that lay behind the disturbances, the government's response has been to push ahead with an educational reform programme wrapped in the rhetoric of high standards for all, but delivering even greater inequalities of achievement between White and Black students. This experience is mirrored in the economy, where Black unemployment rates have risen at twice the White unemployment rate. These patterns have clear historical precedents, and their contemporary incidence is neither accidental nor coincidental. The coalition's approach to English education reform reflects the wider processes of interest-divergence, i.e. its actions appear to embody a belief among White power-holders that a direct benefit can be drawn from even greater exclusion and oppression of minoritised groups. The quotation from the *Mail on Sunday*, above, is highly relevant. The *Mail* is the country's second largest-selling daily newspaper and by far, its most politically influential. The assertion that 'it's time for some stick' encapsulates the aggressive mood among the political elite; a mood reflected in the prime minister's assertion that White people are held to a higher moral standard than minorities, and his rejection of the 'doctrine of state multiculturalism'. At this time, the interests of minoritised groups in general, and Black people in particular, appear to be wilfully sacrificed by reforms that extend academy schools (despite their negative impact on Black student achievement) and by the introduction of a new measure of attainment, the E.Bacc., which demonstrably worsens inequality of achievement. Although these developments have occurred within the English system, there is at least *prime facie* evidence to suggest they operate internationally also. This suggests that the concept of interest-divergence has potential to inform our analysis of current inequities and our struggles to achieve greater race equity in the future.

Notes

1. Verbatim transcript, by the author, from BBC News night, TV broadcast.
2. By 'Black' I mean people who would generally self-identify in relation to that term, especially where they identify their family origins as – at least in part – in Black Africa and/or the Caribbean. In UK census categories, this would include 'Black Caribbean', 'Black African', 'Mixed: White and Black Caribbean', and 'Any Other Black' Group.
3. Although the majority of funding for academies comes directly from the national government, they enjoy freedoms usually associated with private schools and are entirely independent of local authority control. The number of academies has risen from 203 in May 2010 (when the coalition came to power) to 2309 just over two years later (BBC News, 2013).
4. The general category 'Asian' became much less prominent in official statistics from the late 1990s until the coalition's election in 2010. The category is especially unhelpful because it lumps together particularly diverse demographic groups (Indian, Pakistani, Bangladeshi) whose political, economic, cultural and educational profiles are markedly different. Indian students, for example, generally achieve above the national average, whereas Pakistani students tend to achieve below the average. For an extended analysis of Indian students' educational experiences and achievement, see Gillborn (2008), especially Chapter 7.
5. The GCSE is the dominant form of assessment for young people in England at the end of compulsory schooling, aged 16. Students are assessed for separate GCSEs in each curriculum subject that they follow throughout their secondary schooling.
6. These are the distinct ethnic census categories with a minimum of 5000 students in the annual cohort: together they account for 89.7% of the student population in 2010–2011.

References

Apple, M. W., Kenway, J., & Singh, M. (Eds.). (2005). *Globalizing education: Policies, pedagogies, and politics*. New York: Peter Lang.

Applied Research Center (ARC). (2009). *Race and recession: How inequity rigged the economy and how to change the rules*. Oakland, CA: Author.

Araujo, M. (2007). Modernising the comprehensive principle: Selection, setting and the institutionalisation of educational failure. *British Journal of Sociology of Education*, *28*(2), 241–257. doi:10.1080/01425690701192752

Ball, S. J. (2006). *Education policy and social class*. London: Routledge.

BBC News. (2011a). *England riots: Maps and timeline*. Retrieved from http://www.bbc.co.uk/news/uk-10321233

BBC News. (2011b). *Row over David Cameron multiculturalism speech timing*. Retrieved from http://www.bbc.co.uk/news/uk-politics-12376304

BBC News. (2012). *Cameron 'calls time' on labour's equality impact assessments*. Retrieved from http://www.bbc.co.uk/news/uk-politics-20400747

BBC News. (2013). *Academies could 'fuel social segregation'*. Retrieved from http://www.bbc.co.uk/news/education-20960500

Bell, D. (1980a). Brown v. Board of Education and the Interest-Convergence Dilemma. *Harvard Law Review*, *93*(3), 518–533. doi:10.2307/1340546

Bell, D. (1980b). *Race, racism and American law*. Boston, MA: Little Brown.

Bradbury, A. (2011). *Learner identities, assessment and equality in early years education* (Unpublished doctoral dissertation). Institute of Education, University of London.

Cameron, D. (2011a). *Leadership for a better Britain, Speech to the Conservative Party Conference*. London: Conservative Party. Retrieved from http://www.conservatives.com/News/Speeches/2011/10/David_Cameron_Leadership_for_a_better_Britain.aspx

Cameron, D. (2011b). *PM's speech at Munich Security Conference*. Retrieved from http://www.number10.gov.uk/news/speeches-and-transcripts/2011/02/pms-speech-at-munich-security-conference-60293

Cameron, D. (2011c). *Prime Minister's Statement to the House of Commons, 11 August 2011*. Hansard. Retrieved from http://www.publications.parliament.uk/pa/cm201011/cmhansrd/cm110811/debtext/110811-0001.htm

Commission for Racial Equality (CRE). (1992). *Set to fail? Setting and banding in secondary schools*. London: Commission for Racial Equality.

Crenshaw, K., Gotanda, N., Peller, G., & Thomas, K. (Eds.). (1995). *Critical race theory: The key writings that formed the movement*. New York: New Press.

Delgado, R. (1996). *The coming race war? And other apocalyptic tales of America after affirmative action and welfare*. London: New York University Press.

Delgado, R. (2003). *Justice at war: Civil liberties and civil rights during times of crisis*. New York: New York University Press.

Delgado, R. (2007). Rodrigo's corrido: Race, postcolonial theory, and US civil rights. *Vanderbilt Law Review*, *60*, 1689–1745.

Delgado, R., & Stefancic, J. (1997). *Critical white studies: Looking behind the mirror*. Philadelphia: Temple University Press.

Delgado, R., & Stefancic, J. (2001). *Critical race theory: An introduction*. New York: New York University Press.

Department for Education (DfE). (2010a). *The importance of teaching white paper equalities impact assessment*. London: Author.

Department for Education (DfE). (2010b). *The importance of teaching: The Schools White Paper 2010*. London: Author.

Department for Education (DfE). (2012). *GCSE and equivalent attainment by student characteristics in England, 2010/11*. London: Author.

Dorling, D. (2009). Race and the repercussions of recession. *Bulletin: Runnymede Quarterly*, 1–3.

Dudziak, M. L. (2000). Desegregation as a Cold War imperative. In R. Delgado & J. Stefancic (Eds.), *Critical White studies: Looking behind the mirror* (pp. 106–117). Philadelphia, PA: Temple University Press.

East of England Black & Minority Ethnic Network. (n.d.). *The regional race equality council partnership (RRECP)*. Retrieved from http://www.menter.org.uk/content/regional-race-equality-council-partnership-rrecp

Equality & Human Rights Commission. (2009). *Commission and GEO research shows impact of recession on equality groups*. EHRC press release. Retrieved from http://www.equalityhuman rights.com/news/2009/december/commission-and-geo-research-shows-impact-of-recession-on-equality-groups

Gillborn, D. (2005). Education policy as an act of white supremacy: Whiteness, critical race theory and education reform. *Journal of Education Policy, 20*(4), 485–505. doi:10.1080/02680 930500132346

Gillborn, D. (2008). *Racism and education: Coincidence or conspiracy?* London: Routledge.

Gillborn, D. (2010). The White working class, racism and respectability: Victims, degenerates and interest-convergence. *British Journal of Educational Studies, 58*(1), 3–25. doi:10.1080/01425690701192752

Gillies, V., & Robinson, Y. (2012). 'Including' while excluding: Race, class and behaviour support units. *Race Ethnicity & Education, 15*(2), 157–174. doi:10.1080/13613324.2011.578126

Gove, M. (2010, June 16). *Michael Gove to the National College Annual Conference, Birmingham*. DfE Speeches. Retrieved from http://www.education.gov.uk/inthenews/speeches/a0061371/michael-gove-to-the-national-college-annual-conference-birmingham

Guinier, L. (2004). From racial liberalism to racial literacy: Brown v. Board of Education and the interest-divergence dilemma. *Journal of American History, 91*(1), 92–118. doi:10.2307/3659616

Hallam, S. (2002). *Ability grouping in schools: A literature review*. London: Institute of Education, University of London.

Hallam, S., & Toutounji, I. (1996). *What do we know about the grouping of pupils by ability? A Research Review*. London: Institute of Education, University of London.

Harrison, A. (2012). *More teenagers Neet – not in work or education*. Retrieved from http://www.bbc.co.uk/news/education-18623398

John, G. (2011). *Black, Asian, minority ethnic communities and inner city riots*. Retrieved from http://www.gusjohn.com/2011/11/black-asian-minority-ethnic-and-refugee-communities-and-inner-city-riots/

Julian, L. (2009). 'Raza studies' defy American values, *CBS News Opinion*. Retrieved from http://www.cbsnews.com/2100-215_162-4227721.html

Leonardo, Z. (2009). *Race, Whiteness, and education*. London: Routledge.

Lewis, P., Newburn, T., Taylor, M., & Ball, J. (2011, December 5). Rioters say anger with police fuelled summer unrest: Reading the riots. *The Guardian*. Retrieved from http://www.guardian.co.uk/uk/series/reading-the-riots

Lipman, P. (2004, March). Education accountability and repression of democracy Post-9/11, *Journal for Critical Education Policy Studies, 2*(1), 1–39. Retrieved from http://www.jceps.com/?pageID=article&articleID=23

Lipsett, A. (2007, November 13). What are academy schools? *The Guardian*, http://www.guardian.co.uk/education/2007/nov/13/newschools.schools

Mail on Sunday (2011, August 14). We've had 50 years of carrot … Now it's time for some stick. Retrieved from http://www.dailymail.co.uk/debate/article-2025816/UK-riots-Weve-50-years-carrot–time-stick.html

Martinez, G. A. (2010). Race, American law and the state of nature. *West Virginia Law Review, 112*, 799–838.

Martinez, G. A. (2012). Arizona, immigration, and Latinos: The epistemology of Whiteness, the geography of race, interest convergence, and the view from the perspective of critical theory. *Arizona State Law Journal, 44*, 175–211.

Mills, C. W. (1997). *The racial contract*. London: Cornell University Press.

Morrell, G., Scott, S., McNeish, D., & Webster, S. (2011). *The August riots in England: Understanding the involvement of young people*. Report for the Cabinet Office. London: NatCen.

Newburn, T., Lewis, P., Addley, E., & Taylor, M. (2011). 'David Cameron, the Queen and the rioters' sense of injustice': Reading the Riots. *The Guardian*. Retrieved from http://www.guardian.co.uk/uk/2011/dec/05/cameron-queen-injustice-english-rioters

Rizvi, F., & Lingard, B. (2009). *Globalizing education policy*. London: Routledge.

Rollock, N. (2007). *Failure by any other name? Educational policy and the continuing struggle for Black academic success*. London: Runnymede Trust.

Romero, A., & Arce, M. S. (2010). Culture as a resource: Critically compassionate intellectualism and its struggle against racism, fascism, and intellectual apartheid in Arizona. *Hamline Journal of Public Law and Policy, 31*, 179–217.

Strand, S. (2012). The White British–Black Caribbean achievement gap: Tests, tiers and teacher expectations. *British Educational Research Journal, 38*(1), 75–101. doi:10.1080/01411926. 2010.526702

Sukhnandan, L., & Lee, B. (1998). *Streaming, setting and grouping by ability*. Slough: NFER.

Sveinsson, K. P. (Ed.). (2009). *Who cares about the White working class?* London: Runnymede Trust.

Taylor, E. (1998). A primer on critical race theory. *The Journal of Blacks in Higher Education, 19*, 122–124. doi:10.2307/2998940

Tikly, L., Haynes, J., Caballero, C., Hill, J., & Gillborn, D. (2006). *Evaluation of aiming high: African Caribbean achievement project*. Research Report RR801. London: DfES.

Zamudio, M. M., Russell, C., Rios, F. A., & Bridgeman, J. L. (2011). *Critical race theory matters: Education and ideology*. London: Routledge.

A political investment: revisiting race and racism in the research process

Nicola Rollock

Department of Education & Social Justice, School of Education, University of Birmingham, Birmingham, UK

This paper draws upon a two-year Economic and Social Research Council (ESRC) funded study into the educational strategies of the black middle classes to examine the role of race and racism in the research process. Specifically, it explores how my political positioning and experiences of racism, as a black female scholar, shaped not only my engagement with the research but also how I was perceived and positioned by others. This is analysed in terms of three areas: the recruitment and identification of research participants, the interview process and the dissemination of the project findings. While consideration of the researcher's race and racial politics tended to run parallel to or quietly intersect with the project development, fieldwork and analysis, it is argued that these factors, in actuality, play a significant and highly informative role in shaping a broader, nuanced conceptualisation of race and racism that is too often silenced and neglected in race research and the academy as a whole. Informed by Fanon and Critical Race Theory, it is posited that these seemingly peripheral race moments need to be foregrounded, named and analysed not just by scholars of colour but also by white colleagues electing to do race research. Such call to action remains fundamental within a wider socio-political context that increasingly is devoid of meaningful engagement with race and racism.

Introduction

A growing number of Black feminists have documented their experiences in the academy as a means of drawing attention to and working to disrupt hegemonic paradigms of knowledge and knowledge production which claim to be the only legitimate ways of viewing the world (Egharevba, 2001; Ladson-Billings, 2003; Mirza, 2009; Reynolds, 1997). These accounts from the 'liminal space of alterity' (Rollock, 2012a, p. 65) not only help to highlight the complex, intersectional nature of identities and the centrality of whiteness in informing our understanding of racism and feminism (Ladson-Billing & Donnor, 2008; Wynter, 1992) but also to reveal how the centre operates often in subtle yet sophisticated ways to maintain an inequitable status quo (Brah & Phoenix, 2004; Crenshaw, 2009; Rollock, 2012a). It is important to note that in 'speaking back' from the margins, scholars of colour seek not to enter or become part of the central 'norm', rather they endeavour to reveal how the power and the privileges of whiteness can be disrupted and an equitable landscape secured.

However, as I have argued elsewhere (Rollock, 2012a), 'speaking back' carries risks. It is to challenge and seek to undo the unexamined, taken-for-granted comforts and privileges on which institutional norms and practices and the individual actions of the dominant group are based. Rather than consciously engaging with the experiences of racially minoritised scholars with the view that their experiences can offer meaningful insights into inequities of race (Delgado, 1989; Tate, 1997), race and racism become a 'no go' subject area, leaving fundamental issues around the recruitment, progression and experiences of Black and minority ethnic staff unaddressed. Ahmed (2009) details the challenges of naming race in academic spaces which refuse to – choose not to – see race but simultaneously want to celebrate one's (often isolated) presence as a scholar of colour and as a major advance in 'diversity':

> The organisation becomes the subject of feeling, the one who must be protected, the one who is easily bruised or hurt. To speak of racism is to introduce bad feeling. It is to hurt not just the organisation, re-imagined as a subject with feelings, but also the subjects who identify with the organisation, the 'good white diversity' subjects, to whom we are supposed to be grateful. (p. 46)

To occupy the academy as a scholar of colour and, moreover, to be racially aware *and* specialise in race and racism presents multiple layers of complexity. Maylor (2009), a Black British female scholar, describes the hurt and frustration she endures when white academics and research participants refuse to engage with her or acknowledge, during the course of fieldwork or conferences, that she is actually an academic[1] as opposed to a junior or a non-academic member of staff. Maylor explains that white team members and colleagues often fail to notice these incidents, and even when the details have been carefully explained to them, they fail to comprehend their significance and the emotional toil they incur. In not seeing racism, and by not attempting to work to see it, white colleagues are also implicated in committing acts of injustice and psychic violence to the minoristised staff (Leonardo & Porter, 2010). And racism, rather than being understood as including attitudes and behaviours of 'unwitting prejudice, ignorance and thoughtlessness' (Macpherson, 1999, section 6.34) often becomes remade as a random individual act of deficient thinking on the part of the minoritised staff, a 'fantasy of paranoia' (Ahmed, 2009, p. 47). Alternatively, the minoritised staff may also experience what Delgado (1996, p. 70) describes as 'false empathy', when recounting incidents of racism to whites. This relates to an emotional state in which a white person believes he or she is identifying or connecting with a person of colour but in fact is doing so only in a facile, superficial way. An example of this might be when white female staff attempt to signal their understanding of racial discrimination by speaking about gender or social class as being the same; an act which in fact obfuscates race.

This paper is interested in how scholars of colour engage with research which has race and racism as its focus and how they carry it out within academic spaces which deny and subjugate race and their experiences as a reality. This includes considerations not only around race matching but also extends beyond this. While Ali (2009) and Maylor (2009) both point, for example, to the burden of being marked within the academy by the colour of their skin – a 'corporeal malediction' (Fanon, 1967, p. 84) – they respond positively to the discernible joy that their presence brings to students and the research participants who are also from Black and minority ethnic backgrounds. The presence of Black scholars can often serve as an unspoken, humanising act of recognition for participants and students. Their presence through the colour of their skin serves as a kind of signal – a connection – reminding them that there are others like them, who may share similar experiences within a society that otherwise marks them as invisible. However, as Phoenix (1994) incisively reminds us, sharing a racial identity does not necessarily equate to matched perspectives or politics. Within the research context, a shared racial identity does not inevitably guarantee ease of access or rebalance unequal differences in the distribution of power between researcher and participant. Writing about her experiences during two studies with young people (one group were mothers under the age of 20), Phoenix recalls an incident where a Black teenager refused to take part in the research due to concerns about how the findings and her comments might be used. Phoenix points out that sharing a racial identity in this context did not mean that the young woman was readily reassured that this would prevent the research from being exploitative. An awareness of the way in which research has traditionally been exploitative of people of colour, clearly outweighed any possible impact that the presence of a single Black researcher may have played.

Egharevba (2001), who is of Black African heritage, contends that despite the differing ways in which social identities intersect a common understanding and experience of racism – characterised by a perspective that is 'Black, postcolonial and antiracist' (Mirza, 2009, p. 3) – frequently plays a major role in shaping the research dynamic. However, despite this, she does also acknowledge that there were moments during her interviews with South Asian heritage women in which she was cross-examined about her hair, language and culture. Shared experiences of racism while providing moments of connection were not sufficient to ensure that she was regarded as 'one of us'.

This paper draws upon a two-year study into the educational strategies of the Black middle classes, to examine the role of race and racism in the research process. Specifically, it explores how my political positioning and experiences of racism intersected with my role as a Black female scholar and shaped my engagement with and connection to the research. As I will argue, these aspects of my identity were fundamental to the ways in which I was perceived and positioned not only by project participants but also by those on the periphery of the study. Taken together, it is argued that these race processes form an integral role in revealing the nuanced complexities and significance of race and racism within the research project and within British society more broadly. Further, these aspects of racial identity, race politics and positioning ought not to be limited to the reflections and analyses of scholars of colour, but crucially, should also be named, foregrounded and addressed by white colleagues electing to carry out race research.

The research process

The paper begins with a brief overview of the research project (sometimes referred to as the 'Black middle classes project') and its aims. I then summarise my personal and political positioning as a Black female scholar. I am particularly interested here in drawing attention to the elements of my identity that mirrored the selection criteria for project participants since, as will become apparent, this was pertinent to the relationship that I established with others (members of the research team, participants and third parties) and, in turn, informed the sense of responsibility I developed in ensuring the wide dissemination of the project findings and its subsequent impact. These issues are examined in relation to three principal areas: the recruitment and identification of research participants; the interview process and the dissemination of the project findings.

Project overview

'The Educational Strategies of the Black middle classes' is a two-year study, carried out between 2009 and 2011, which examines the educational perspectives and strategies of

Black Caribbean[2] heritage families. The project sought to bring together an analysis of race and social class in shaping the experiences of participants. Black Caribbean families were considered particularly relevant as a focus of study since available research evidence continues to indicate that pupils from these backgrounds experience some of the lowest levels of academic attainment compared with other ethnic groups irrespective of their class position. Black Caribbean pupils from non-manual backgrounds are the lowest attaining of the middle-class groups (Gillborn, 2008; Strand, 2008). Further, research has tended not to differentiate this ethnic group by social class. As researchers we were keen, therefore, to provide a detailed exploration of how race and social class intersect in the educational decisions and choices of these families.

Aware of the increasing number of Black Caribbeans who have a partner outside of their ethnic group, we decided to include families where both or just one of the parents is Black Caribbean (Platt, 2009). Participants were recruited through a range of sources that included family and education websites, Black professional networks and social groups as well as through extensive use of snow-balling via existing contacts within the Black community. Participants were selected following the completion of a brief filter questionnaire that asked specific questions about their ethnic group identification, the age of their children and their occupation. We were interested in speaking with parents who had at least one child between 8 and 18 years, age groups which encompass key transition points in the English school calendar and which would, therefore, yield potentially useful information about the process of school selection, choice and decision-making. With regard to class categorisation, we identified parents in professional or managerial occupations (i.e. NS-SEC[3] 1 and 2) – that is at the highest end of the occupational grading scale – using Government Standard Occupational Classification manuals. Sensitive to debates that centre on the absence of Black men as fathers (Reynolds, 2009), we explicitly sought to include them in our sample. Thirteen of our interviews were carried out with Black Caribbean fathers.

In total, we carried out 62 initial interviews with parents and returned a year later to conduct follow-up interviews with 15 of our original sample, 77 interviews in total. This process was found to be extremely effective in enabling us to explore in more detail themes and patterns in the data that had been revealed from our first set of interviews.

Political blackness

The research team comprised four members – myself and three colleagues who are white professors. Two are male. Despite the importance of me being a co-investigator[4] on the project, as professors, they held permanent positions in the university compared to my fixed-term, full-time position as the project researcher. This team profile reflects directly the unequal distribution by race and gender of academic staff in higher education (Equality Challenge Unit, 2011) and also speaks of the differences in status and power that often require acknowledgement and ongoing negotiation for the minoritised staff. Statistical data published by the Equality Challenge Unit (ECU) reveal that Black staff are more likely than other ethnic groups to be employed on short-term research contracts, posts that tend to provide limited opportunities for writing and the development of precisely the type of skills (e.g. grant-writing and teaching) which serve as the criteria for successful career progression. This data also tells us that a significantly higher percentage of white academics occupy professorial roles (11.1% of the white academic population) when compared with the percentage of Black academics at the same level (3.6% of Black academics are professors). The team acknowledged and discussed these inequities early in the development of the research, coming to an agreement about how journal articles would be authored and, clearly, stating our position in the research proposal:

> We are of course acutely aware of the dishonourable history of research undertaken by White researchers which has offered pathological representations of Black communities. Such portrayals arose from a research focus on the perceived differences, inadequacies and exoticisms of Black people rather than a focus on White racism. We are also aware of the impossibilities of stepping away from our raced, classed and gendered identities, and will remain sensitive to the way in which we view the world through these lenses ... We are also sensitive to the way in which the project team reflects the raced and gendered hierarchy within the academy. We have discussed the possible implications for our team dynamics and will continue to reflect on these issues throughout the course of the research. We will ensure that there are opportunities for joint writing as a project team, and that the research officer is lead author on some publications. (Vincent, Rollock, Ball, & Gillborn, 2008 – ESRC research proposal, p. 4)

As a team, we presented with varying biographies and conceptualisations of our own raced and classed identities. I am Black, of Caribbean heritage, my parents arriving to the UK from Barbados in the late 1960s. I often visited Barbados as a child with my parents. My Caribbean heritage, therefore, forms a quietly significant part of my identity, and I often refer to Barbados as home even though I was born in the UK. Had my parents pursued their career interests 'back home', they would have been classified as middle class. However, their journey of migration saw them take up working-class and lower middle-class occupations in the UK that seemed poised in perilous uncertainty in the face of ongoing racism.

I initially attended a state primary school, but being strongly committed to the possibilities that education offered (and following the recommendation of a Black teacher who noted that I was being held back by her white colleagues), I was moved to a private girls' school when I was about 8 years old. I have already discussed, at some length, the awkward and oft painful ways in which I came to race and class awareness in that space and how those moments of otherness continue, albeit dressed in the apparent liberal attire of post-racial progression, into the world of the academy (Rollock, 2012a, 2012b). My understanding of myself as a Black woman in the British context is one which is marked by experiences of racism and otherness. The starkness of this is made all the more apparent when I return 'home' to Barbados where the colonial gaze, while present in the island's history, economy and tourism, is replaced by a discernible lightness of being and sense of belonging.

I would describe myself as having a consciousness or political and lived awareness and experience of race and racism, and I am alert to and work to challenge white privilege and power inequities (Fanon, 1967; Ignatiev, 1997). These processes inform my thinking and practice and, increasingly, shape my reasons for pursuing particular lines of research enquiry. I use the term 'political blackness' or 'consciousness' to encapsulate these identities, practices and ideologies. It is, of course, possible to be Black and sit outside of or not be committed to race consciousness and activism in this way.

With regard to race and racism, my colleagues were each at different stages in understanding their own whiteness and issues of race inequity. While we acknowledged these differences sometimes, as the project progressed, we struggled to negotiate and hold on to them as a team. On occasion, it became clear that our raced positionalities meant that we recognised different processes and meanings as 'normal' or reasonable. For example, while my colleagues pondered over how we might access a large number of

Black middle-class respondents, this quite simply did not present itself as a question in my mind and, moreover, seemed relatively straightforward since not only was I part of that demographic but they – 'the Black middle classes' – were an unremarkable and normal part of my personal and professional networks.

Identifying and recruiting participants

Deciding how we would phrase the advertisement which would invite participants to take part in the study resulted in much debate with regard to conceptualisations of ethnicity and social class.

The significance of ethnicity

To simply use 'Black' to refer to ethnicity was problematic since, in the UK, it encompasses those of Caribbean *and* African heritage and, sometimes, also those of mixed (i.e. biracial) heritage. We explored whether it was the ethnicity of the child that mattered or the ethnicity of the parent. For example, would we include a white father of a Black child in our sample? In addition, we noted that there was also a small but growing body of activists who rejected the term 'Black' altogether as being steeped in a divisive post-colonial discourse that lacked any meaningful cultural connectivity.[5] We questioned whether by using the term 'Black' we might exclude those who rejected self-identification in this way. Our debates were important in revealing something of the messy complexities of identities in the UK context.

Yet while the final advertisement specifically invited response from 'Black Caribbean' parents, we were struck by the number of enquiries we received from those of Black African[6] heritage also wanting to take part. We even received an inquiry from the white middle-class mother of a (adopted) Black middle-class child asking for advice and guidance regarding her daughter's schooling. I suggest that these additional responses speak to the dire political silence around the schooling of Black children in the UK and parents' deep concern about their children's experiences within the education system.

Despite having previously worked on several projects which have focused on race, I was struck by the extent of interest that the project garnered with some people even taking the time to detail their views by email. These were often lengthy, passionate and sometimes irate communications from Black members of the public not seeking to take part in the project necessarily but querying and objecting to our proposed examination of a discernible Black middle class:

> The matter of middle class education concerns me, the reason being that it starts from a divisory basis, and therefore in my humble opinion, misses the point of undertaking this type of study ... class is laced with severe oppression and (...)[7] any form of oppression is wrong. (Project Communication, Mr A, June 2009)

> There are several points I wish to raise and the first one is why would you assume that only middle class black 'Professional Caribbean' which itself is a stereotypical viewpoint, make decisions around their children's education, as opposed to what? Those who are not middle classed and are not making any decisions? (Project Communication, Mrs X, June 2009)

There are, of course, several ways in which such correspondence can be read. As an academic, I found these communications unusual since there seemed to be an enduring assumption that the issues raised had not already been given careful consideration by the team during the design stage of the study. The emails tended to come from Black parents and/or activists deeply concerned about issues affecting their children and the Black community more broadly. Their messages, therefore, can be interpreted as being embedded within personal biographies and an historical context which has seen Black families continually disadvantaged within the education system (Coard, 1971; Gillborn, 2008; Gillborn, Rollock, Vincent, & Ball, 2012; Tomlinson, 2008) and within society more broadly (Clark & Drinkwater, 2007).

It is also likely, given the history of being studied and observed by white researchers, that there may have been an apprehension and expectation that the study was being carried out by ill-informed white academics driven by an uncritical post-colonial gaze. As Ladson-Billings pointedly reminds us, people of colour are 'often the objects but rarely the beneficiaries of research ...' (2003, p. 416). Understandably, they may not have anticipated that there would be a conscious Black researcher involved in the research or that any white researchers leading in such research would actively demonstrate a critical awareness of race. Finally, it is also feasible that some members of the public simply are not familiar with the various stages and procedures that inform academic research.

Social class as a tool of division?

The accusation that the research is focused on Black *middle class* was divisive both interested and concerned me. Claims about creating boundaries amongst Black people spoke, to my mind, to an unhelpful and outdated essentialist analysis that presupposed all Black people were the same. As the study progressed, Black colleagues, friends and even strangers, who were aware of my involvement in the research, would approach me to share their views or experiences about being Black professionals, about social class, racism or white people. Those critiquing the focus on Black middle class insisted that any such differences amongst us faded into insignificance in the light of the pervasive experiences of racism that bound us and shaped our experiences. To speak of differences not only detracted from the centrality of racism but also played into the open arms of a white society which was only too ready to embrace any argument that might minimise or trivialise the prevalence and significance of racism.

However, my most common experience was of being approached at both professional and social events[8] and congratulated for carrying out what was regarded as a highly significant piece of research that not only had historic import in terms of the experiences of Black Caribbean people in the UK but would also demonstrate to a naïve white society how the terrors of racism paid little attention to middle-class status. The project would, to their minds, make visible our otherwise invisible experiences. It would highlight the existence of a Black demographic beyond the delinquent criminalised media stereotype with which we had to contend via the low expectations and limiting assumptions of mainstream white society.

Even though I would remind people that there were other members of the team, the fact that they were white meant that they were regarded as unable to ever comprehend the complexities of racism and this, coupled with a recognition of class status and my racial politics or consciousness, meant that I was seen by Black friends and colleagues as having particular responsibility to ensure the successful completion of the study and dissemination of its findings.

Reflections about race during the interview process

Race and racism were a central aspect of the project and, hence, the research questions. As such, the team spent much time discussing how, beyond logistic considerations, we would decide who would carry out the interviews and how my white colleagues would approach (if at all) or rephrase the specific questions that asked about experiences of racism.

The race of the interviewer

While we agreed that attempts to establish 'race symmetry' between researcher and respondents would be suggestive of an narrow, essentialist interpretation of race (Phoenix, 1994), we remained sensitive to the fact that given the study's explicit focus on race, racism and social class that it was highly possible that there would be issues that some participants might feel less comfortable discussing with white researchers. We finally resolved this by offering participants two choices at the point of arranging the interview. They could tick a box indicating that they had 'no preference' with regard to the ethnicity of the researcher or they could tick to state that they preferred to 'speak with a Black researcher'. Of the 51 respondents who answered this question, the majority (37 participants) indicated they had no preference, while 14 specified wanting to speak with a Black researcher.

In hindsight, I wonder whether we ought to have been surprised at these responses since we were, in effect, presenting participants with options that due to prevalent patterns of race inequality within society, they would not necessarily have expected to have had in the first place. In other words, they would know from first-hand experience that there is a lack of diversity across the professions and would not necessarily have expected to have had the luxury of being able to choose with whom they spoke. In addition, there were a range of cultural signifiers in the leaflet that advertised the project that would have highlighted, albeit tacitly, evidence of power, status and whiteness. For example, the research was based at a high status London university, whose logo (and that of our funder) was clearly positioned at the head of the recruitment leaflet. Our respondents are used to operating in a context in which they are in a minority, and it is highly probable that this shaped their responses to our question about researcher preference. This is a subject that we explored with them during the course of the interview itself. One of our participants, Femi, had originally indicated that she had 'no preference' in terms of with whom she spoke. I asked her at the end of the interview to reflect on whether, bearing in mind her original choice, it had made a difference speaking with a Black researcher. This is her response:

> Because I studied and worked with majority white people most of my life, I probably feel as at ease talking to a white researcher as I would a Black researcher because that's what I'm used to really. It may be that I may have couched some of my comments differently had it been a white researcher. I may not have been as explicit about some of my comments. If it had been a white researcher, I think I would have wanted to maintain an image of neutrality, objectivity when it came to race, not necessarily being seen to be as pro-Black as I am, possibly, if it had been a white researcher, I might have toned it down a bit. (Femi, Psychologist)

Femi's response speaks to the tragic, inescapable relationship between whiteness and blackness, between the oppressed and the oppressor (Fanon, 1967). While stating that she would be comfortable talking to a white researcher, she, nonetheless, explains that had she been faced with that option, she would have endeavoured to moderate her responses when it came to the subject of race. This is interesting, significant and yet – if we are to analyse this through the eyes of Fanon and Critical Race Theory, both of which emphasise the role of race in shaping our acts and our consciousness – is not at all surprising. While Femi would have acquired a mask of neutrality and attempted objectivity with white researchers, we should understand this 'act' as an entirely ordinary and natural mode of operation designed to help her navigate white society and to enable her to retain some measure of humanity in a wider context in which she is minoritised. White researchers, therefore, are not neutral enquirers in conversations about race. They sit within and are part of a wider system of race inequity characterised by performances of privilege, power and entitlement. To be 'pro-Black' in this space is to display evidence of race consciousness that seeks to break free of whiteness. It is to reveal whiteness, to upset and disrupt the status quo. And as I have already intimated earlier, disruption is risky work, the reason for which Bergerson (2003) summarises thus:

> The underlying problem is that whites do not want to consider race and racism as everyday realities, because doing so requires them to face their own racist behaviors (sic) as well as the privileges that come from being white. (p. 53)

With this in mind we can, therefore, consider Femi's actions as a shrewd and highly strategic means of survival within mainstream white society (Rollock, Gillborn, Vincent, & Ball, 2011). I say more about this topic later.

Discussing race during the interview

The interview data also allowed us to consider how discussions about race and racism might vary or be differently inflected according to the race of the interviewer. There are, as Leonardo and Porter (2010) maintain, rules and regulations often unspoken that surround and infuse conversations about race between whites and people of colour; Femi's comment (above) speaks to just some of the acts of compromise and identity management that are required. She is not alone, amongst our participants, in her awareness and navigation of these race rules. Simon, who works as a school teacher, explains that an understanding of what he characterises as a 'unique Black experience' plays a significant role in shaping the interaction and tone between interviewer and interviewee:

> A Black researcher knows what you are talking about and that is (…) not a Black glove in your hand, [this is not] the 1968 Olympics. It's not anything like that (…) there is a big thing about the Black experience. And even if we all have individual experiences you know as Black people in general, the Black experience is unique, obviously. My experience as a Black person is not exactly the same [as yours] but there are definitely connections in terms of Black experience. I'm not necessarily saying that a white researcher can't research Black issues because I think that would be ridiculous and that is not what I am saying but I think, I just think it's different (…) if there was a white man sitting there I wouldn't change my answers but perhaps in some of the way I answered the questions … the question that comes back might not have been the same (…) it may be that the questions when I came back with some of the answers you may have understood the answer and then take it in a direction knowing that you are talking to Black male. And you may be able to relate to some of the experiences.

Simon's comment is particularly pertinent because it attends rightly to the fluidity of Black identities while, simultaneously, emphasising the unifying impact of racism. Again, we are alerted to the possible dangers of talking about race with whites. In evoking the image of the Black Power salute at the 1968 Olympics, Simon like Femi recognises that he could be positioned – misrecognised – as being 'overly' Black or militant in his analysis of race because it sits outside of and challenges the comforts of whiteness. While this does not mean that white researchers should avoid race research, he insists that there is likely to be a qualitative difference in the detail, essence and direction of their work. A similar observation is made by Duster (1999) writing in the foreword of 'Race-ing Research, Researching Race'. Commenting on research, involving white and African-American researchers, carried out with African-Americans about sickle-cell disease, he notes that:

> Some of the most important 'concerns and issues' never surfaced for exploration with white interviewers, because the group being interviewed never headed down the road to frame the question such a manner in the first place. (Duster, 1999, p. xiii)

This is an interesting and important observation. The inequalities and regulations of race that govern society also come to bear in the context of the interview, shaping its richness and direction. There are common responses to racism that can also take place within the interview setting and of which many of our participants were aware. I mentioned false empathy earlier. Another, common response when talking with whites about racism is that such blatant and irrational injustice must provoke anger.[9] While this obviously can be the case, I contend that racism is such a normal and unremarkable aspect of our lives that many people of colour in fact work to develop a repertoire of strategies and responses (anger may well be amongst them) – a unique form of cultural capital – in order to stay sane. Anger simply does not hold as a long-term strategy:

> People of color (sic) sometimes overlook white violence *so they can get through their daily life* [emphasis in original]. Like a child who has been abused, people of color avoid white violence by strategically playing along, a practice that whites, whose racial development stunts their growth, underestimate when they mistake consensus as the absence of coercion. Like abused children who do not possess the ability to consent and defend themselves against the verbal and physical power of a parent, *people of color have become masters at deflection. This is how they secure safety in violent circumstances.* (Leonardo & Porter, 2010, p. 151, emphases added)

Therefore, respondents' claims that they have no preference with regard to researcher ethnicity – and even in one case retorting to a white colleague who queried this that 'I would talk to a brick' – must be understood within this wider context of race politics. Rather than, as Leonardo and Porter contend, not possessing 'the ability to consent and defend' ourselves, sometimes we must make a conscious choice about the inevitable pitfalls of acting. Ability may be suppressed and not used because it is dangerous to do otherwise. As Fanon (1967, p. 23) pointedly reminds us 'it is understandable that the first action of the black man is *reaction* (…) since the Negro is appraised in terms of the extent of his assimilation'. The 'Black man' to borrow from Fanon, therefore, learns early on the rules that govern his existence and assimilation in white society. My point here is that discussing race with a white person is fraught with risk. Therefore, for a white researcher to ask a Black respondent whether speaking with them has made a difference is to overlook this politics – to pretend that the regulations and rules of race as conceived, imposed and enforced by whites, do not in fact exist. It is to imply that it is possible to speak freely or to act independently from the bounds of white violence. Since such violence comes in many guises – even in the form of seemingly innocuous research questions about race – the best means for survival, to outdo the introduction of this potentially new violence, this trickery, is to deploy the highly accomplished skill of deflection. This strategic calculation enables people of colour to retain some degree of safety, something near to a humanising existence within white society.

These are calculations and assessments that I too have depended upon for survival. I speak, colloquially, of 'sussing out' whites to determine where they have reached in their journey of race consciousness. I pay attention to the tendency to revert to other inequalities when race is raised, to the willingness to discuss their own whiteness, the preparedness to acknowledge privilege and racial differences and to be proactive in the face of racism. Such experience was present and came to bear during my interviews with Black middle-class respondents. My reaction and subsequent questioning was borne from the positioning of my political blackness even while I retained a rigorous academic lens. Sometimes when some act of racism was mentioned, I simply nodded in empathetic acknowledgement, but even this – a well-placed and paced nod – can be enough to signal a profound understanding of and connection with the issues. Even when I sought to leave my political positioning, quietly observing from the corner of the room, participants' accounts of their schooling forced it back, demanding involvement in the conversation. This was especially the case with female respondents whose retrospective accounts of their schooling, recalled in me a familiar white gaze that inquired about my hair, my bottom and the colour of my skin. I noted the energy, the passion and the expressions that accompanied the retelling of these formative episodes; their code-switching – moment-arily lapses into Patois – to drive home more effectively some historic account. I actively reminded myself to ask respondents to state – for the purposes of the tape and, hence, the doubting or invisible white listener – who they meant by 'we', by 'our', by 'they' and 'them' even though we both knew who 'we' and 'they' were.

As Simon earlier describes, the interview takes its direction from this understanding. Ray, one of the fathers in the project, was one of the small numbers who requested to speak with a Black researcher. He explains, when prompted, his reasoning for this towards the end of his interview:

> [It felt justified] in as much as I didn't feel either patronised or the subject of some kind of false empathy. And very often we … I find myself in the situation where people think, that's the truth of what happened to you and [I'm] telling you because I want you to empathise and to [feel] sorry for me (…) because I feel the people who [are like] that haven't actually experienced and … or have no true understanding of what it's like to experience racism or different forms of disadvantage in society. So it's just a demonstration of the differences in reality and what I didn't get from you … I didn't' get a sense of some of the things that I said you were shocked by them or found it disbelieving that in this day and age you have these attitudes and [that] people are still experiencing these things. Because sometimes despite their best intention, I find researchers exist in this little cocoon and they see the world as they desire it rather than as it is.

The solution to this is not simply about race matching. That misses the complexity of racism and raced identities. From a critical perspective, this is about whiteness and blackness both of which are at the dualistic core of racism and race inequality. Thus, we can move away from conceptualising 'blackness' and 'whiteness' as mere representations of colour, to thinking instead about them as concepts of political investment and activism:

> Politically, whiteness is the willingness to seek a comfortable place within the system of race privilege. Blackness means total, implacable, and relentless opposition to that system. To the extent so-called whites oppose the race line, repudiate their own race privileges, and jeopardize their own standing in the white race that can be said to have washed away their whiteness and taken in some blackness. Probably a black person should not accept a white person's claim to have done that, but should watch how that person acts. (Ignatiev, 1997, p. 609)

This political standpoint moves us beyond an essentialist conceptualisation of race and raced identities. Therefore, my articulation of 'sussing out', in fact, means seeking to determine not only the awareness whites have of their privilege but also as a non-negotiable implicated aspect of this, whether they endeavour to act in ways that problematise and lessen their power and privilege; in short, whether they are moving towards being 'traitors' to their race (Ignatiev, 1997). Racism through this lens recognises that becoming politicised – becoming Black – is an ongoing journey or process of growing, awareness and reflection. It requires a preparedness to become immersed in the discomforts of racism and to move beyond a liberal stance. And just as we can speak of whites as being traitors to their race and investing in blackness, it is possible to do the same in relation to people of colour.

Fluidity of black identity

So far, I have set out an argument that centres on a notion of race consciousness and awareness of racism. However, it is important to note that not all participants in the Black middle classes study positioned themselves in this way. Some (a minority) downplayed any personal awareness or experience of racism and regarded the colour of their skin as a mere incidental, non-consequential aspect of their person. The ways in which these particular respondents spoke about race was discernibly less rich and detailed than those who were more closely located within a political notion of blackness.

These less-conscious participants tended to valorise the merits of hard work which they saw as directly and unequivocally leading to reward and success. There was less or no evidence in their interviews of a collective notion of a Black 'we' and nor was there much acknowledgement or discussion of inequality and discrimination. I also noted that I felt differently in these interviews; they had a different energy about them. There was no sense of connection which had resulted in invitations to dinner or long heartfelt hugs at the end of other interviews as had been the case with some other participants. Consider, for example, the extract in which I have just asked Miles (senior manager) about the role of ethnicity in shaping his experiences:

> I don't put it [ethnicity] high on my agenda (...) I will give you an example (...) I must have been, about 17 or 18 I was a (...) and we were serving at [a prestigious dinner] with (...) 3000 people at [grand historic venue in Central London] and there were a couple of guys with me who said, 'Miles do you realise you are the only Black bloke here?' and I kind of looked around and went, 'Oh yeah you're right'. That is because I don't see myself as being a colour, I don't see people as being White or Black (...) I don't tolerate racist jokes but at the same time I am not somebody who sits there and thinks I should be acting like a stereotype of this or that, I just act in the way that I want to in any situation.
>
> Researcher: And so how do you manage situations that are racist. I mean you talked about that incident when you were 17, but as an adult, how do you manage situations that are about your race?
>
> Very rarely do I feel that there is a racist incident that comes up.

There are several aspects of this extract which warrant comment. However, for the purposes of this paper, I am interested in the way in which Miles not only minimises awareness of his racial identity but, in stating that he does not see colour, actively assumes a colour-blind position that is frequently associated with whites. After all, in order to not see colour he must be aware it is there in the first place.[10] This denial is reinforced by his declaration that he rarely – despite his workplace being majority white – experiences racism. Within politically Black spaces, he would be regarded as being only symbolically or superficially Black. He lacks race consciousness. If we take as the starting point of our analysis, the prevalence of racism within white society and acknowledge the symbiotic relationship been the coloniser and colonised, then we must view Miles' response as embedded within this same dialectic. Fanon again proves useful here:

> Fanon's anger is directed not towards the 'black man' but the proposition that he is required not only to be black but he must be black in relation to the white man. It is the internalization or rather as Fanon calls it epidermalization, of this inferiority that concerns him. When the black man comes into contact with the white world he goes through an experience of sensitization. His ego collapses. His self-esteem evaporates. He ceases to be a self-motivated person. The entire purpose of his behaviour is to emulate the white man, to become like him, and thus hope to be accepted as man. (Sardar, 2008 p. xiii)

Therefore, rather than being free of binds of colour and racism, Miles' reaction is precisely that – a relational act, perhaps originally conceived as a strategy to survive and be successful – within the context of whiteness.

Participants' investments

The 'sussing out' or calculations I described earlier are not simply directed at whites. It is also an act carried out between people of colour to determine their extent of political awareness. Participants knew there was a Black researcher on the project (and in some cases had elected to speak with me), yet this was not enough to give them key information about my political leanings. Therefore, when I arrived to carry out their interview and while formal hellos were being exchanged, I was silently 'checked out'. My natural hair which I tended to wear in twists drew assumptions about my politics and blackness long before I even sat down and interspersed the conversation with empathetic nods (Lorde, 2009; Weekes, 1997). Interviews had been set up by email or, in some instances, over the telephone, so it was only on meeting me that participants who had indicated that they had no preference with whom they spoke knew I was Black. Then, meanings were read into my Black skin, assessments were about my age and, hence, my biography and even my professional status to establish a picture of the kind of blackness that I might embody and the kind of life that I might have had:

> It's been easier [having a Black researcher] … I've made an assumption that your parents are first generation migrated here and I've made an assumption that you've had probably some of the same kind of hardships that I've had. And you might not have. You might've been one of the ones that got dropped off and then put into foster care. You could've had any manner of things (…) Wherever your background was in this country, it's very difficult for it to be easy. (Patricia, Resources Manager, Local Government)

Patricia's comment is interesting precisely because it is an assumption. At no stage during the interview did I share with her aspects of my politics or biography. Yet, in this case, her assumption and the various readings she made of me granted her an ease during the interview. Another participant spoke emphatically of her pride in seeing a 'young' female Black doctor carrying out this research and how this inspired her. In this case, inequalities of gender and race intersect so that within the context of a racist, patriarchal society, my achievement became not the achievement of an individual but instead was imbued with a wider political significance that overrode the fact that we were strangers and that it was the first time that we had met.

My political blackness and embodied Black identity worked alongside my academic status (i.e. holding a Ph.D.) to facilitate in participants a degree of investment and trust in the project. My presence, connection and blackness minimised, to their mind, the element of risk associated with being 'the researched'. As the project developed, so did the expectation that I would bring the findings to the attention of mainstream white society. I became the conduit for delivering the message – our message – accurately to the masses. This was both a privilege and a simultaneous weight on my consciousness:[11] The emotional profundity of this investment is exemplified by Margaret:

> I don't put my heart on the line for anyone and unfortunately (…) there is that degree of trust that I have with someone who comes from a very similar background to me who I'm hoping will be able to say, 'you know what, when she said that, I can't pretend to get into her head but some of the stuff she said resonates with me, so actually when we're digesting this, editing this, I understand what she meant by that'. (…) I don't think that someone from another ethnic background could have understood that. (Margaret, Senior Corporate Manager, Private Sector)

While I was honoured and humbled by the hopes that participants like Margaret and Black colleagues and friends had invested in me as an advocate for our experiences, there were moments during the course of the project that I found this expectation difficult to manage. While I largely understood and had endured similar experiences as those described by participants, I also existed and was carrying out the research within a predominantly white academic space which tended to demonstrate very little proactive engagement with race. I often felt as though I was oscillating between two starkly contrasting worlds. As such, it would feel like a disservice and betrayal to participants, to bring their pained, raced experiences to this world that seemed only interested in race as the subject of voyeuristic research. I shared some of these concerns with my colleagues who reminded me that the study was important precisely because it was naming the experiences of an otherwise invisible Black middle class. While I agreed with them, I retained a burning discomfort about merely sharing our findings through academic journal articles and conferences that would be attended by simply other academics. To my mind, we needed to do more than simply report the findings; we needed to do something that would have a wider significance to the lives of Black middle-class families.

Dissemination and impact

The central finding of the Black middle-classes project was that despite possessing the resources, knowledge and capitals to engage with the education system, Black middle-class parents, nonetheless, encounter resistance, low expectations and a lack of support from teachers and school staff. Their class status served to provide some though limited protection from incidents of racism (Vincent, Rollock, Ball, & Gillborn, 2011).[12]

While the project's findings did not surprise me, they disturbed me. The countless stories of pain, of determination, of frustration in the face of low teacher expectations and stereotyping as recounted by Black families we spoke with across England, frustrated me. I was struck by the countless ways in which parents had sought to engage with their child's schooling but had been met with surprise or resistance. Mainly, I was moved and saddened by the desperate isolation of these Black middle-class parents who were, by and large, working hard to offer the best for their children irrespective of racism. So while we had plans to publish in various high-status journals and also held two seminar events, for me, this was not enough, and I set about exploring ways of sharing the findings more broadly.

Months before we sent out a press release, I spoke regularly and off the record with select journalists, with whom I had an existing relationship, to alert them to the imminent findings. I managed to secure exclusive coverage of the research in *The Guardian* (a widely read, left of centre national broadsheet). This coverage provoked a flurry of debate largely from a Black professional readership who had not, *The Guardian* latter told us, previously engaged in their online discussions in such high numbers. In fact, such was the response that *The Guardian* ran a special pull-out section the following day, featuring a selection of readers' comments.

My frustration not yet abated, I also contacted two prominent Black politicians, each of whom had a particular passion for education and met with them individually to discuss the research. I worked closely with one to co-host a private event comprising leading Black business people, activists and parents to discuss the research findings and to come up with specific ideas that could be implemented to support Black families in their attempts to successfully educate their children.

I then took those ideas and developed a small pilot study called Parents' Strategies into Education and Employment (SEE), which I am running with the Runnymede Trust. Through this action research, we hold small conversation groups with Black parents to find out from them what their challenges have been when engaging with the education system and how they have addressed them. Parents share ideas and strategies with each other, the ultimate aim being to help them connect with and support one another to eventually develop a wider network of support for Black parents across the country.

It was important to me that the Black middle-classes project did not simply state what I and many other Black middle classes already know – that we experience racism. While this might be news to mainstream white society, I was concerned that the legacy of the project was more than this. The research needed to be *for* us, not simply *about* us. This, in part, is my response to the investment and trust that was placed in me and also is informed by my political positioning.

Concluding thoughts

I have sought, in this paper, to reveal some of the behind-the-scenes deliberations, reflections and complexities that shaped the development of a two-year study into the educational experiences of the Black middle classes. In particular, I have considered my role as the only researcher within the team who not only shared the same race and class position as our respondents but also would describe myself as being politically conscious or aware. These considerations led me to revisit the debate on interviewer–interviewee race matching, paying particular attention to key factors such as the interview topic and the extent of race awareness or consciousness on the part of the researcher. I have argued that the concern in such debates ought not to be solely fixed on race symmetry per se, rather should focus on the political awareness of the researcher and their proactive engagement with the notion of whiteness and blackness.

Having said this, bearing in mind that whiteness is usually evidenced in white people, white researchers electing to carry out race research have a particular responsibility to critically reflect upon and demonstrate awareness of these issues. They must remain alert to and report on the dynamics of race and their responses to it. To do so not only ensures the development of critically reflexive practice but also remains crucial to making the processes of whiteness visible. To do otherwise, to remain silent about these processes even while researching race is to enact and endorse a paradigm interred in racial division and hierarchy:

> Trendy cultural critique that is in no way linked to a concern with critical pedagogy or liberation hinders this process [of decolonization]. When white critics write about black culture 'cause it's the "in" subject without interrogating their work to see whether or not it helps perpetuate and maintain racist domination, they participate in the commodification of 'blackness' that is so peculiar to postmodern strategies of colonization. (Hooks, 1990, p. 8)

Coming from the radical position of my blackness, the Black middle-classes project needed to live beyond the white ivory towers of the academy, to be more than journal articles to be read by other academics and to be more than the focus of debates at seminars and conferences. It needed to be political; about changing the lives of those of us in the margins.

Acknowledgement

Economic & Social Research Council Project Reference RES-062-23-1880.

Notes

1. That is, member of faculty.
2. Within the UK, the term 'Black Caribbean' is used to refer to Black families who can identify their heritage as being from the Caribbean. It is a term that can be applied to first-generation Caribbean families (who migrated to the UK in significant numbers in the 1950s and 1960s) as well as to subsequent, younger generations.
3. National Standard, Socio-Economic Classification.
4. In other words, contributing equally to the project development, design and funding application.
5. These campaigners seek to reclaim the use of 'African' as more appropriately defining the identities of those of Caribbean and African heritage (The African Or Black Question http://taobq.blogspot.co.uk/search/label/TAOBQ, accessed 17 November 2012).
6. That is those Black families who can identify their heritage as being from the continent of Africa. As with 'Black Caribbean', 'Black African' can apply across generation and is not limited to those born in Africa per se.
7. Within quoted text, '...' denotes a pause while '(...)' indicates where text has been edited for brevity or clarity.
8. These social events included dinner parties, public talks and gatherings that largely attracted a Black middle-class demographic mainly of whom had initially met through professional circles. Sometimes the boundaries between my professional and social networks blur. Experiences of racism and class position serve or inform, in some ways, the boundaries of Black middle class space.
9. This in itself can be regarded as a type of false empathy.
10. Although clearly due to issues of power, this has different implications for a white person compared to Black.
11. One Black colleague laughed when I explained the situation to him, referring to it as the 'Obama effect' to denote the high expectations that many Black people across the world had invested in the first, then recently elected, Black President of America. The Black middle-classes project began in 2009, the same year that Barack Obama began his first term.
12. While the definition of middle class varies, quite fundamentally, these findings echo research about the African-American middle class carried out in the USA (e.g. Lacy, 2007; Moore, 2008; Patillo-Mckoy, 1999).

References

Ahmed, S. (2009). Embodying diversity: Problems and paradoxes for Black feminists. *Race, Ethnicity & Education, Special Issue Black Feminisms and Postcolonial Paradigms: Researching Educational Inequalities, 12*(1), 41–52. doi:10.1080/13613320802650931

Ali, S. (2009). Black feminist praxis: Some reflections on pedagogies and politics in higher education. *Race, Ethnicity & Education, Special Issue Black Feminisms and Postcolonial Paradigms: Researching Educational Inequalities, 12*(1), 79–86. doi:10.1080/13613320802650998

Bergerson, A. A. (2003). Critical race theory and white racism: Is there room for white scholars in fighting racism in education? *International Journal for Qualitative Studies in Education, 16*(1), 51–63. doi:10.1080/0951839032000033527.

Brah, A., & Phoenix, A. (2004). Ain't I a woman? Revisiting intersectionality. *Journal of International Women's Studies, 5*(3), 75–86.

Clark, K., & Drinkwater, S. (2007). *Ethnic minorities and the labour market*. York: Joseph Rowntree Foundation.

Coard, B. (1971). *How the west Indian child is made educationally subnormal in the British school system: The scandal of the black child in British schools*. London: Beacon Books.

Crenshaw, K. (2009). Mapping the margins: Intersectionality, identity politics and violence against women of color. In E. Taylor, D. Gillborn, & G. Ladson-Billings (Eds.), *Foundations of Critical Race Theory in education* (pp. 213–246). New York, NY & London: Routledge.

Delgado, R. (1989). Storytelling for oppositionists and others: A plea for narrative. *Michigan Law Review, 87*(8), 2411–2441. doi:10.2307/1289308

Delgado, R. (1996). Rodrigo's eleventh chronicle: Empathy and false empathy. *California Law Review, 84*(1), 61–100. doi:10.2307/3480903

Duster, T. (1999). Foreword. In J. W. Twine Warren & F. Winddance (Eds.), *Race-ing research, researching race: Methodological dilemmas in Critical Race Studies* (pp. xi–xiv). New York: New York University Press.

Egharevba, I. (2001). Researching an-'other' minority ethnic community: Reflections of a black female researcher on the intersections of race, gender and other power positions on the research process. *International Journal of Social Research Methodology, 4*(3), 225–241. doi:10.1080/13645570010023760

Equality Challenge Unit. (2011). *Equality in higher education: Statistical report, 2011*. London: Author.

Fanon, F. (1967). *Black skin, white masks*. London: Pluto Books.

Gillborn, D. (2008). *Race and racism: Coincidence or conspiracy*? New York, NY & London: Routledge.

Gillborn, D., Rollock, N., Vincent, C., & Ball, S. J. (2012). 'You got a pass, what more do you want?' Race, class and gender intersections in the educational experiences of the black middle classes. *Race, Ethnicity & Education, Special Issue on Critical Race Theory in England, 15*(1), 121–139. doi:10.1080/13613324.2012.638869

Hooks, B. (1990). *Yearning: Race, gender and cultural politics*. Boston, MA: South End Press.

Ignatiev, N. (1997). Treason to whiteness is loyalty to humanity: An interview with Noel Ignatiev of Race Traitor Magazine. In R. Delgado & J. Stefancic (Eds.), *Critical white studies: Looking behind the mirror* (pp. 607–612). Philadelphia, PA: Temple.

Lacy, K. (2007). *Blue-chip black: Race, class and status in the new black middle class*. Berkeley, Los Angeles: University of California Press.

Ladson-Billings, G. (2003). Racialised discourses and ethnic epistemologies. In N. K. Denzin & Y. S. Lincoln (Eds.), *The landscape of qualitative research: Theories and issues* (pp. 398–432). London: Sage.

Ladson-Billing, G., & Donnor, J. (2008). The moral activist role of Critical Race Theory scholarship. In N. K. Denzin & Y. S. Lincoln (Eds.), *The landscape of qualitative research* (3rd ed., pp. 279–302). London and Los Angeles, CA: Sage.

Leonardo, Z., & Porter, R. K. (2010). Pedagogy of fear: Toward a Fanonian theory of 'safety' in race dialogue. *Race, Ethnicity & Education, 13*(2), 139–157. doi:10.1080/13613324.2010.482898.

Lorde, A. (2009). Is your hair still political? In R. P. Byrd, J. B. Cole, & B. Guy-Sheftall (Eds.), *I am your sister: Collected and unpublished writings of Audre Lorde*. New York, NY: Oxford University Press.

Macpherson, W. (1999). *The Stephen Lawrence inquiry*. London: TSO.

Maylor, U. (2009). Is it because I'm black? A black female research experience. *Race, Ethnicity & Education, 12*(1), 53–64. doi:10.1080/13613320802650949

Mirza, H. S. (2009). Plotting a history: Black and postcolonial feminisms in 'new times'. *Race, Ethnicity & Education, Special Issue Black Feminisms and Postcolonial Paradigms: Researching Educational Inequalities, 12*(1), 1–10. doi:10.1080/13613320802650899

Moore, K. S. (2008). Class formations: Competing forms of black middle-class identity. *Ethnicities, 8*(4), 492–517. doi:10.1177/1468796808097075

Patillo-McKoy, M. (1999). *Black picket fences: Privilege and peril among the black middle class.* Chicago, IL: University of Chicago Press.

Phoenix, A. (1994). Practising feminist research: The intersection of gender and 'race' in the research process. In M. Maynard & J. Purvis (Eds.), *Researching women's lives from a feminist perspective* (pp. 49–71). London: Taylor & Francis.

Platt, L. (2009). Ethnicity and family: Relationships within and between ethnic groups. In *An analysis using the Labour Force Survey.* Essex: University of Essex, Institute for Social & Economic Research.

Reynolds, T. (1997). Class matters, 'race' matters, gender matters. In P. Mahony & C. Zmroczek (Eds.), *Class matters: 'Working class' women's perspectives on social class* (pp. 9–18). London: Taylor & Francis.

Reynolds, T. (2009). Exploring the absent/present dilemma: Black fathers, family relationships, and social capital in Britain. *The Annals of the American Academy of Political and Social Science, 624*(1), 12–28. doi:10.1177/0002716209334440

Rollock, N. (2012a). The invisibility of race: Intersectional reflections on the liminal space of alterity. *Race, Ethnicity & Education, Special Issue on Critical Race Theory in England, 15*(1), 65–84. doi:10.1080/13613324.2012.638864.

Rollock, N. (2012b). Unspoken rules of engagement: Navigating racial microaggressions in the academy terrain. *International Journal of Qualitative Studies in Education, 25*(5), 517–532. doi:10.1080/09518398.2010.543433

Rollock, N., Gillborn, D., Vincent, C., & Ball, S. (2011). The public identities of the black middle classes: Managing race in public spaces. *Sociology, 45*(6), 1078–1093. doi:10.1177/0038038511416167.

Sardar, Z. (2008). Foreword to the 2008 edition. In F. Fanon (Ed.), *Black skin, white masks* (pp. vi–xx). London: Pluto Books.

Strand, S. (2008). *Minority ethnic pupils in the longitudinal survey of young people in England: Extension report on performance in public examinations at age 16.* DCSFRR029. London: DCSF.

Tate, W. F. (1997). Critical Race Theory and education: History, theory and implications. *Review of Research in Education, 22*(1), 195–247. doi:10.3102/0091732X022001195.

Tomlinson, S. (2008). *Race and education: Politics and policy in Britain.* Berkshire: Open University Press.

Vincent, C., Rollock, N., Ball, S., & Gillborn, D. (2008). *The educational strategies of the black middle classes.* Economic & Social Research Council Final Grant Proposal.

Vincent, C., Rollock, N., Ball, S., & Gillborn, D. (2011). *The educational strategies of the black middle classes.* Project report. London: Institute of Education.

Weekes, D. (1997). Shades of blackness: Young female constructions of beauty. In H. S. Mirza (Ed.), *Black British feminism: A reader* (pp. 113–126). London: Routledge.

Wynter, S. (1992). *Do not call us Negros: How 'multicultural' textbooks perpetuate racism.* San Francisco, CA: Aspire Books.

Race talk and school equity in local print media: the discursive flexibility of whiteness and the promise of race-conscious talk

Sofia A. Villenas[a] and Sophia L. Angeles[b]

[a]Department of Anthropology, Cornell University, Ithaca, NY, USA; [b]Department of Counseling and Educational Development, University of North Carolina-Greensboro, Greensboro, NC, USA

This article examines how a progressive, rural/small city community in the USA wrestles with race, racism, and school equity in the public arena of print media. It inquires into the tensions, limitations, and possibilities for race-conscious discourse in the face of both explicit racist hate speech and benevolent liberal race talk. Based on ethnographic and cultural discourse analyses of local print media, this article draws from critical race and whiteness theories to examine how racist hate speech, occurring in a non-education context of a police-related tragedy, and benevolent liberal race talk on school equity issues mutually reinforce the logic of white racial dominance. It also locates the possibilities of race-conscious talk as generative speech that demands a response.

Introduction

Print media is a site of production and contestation for race and equity talk in local communities. It produces and reproduces, constitutes and re-inscribes ideas about how the world is racially organized, and about how race and racism are to be understood and acted upon, particularly in the arenas of education and schooling. Print media professionals powerfully shape public discourse through choice of words, pictures, topics, placement of articles, and framing of storylines (Richardson, 2007). Local community members also work hard to shape this discursive arena through opinion pieces and letters to the editor, and through direct communication of their criticism and demands for journalistic integrity, as well as by bestowing their praise and recognition. This article examines how a liberal-progressive college town community in the USA wrestles with race, racism, and school equity in the public arena of print media. Specifically, we examine how two local newspapers represent and constitute race and racism through various forms of race talk. We inquire into the tensions, limitations, and possibilities for race-conscious and social justice-oriented discourse to exist in the face of both explicit racial hate speech and benevolent liberal race talk.

On 10 December 2010, the *Ithaca Times* printed an unsigned opinion piece in its local weekly newspaper serving Ithaca, a small/rural city in central New York. The title of the editorial, '$175K is too much', referenced the salary of the newly appointed superintendent of the Ithaca City School District (ICSD). The opinion piece criticized the district's appointment of an African American man, arguing that race played a role in his selection. 'To the school board: Please, please, don't tell us you bent over backward to hire this guy just because he's black'. The piece went on to make the argument that poverty and class were the real issues, and ended with an unsubstantiated projection of the new superintendent: 'Real equity is going to have to start with making sure all the kids in the district get an equal shot, whether black, white, immigrant, or any other minority. This move doesn't do it'.

This opinion piece drew community outrage. In the seven letters to the editor that were published on 15 December 2010, the editorial was referred to as 'racist', 'race-baiting', 'offensive', and 'unacceptable'. Quotes from three of the letters are excerpted below:

- Your editorial '$175,000 Is Too Much' is offensive, racist, race-baiting, and poorly researched ... To claim that the school board hired him only because he's black is deeply offensive and presumptuous ... It sounds a lot to me like you are suggesting Black people should step back quietly into their 'place' because even when they rise to positions of leadership and power it won't change anything.
- I felt my gut sink at the racist and inaccurate statement .... I'm not as eloquent a writer as many here in Ithaca, and others will be able to articulate better than I can, but I felt it was important to let the author of this offensive article know that there are more people like myself (more white people, that is) that found this article disturbingly racist and off base for a public newspaper.
- Despite [his] doctorate from a very prestigious university and school of education, despite his strong overall credentials and experience working with and in a community similar to Ithaca, and despite his overwhelmingly popular candidacy for the position, he is still treated in the editorial purely on the basis of his race!! The editorial suggests he was hired only because he is black. This reveals that a highly accomplished, appropriately credentialed, professional, middle-class African American can't get respect on the basis of his record in one of the main newspapers of supposedly enlightened Ithaca! This is offensive and unacceptable!! It's also very bad journalism!!

Importantly, these letters to the editor placed full responsibility on the newspaper and its editor, referring to the publication of the opinion piece as 'very bad journalism'. They emphasized the newspaper's obligations to the community and its importance as a forum for community dialogue about race and equity. A co-written letter called for an apology and an explanation by the publisher 'as to why this community should continue to support a publication that exhibits such wanton disregard for journalistic ethics and our community's standards'. Another letter, signed by leaders of the Chamber of Commerce, invited the *Ithaca Times* to 'consider becoming a partner in the Chamber's efforts to work for equity in our community' and to take part in workplace conversations about 'equity, discrimination, cultural competence'.

Along with the letters, the *Ithaca Times*' managing editor published a 'sincere apology' to its readership, stating: 'The intent was to open dialogue about the way the Ithaca City School District proceeded with its search' and that 'the racially-insensitive language used and factual inaccuracies in the editorial undercut the true intent of the editorial and was irresponsible'. He went on to say, 'While there are race and class issues evident in both the Ithaca City School District and City of Ithaca, the approach taken in the editorial not only produced non-constructive commentary, it confused the true purpose of the piece', and that it also did a great disservice to the newly arriving superintendent. The managing editor also explained that unusual circumstances prevented him from vetting the editorial prior to publication. He then affirmed the mission of the *Ithaca Times* as a community newspaper with a duty to have 'the difficult discussions about the tough issues that face the City of Ithaca and the surrounding communities'. He concluded by inviting the public to help the *Ithaca Times* in this endeavor.

A year and half later, the *Ithaca Times* featured an article entitled '*Ithaca Times* Editor among ... Community Award Honorees' (Hart, 2012). Following a detailed description of the joint anniversary celebrations of two community organizations, the article reported that the *Ithaca Times*' managing editor was a recipient of the Rere Sojourner Hassett Social Justice Award, given to a community member 'who is an advocate for social and racial justice'. The presenter of the award is quoted as saying, 'The change that he has made in this community is phenomenal ... We went from newspaper after newspaper of white people only on the cover, only white people in the inquiring photographer, to this'. The presenter then noted a host of articles covering events and issues about race and diversity. The editor accepted the award and thanked community members for communicating regularly with the paper and for providing ideas and stories.

We begin with this somewhat lengthy story concerning the *Ithaca Times* because it serves to highlight two important ideas and arguments in this article. First, print media provides a site for a full range of sanctioned and unsanctioned race talk to circulate – in articles, letters, and online forums. Indeed, it is precisely this range of race talk that provides an opportunity to identify, even if momentarily and quite locally, the constitutive elements of race talk and how it works. In the above opinion piece and the rejoinders, we see at least three different kinds of race talk taking place simultaneously in Ithaca's print media – racist hate speech, race-conscious talk, and benevolent liberal race talk.

To summarize from the story above, explicit, racially motivated speech that positions People of Color as inferior and Whites as superior, or *racist hate speech* (see Delgado & Stefancic, 2004), drew public outrage, particularly among community leaders. The managing editor of the *Ithaca Times* publically declared the '$175K' opinion piece to be 'unconstructive' to a dialogue on race issues. In a progressive community, this kind of race talk in print media is usually relegated to the margins of online replies and commentaries. Next, *race-conscious talk* was evident in the letters to the editor. Race consciousness, as community leader Ms. Michelle-Nunn explained on the locally syndicated radio show 'All Things Equal' on WHCU, 'requires an understanding of how, historically, racism has been structured over the years and how it has been built into our institutions' (8 May 2012) (see also Peller, 1995). The race-conscious speech in the letters to the *Ithaca Times* unmasked the racist hate speech and the systemic nature of racial discrimination. We also see how speakers of race-conscious talk, including the letter writers and the award presenter above, have acted in explicit ways to influence changes in newspaper content, to feature more people of color and events taking place in communities of color, and to keep critical conversations about race and racism on the table. Lastly, *benevolent liberal race talk* exemplifies the 'new racialism' perspective (Chang, 2002). The '$175K' opinion piece used racist hate speech, but it also drew on benevolent liberal racism to make the case for a class-trumps-race perspective in the name of advocating for all kids' success. Racial disparities were thus explained as natural outcomes of a meritocratic and free market society, and the responsibility for success and failure was individualized. In the benevolent version, families and youths need to be helped in assimilating and changing their culture, language, habits, and outlook (see Villenas, 2002). Race is used to describe, recognize, and care for minoritized youth, but is then decontextualized from structural racism. This sanctioned discourse has dominated local media.

The *Ithaca Times* example also illustrates another point. These various race discourses are connected and interdependent in ways that may limit the discursive power of race-conscious talk for directing school equity and other racial justice efforts. As we shall see, benevolent liberal race talk works in tandem with racist hate speech on the margins. The '$175K' opinion piece used both racist hate speech and benevolent liberal race talk, but the latter did not receive attention in the race-conscious letters to the editor, which were focused on addressing the more blatant racist hate speech. As will later be explored, similar benevolent liberal race arguments have appeared in many other opinion pieces and articles about school equity issues in the local newspapers. These have not generated print controversy except as the target of racist hate speech in the online forum, thus adding credence to the 'non-racist' positioning of benevolent liberal race talk. We argue that in a progressive community, racist hate speech on the margins and benevolent liberal race talk are mutually reinforcing in ways that may limit the power of race-conscious talk; benevolent liberal racism draws its discursive power precisely from the silencing and distraction that marginalized hate speech generates. In comparison with racist hate speech, benevolent liberal race talk is perceived as objective, caring, and empathetic, even as it responds in varying ways to race-conscious speech.

This article is based on an ethnographic and cultural discourse analysis of local print media in Ithaca, New York. We draw from critical race and whiteness theories – in particular, the ideas of flexible whiteness (Leonardo, 2009), and racist hate speech (Delgado & Stefancic, 2004; Lawrence, 1990; Matsuda, 1989) – to examine how a progressive community actively accommodates race-conscious speech and tolerates marginalized racist hate speech in local media in ways that reinforce the discursive power of white racial dominance. We explore these questions by highlighting how racist hate speech occurring in a non-education case of a police-related tragedy and benevolent liberal race talk occurring on school equity issues mutually constitute the logic of white racial dominance. We found that in a small city/rural community, it is important to study race talk in education alongside race talk concerning other institutions, such as law enforcement. In these instances, we also locate the possibilities of race-conscious talk – which gains momentum across issues of law enforcement and education – as generative speech that demands a response.

An 'enlightened' community: race-conscious talk in a liberal-progressive college town

In order to contextualize race talk in a liberal-progressive community, we highlight Ithaca's characteristics as a college town, which, according to Gumprecht (2003), is a peculiarly US American phenomenon. Like many college towns across the USA, Ithaca's economy and social life have been profoundly shaped by the education industry and collegiate culture (Gumprecht, 2003). Gumprecht notes that college towns are different from other types of cities or towns in that they are youthful places with a highly educated population. They are also transient places, comparatively cosmopolitan and unconventional, and characterized by 'higher concentrations of people who listen to National Public Radio, vote Green or belong to a food co-op' (Gumprecht, 2003, p. 55). Importantly, college towns are viewed as bastions of liberal politics, particularly those with flagship or elite private universities. Ithaca, with its city population of 30,000 and county population of 101,564, is considered to be the center of left-leaning politics in the region and surrounding counties. It is embedded in a long history of social movements for racial justice (most notably the underground railroad during slavery), and women's rights.

Current left-leaning political movements in Ithaca include activism for environmental sustainability, food justice, labor, human rights and racial justice, immigration/refugee sanctuary, and educational equity. As opposed to conservative cities, public talk (or tolerance of talk) about diversity and race/racism is part of what it means to be liberal-progressive in Ithaca. Race-conscious talk is amplified in Ithaca because of both its small size and its cosmopolitanism. Furthermore, Ithaca's designation as the most 'enlightened' city in the USA (see Spayde, 1997) provides a shared point of reference that begins many public conversations across the political spectrum. Conservative voices in newspaper commentary forums issue harsh critiques against 'left-leaning libs', mocking their liberal intolerance and 'unenlightened' adherence to political correctness at the expense of Whites. Other voices articulate what is felt to be the hypocrisy of maintaining the veneer of an 'enlightened' community despite Ithaca's economic and racial inequities. Ithaca's 'enlightened' label is one thing people agree to argue about.

Ithaca's specific history and status as a liberal-progressive college town affords it a larger platform, one from which race-conscious talk is amplified in comparison with other more conservative or mainstream cities of similar size. Relatively speaking, race-conscious talk has a presence in local city government, the school board, the media, and other institutions. At the same time, Ithaca is typically US American in its race talk. For example, people of color are racialized in the contexts of both a Black–White binary and strict White and non-White racial categorizations, as compared to other countries such as Brazil or South Africa, which have more fluid race-class identifications (see Laurie Olsen, 2008, on immigrant students' racialization in a California high school). Ithaca's race talk also fits patterned cultural practices typical of the USA in the twenty-first century (see Pollock, 2004). People *expect* a racialized social order that favors Whites and disenfranchises people of color – particularly in terms of wealth, schools, and prisons – but simultaneously *refuse* to talk in racial terms (see Pollock, 2004). Finally, liberal talk regarding diversity and equality – and simultaneous silence about inequities in outcomes – is similar to that in other communities (see Brantlinger, 2003; Castagno, 2009; Kailin, 1999). As we shall see, however, Ithaca's unusually amplified race-conscious talk explicitly works to present a challenge to white dominance or whiteness-as-usual.

Flexible whiteness and racist hate speech: a conceptual map

In a community that, relatively speaking, regularly engages in public conversations about race, racism, and equity, how is it that the great majority of economically secure White community members do not have to talk about it at all, yet still accrue the material benefits from benevolent liberal discourse and 'low grade racism' (Delgado & Stefancic, 2004) that are maintained by marginalized racist hate speech? In a historical and qualitative study of the ICSD, Eversley Bradwell (2009) conceptualized the cyclical nature of violent racial conflicts in the community, including interracial conflicts in the secondary schools, and the enduring systemic racial disparities within ICSD as a repeating time-loop of educational excellence, educational failure, and paradoxical resistance. The paradox, he explains, refers to a continuing history of *resistance to oppression* via cross-racial and cross-class coalitions, and an even more powerful *resistance to equity*. Eversley Bradwell argued that educational reform efforts 'will be ineffective unless they address the fact that racial disparities are often linked to and rooted in institutionalized policies and practices that are deeply entrenched and *protected at the community level* [emphasis added] (2009, p. ii). This community-level protection requires the discursive flexibility of white racial dominance through accommodation of race-conscious talk, passive tolerance of racist hate speech on the margins, and active promotion of benevolent liberal racism. In this section, we present the ideas of 'flexible whiteness' (Leonardo, 2009) and 'racist hate speech' in order to later examine how this 'protection' endures ideologically and discursively as it is (re)produced and contested in print media.

Flexible whiteness and benevolent liberal racism

'Late whiteness', like late capitalism, argues Zeus Leonardo (2009, p. 168), evolved as a global racial force that is necessarily adaptable, flexible, and fragmented so that it can exploit various material conditions. Importantly, it is buttressed by a process that mystifies both its workings and its global coherence. Leonardo likens finance capital's evolving response to economic crises and recessions to whiteness' need to exhibit signs of flexibility in the face of its own discursive crises. From the late twentieth and into the twenty-first century, the old narratives of biological and colonial cultural racism, which had previously supported modernity's projects of colonization, slavery, empire, and state-sponsored segregation, have not carried the same weight that they did in previous eras. They have been challenged by various social forces, including social movements and academic attention to race and whiteness (Leonardo, 2009), all of which create an ill-afforded crisis for whiteness' modes of self-masking and mystification. However, as Leonardo argues, new forms of fragmentation and abstraction make whiteness, like finance capital, difficult to locate. Its focus on 'scope, not scales of influence', for example, means that whiteness must accommodate and seduce previously marked 'Others' and 'be able to forsake immediate advantages for long term goals of domination' (Leonardo, 2009, p. 181).

Leonardo's focus in developing this idea of flexible whiteness is to provide a language for discussing the scope of whiteness beyond the nation-state. Here we turn to the local/ global contexts to examine how whiteness as a discourse accommodates race-conscious talk. We might look at the practices and contours of flexible whiteness precisely in terms of its normalization and intense mystification under the logic and practices of color-blindness. What does color-blindness hide and deny, and what does it emphasize? First, as Leonardo (2009) points out, it disavows racial difference as the reigning logic for education, social, and economic policies, and it also denies racial differences as institutionalized outcomes. Second, color-blindness refuses recognition of the history of state-sponsored discrimination and violence toward people of color. It denies the continuing legacy of racial disparities in education and in the workplace, and the disproportionate rates of incarceration and violence in communities of color (see Bell, 2005). Third, race is further denied and its reigning logic masked or hidden when racial disparities are explained away as natural outcomes of a meritocratic and free-market society (Bonilla-Silva, 2006; Chang, 2002). Thus, success and failure are individualized or explained only in terms of social class status. Finally, like the individualization of success and failure, racism is pathologized to the individual (Bonilla-Silva, 2006; Leonardo, 2009). For example, racist hate speech is attributed to acts of an individual racist rather than viewed as ubiquitous and systemic (Lawrence, 1990). (See Bonilla-Silva, 2006; Leonardo,

2009; Zamudio, Russell, Rios, & Bridgeman, 2011, among others summarizing the contours of color-blindness.)

Benevolent liberal race talk works as a discursive form of flexible whiteness in the aforementioned service of color-blindness. As we will discuss in the data sections, benevolent liberal racism seems to address concerns and explicit talk about race, including terms of cultural competency, diversity, and equity used in race-conscious speech. This discourse creates an inclusive 'we' who care about minoritized youth and are acting on their behalf. Its discursive power is fragmented, however, making it difficult to address because it attaches itself to both racist hate speech and race-conscious speech. It also obscures the big picture of how educational inequities are racially structured. Whiteness also flexes and accommodates in the short term (e.g., in conversations about equity and cultural competency) to protect its property in the long term (Harris, 1995). In Ithaca, as elsewhere, these long-term protections have included investments in and prioritizing of mainstream Western curriculum, and differential educational offerings according to merit (tracking) (see Ladson-Billings, 1999; Ladson-Billings & Tate, 1995; and ethnographic examples from Castagno, 2009; Chapman, 2007; Hurd, 2008; Rousseau, 2006; and Vaught, 2011, among others).

Next, we explore the concept of racist hate speech. Our focus will be on examining how benevolent liberal race talk is co-constituted vis-à-vis racist hate speech, and how it can also be viewed as racist hate speech itself when considering its adverse effects and outcomes for people of color (Lawrence, 1990; Vaught, 2011).

Racist hate speech

An important strand in critical race theory focuses on the systems of thought, language, images, and categories that construct racial reality in the USA (Delgado & Stefancic, 2004). Racial depictions, labeling, and imagery of White superiority and People of Color's inferiority, or racist hate speech, do the work that legally sanctioned segregation had performed until only half a century ago. Delgado and Stefancic (2004) explain that hate speech can be considered along various axes including 'direct and indirect, veiled or covert, single or repeated, backed by authority and power or not, and accompanied by threat of violence or not' (2004, p. 11). Hate speech can also be considered in terms of the characteristics of the person or group to which it is directed, and whether it is directed to an individual, a small group such as a Black fraternity, or to a group in general. It also matters who is doing the speaking and whether it is a person in power, such as a teacher or police officer, or someone else like a passerby or 'an educated, genteel author', for example, locating X people's problem in X people's culture and genes (Delgado & Stefancic, 2004, pp. 11–12). Delgado and Stefancic (2004) point out that the effects of direct one-on-one hate speech have been the most intensively studied. Recently, however, there has been growing attention directed to the effects of subtle, indirect, or educated hate speech on individuals and society, and its cumulative effects on the life chances of people who are the targets of such language (Delgado & Stefancic, 2004).

Three important ideas serve to illustrate the discursive interdependence of different forms of racist hate speech and its effects on race-conscious speech. First, racist hate speech is not isolated; critical race theorists argue that it is endemic and represents the tools, processes, and manifestations of white racial dominance (see Bell, 2005; Gillborn, 2008; Matsuda, 1989). Matsuda remarks that all overt and covert forms of racism are mutually reinforcing: 'Gutter racism, parlor racism, corporate racism, and government racism work in coordination, reinforcing existing conditions of domination' and inflicting wounds that are neither random nor isolated (1989, pp. 2334–2335). As Lawrence puts it, racist hate speech is a manifestation 'of a ubiquitous and deeply ingrained cultural belief system, an American way of life' (1990, p. 461). A color-blind understanding of racist hate speech is part and parcel of whiteness' flexibility. It contributes to the broad distribution and tolerance of hate speech, and to a view of democracy as racially color-blind (Leonardo, 2009).

Second, the speakers of racist hate speech often justify its use with the language and discourse of 'free speech' in ways that permit the constant assault of people of color in the public sphere. Gillborn (2008) notes how a call-in radio show focused its discussion on free speech rather than on the controversial racial content and ideas contained in the guest author's book. Gillborn concludes: 'The core of the discussion was about racial domination – about the absolute right of Whites to continue to peddle racist nonsense about Black intellectual inferiority in the name of "freedom of speech"' (2008, p. 179). In this way, 'free speech' explanations often mute race-conscious speech and make racist hate speech more central to public discourse.

Finally, it is also useful to consider the messages delivered by educational practices and labeling as harmful forms of racist hate speech in education (see Vaught, 2011). Drawing from arguments in the Brown v. Board Supreme Court decision to end segregation, Lawrence (1990) makes the case that messages delivered through actions such as segregation, tracking, labeling, and categorizing constitute racist hate speech because they send a message of racial inferiority. In benevolent liberal race perspectives, explanations of racial disparities in education that blame families' cultural and home lives send messages of low regard for students of color and their families (see Vaught, 2011). In sum, flexible whiteness and racist hate speech provide a conceptual road map for exploring the constitutive elements of race talk in local media that normalize color-blind racial discourse.

Methodology

As race-based scholarship, this study is driven by questions that derive from the authors' own racialized experiences and ways of knowing (see López & Parker, 2003), particularly as we have come to *convivir* (co-exist in life affirming ways) and see social life in Ithaca through the words and actions of race-conscious speakers. Following pioneering critical race scholar, Derrick Bell, we believe that it is only by identifying the endemic and systemic nature of racism in our society, and specifically by examining the ways in which the USA is racially constructed, that we can be empowered in our struggles for equity and justice in schools and in society. Ours is necessarily a partial story that has as one aim the eliciting of alternative stories and counter-stories of/from Ithaca and other communities.

The present article is based on an analysis of local print media from 2007 through 2012. Media interpretations are guided by ethnographic observations beginning in mid-2007 of race and school equity conversations in community forums, celebratory public programs and festivals, school events, and other public gatherings. Interpretations are also guided by analysis of selective podcasts of the weekly community radio show, All Things Equal on WHCU, from 2008 through mid-2012. The selection process for specific topics and texts for this article was based on the attention they received as critical and important incidents in the community. The examples of everyday education issues are illustrative of the different ways that these conversations were carried out in print media, as determined by our systematic reading of hundreds of newspaper articles. We collected hard copies of the weekly newspaper, the *Ithaca Times*, sporadically throughout 2008 but systematically from 2009 through 2012. We have archived electronic copies of all relevant news stories, editorials, and opinion pieces from mid-2006 through 2012. Our library for the daily newspaper, the *Ithaca Journal* (*IJ*), is almost entirely electronic and exhaustive of all pieces concerning school equity and race-based news and events from 2007 through 2012. Most pieces were collected in real time so that we also had access to commentaries from the *IJ*'s online forum. In sifting through the relevant media items for this article, we formed a subset of 380 pieces including sets of online replies and commentaries, all of which inform our analysis of the pieces presented in this article. We identified major race events that have polarized the community, and also the ongoing issues on school equity consistently taken up by media.

Our analysis is guided by questions we posed to media text, which we generated from some broad tenets and methodological questions in discourse analysis of media (Fairclough, 1995; Richardson, 2007; Wortham, 2001). Fairclough (1995) argues a first tenet: Effective interdisciplinary work requires that we analyze media language as discourse. A critical analysis of discourse is concerned with social problems and the discursive nature of social and cultural processes and structures (Richardson, 2007). Following Richardson (2007), we asked an overarching critical question: How does the text comment on the community and larger society in which it was produced, and that it was produced for? What influence or impact will it have on social and race relations? Will it reinforce inequalities such as racial disparities in education or help to break them down? We also took for a basic tenet that all critical analysis of discourse is interpretive and can be understood as a systematic study of the relationship between texts, and their social conditions, power relations, and ideologies (Fairclough, 1995; Richardson, 2007).

From the above tenets, we moved on to inquire into how race relations, racial disparities, and educational equity in Ithaca have been discursively taken up through different types of race talk. We asked: How does the conversation around equity and race invoke a larger body of experiences, a larger sense of history, and a sense of identity or position (Hamann & Reeves, 2012)? What are the storylines around major racial events? What discourses about race are taken up and how? What are the *assumed* or mainstream storylines (Hamann & Reeves, 2012)? What is present and what *could have been* but *is not* present, and what choices were made to describe a person, action, or process in a particular way (Richardson, 2007)? The selected media examples in this article are representative in content and form of the different kinds of race talk in the larger subset of media pieces.

Next, we looked more closely at the discursive 'work' of various kinds of race talk. What aims, goals, identities (i.e., rational, objective, enlightened, activist, citizen), and relationships did this race talk work to establish through various forms of language choice (Fairclough, 1995)? How are meanings constructed through the interactions between producer, text, and consumer (Richardson, 2007)? From a dialogic perspective (Bakhtin, 1981), we considered how speakers positioned themselves in relation to other speakers or earlier voices, and how they answered, refuted, or spoke in concert with other, imagined groups of speakers (Wortham, 2001). We also looked at the discursive work of accommodating, validating, disqualifying, or contesting differing perspectives and understandings about race and school equity. In the following two sections, we present data that examine and link (1) racist hate speech in a tragedy concerning a police shooting and (2) benevolent liberal race talk concerning racial disparities in special education. Race-conscious talk and a range of school equity discourses are also parts of these stories. In this way, we illustrate not only the discursive work of flexible whiteness, but also the possibilities for race-conscious talk.

A 'racially polarizing' tragedy: hate speech and race-conscious talk

On 23 February 2010, Ithaca experienced the tragic shooting death of Ithaca native Shawn Greenwood by Ithaca Police Sgt. Bryan Bangs during a narcotics investigation – a black man shot and killed by a white police officer, as it was understood and framed (and contested as such) in the community and the media. On 1 July 2010, a Tompkins County Grand Jury found that Sgt. Bangs was justified in his actions. Nine days later, on 10 July, Sgt. Bangs survived an act of arson that burned down his house. Community leaders recognized this set of events and their aftermath as painful, difficult, and racially polarizing. The daily newspaper, the *IJ*, followed the story and featured community reactions in news articles, editorials, opinion pieces, and online replies from readers. Coverage also included formal statements and comments from local government officials, religious leaders, law enforcement, and from Community Leaders of Color (CLOC, 2010), a coalition that formed to address race relations and racial disparities, including employment opportunities in the region for young African American men. In this section, we use this nonschool-related case to highlight the dominant or media-sanctioned race talk that made room for some – though not all – race-conscious discourse. We also show how non-sanctioned racist hate speech worked from the margins of online replies and through Facebook to maintain its influence in the market of ideas, particularly in connection to education.

Racist and color-blind hate speech (seemingly) on the margins

A set of *IJ* articles and opinion pieces about Mr. Greenwood's memorial service (Drumsta, 2010d), how his family and friends remembered him (Drumsta, 2010d, 2010c), the community forums sponsored by the City (Drumsta 2010b), and later by CLOC (Gashler, 2010), the shooting as history's latest injustice (authored by a community activist) (Bush, 2010), the arson on Sgt. Bangs' home (Drumsta, 2010e), and CLOC's immediate response of condemnation and calls for honest conversations about racism, which was published in the *IJ* on 10 July 2010, all prompted a host of polarizing responses that dominated the online forum. The story about the arson alone received over 300 replies, and the opinion letter on the shooting as history's latest injustice (14 August 2010) received 79 largely racially insensitive responses, racial insults, and accusations by 7.30 p.m. on the day it was published. In this online space, the *IJ* was accused of bias and its legitimacy as a newspaper was questioned. Commentators who believed the shooting was justified felt that there was too much focus on Mr. Greenwood and community concerns about racism, and they accused the *IJ* of reverse discrimination against Whites and 'stirring the pot' with talk of race. One of the only examples of a piece of this nature that appeared in the opinion section of the *IJ*'s print version, published on 10 May 2010, rather than in the form of an online reply, read as follows:

> Regarding Shawn Greenwood: I am sick of your coverage of this event. In your May 1 article, you once again play him as a good human being … In your article you talk with people … who now say they did not have the facts, that they heard things from people on the

street, yet they cry racism, bad shoot, this was just a poor kid who got out of prison and was starting a new life.

Referring to the same letter, an online commentator felt it was tucked away and difficult to locate in comparison with the visibility of stories about Greenwood's life. She wrote: 'If I hadn't known that there was a letter I wouldn't have even found it; but of course Greenwood's story would be plastered on the front pages'. Another commentator wrote: 'I am just amazed that in an educated community everyone sides with crime and the criminal and not the law'. These comments articulate a perception that humanizing Mr. Greenwood and addressing the shooting death in terms of a historical legacy of institutional racism and police brutality signaled clear side-taking along racial lines. These letters were also a response to the *IJ*'s marking of the boundaries of what constituted sanctioned and acceptable race talk in the media of a 'too liberal' community. Racist hate speech and color-blind racism took to the margins, and then to a Facebook page supporting Sgt. Bangs, on which some of the *IJ* articles, editorials, and opinions were shared and discussed among people from Ithaca, Tompkins County, and surrounding counties, and from beyond New York State.

What storylines about race did these online commentators articulate (Bonilla-Silva, 2006)? In the process, who and what were online and Facebook commentators speaking to/with and against? What identities and relationships were thereby created or reinforced? Vitriolic and less-direct racist hate speech was expressed side by side and accepted as part of being on the 'side' of Sgt. Banks and against Mr. Greenwood's 'supporters'. Most commonly, the idea of deservedness versus undeservedness was expressed in words such as 'criminal', 'felon', 'scum', 'dangerous', and 'he got what he deserved'. In contrast to 'law-abiding citizens', this language of deservedness and merit positioned Mr. Greenwood as undeserving of full human rights and of his humanity. As a form of cultural racism (Bonilla-Silva, 2006), this idea encompassed characterizations of his family and upbringing: 'Bad parenting and bad friends leads to bad kids' (*IJ* online forum, 1 May 2010). And 'bad choices' were framed exclusively as individual faults in a world where people made decisions on a neutral, race-free playing field. These views were certainly challenged in online replies by commentators who knew Mr. Greenwood and emphasized that he was a human being who made mistakes and was struggling, a human being who was loved by many people (see also Blas, 2012; Bush, 2010; Drumsta, 2010c).

This language of deserving and non-deserving was also embedded in the racist hate speech concerning the Kearney racial discrimination lawsuit brought against ICSD in 2007, in which a middle school student was racially bullied over many months (see Sanders, 2007; Stern, 2012). The language of deservedness in racist hate speech in this case ranged from culturally racist statements and insults about the child's mother, to claims that she was using the racial incident to bank out on a large sum of money, and that her daughter was thus undeserving of justice. In the context of the US education system, the language of deservedness moves dangerously through racist hate speech, color-blind racism, and benevolent liberal racism to blame children for their own racial bullying and school underachievement, and to normalize the condition of educational inequities. Speech about undeserving individuals easily slips into speech about undeserving groups of people, including the children.

To return to the Greenwood case, the idea that the shooting death of a Black man by a White police officer took place in a racism-free society relied on the simultaneous *rejection* of race as the explanation for continuing racial disparities (i.e., playing the race card) and *recognition* of race in terms of disadvantaging whites (i.e., reverse racism). To see race and racism was to be racist, except when pointing out reverse racism. The following Facebook comment from a resident of a nearby city is illustrative of this point:

> That's all anyone does anymore is throw the race card! It's BS! It's not about race. It's about facts. So what if the kid was black. I don't care if he was purple with pink polka dots. He was in the wrong. Period. End of story. But the real question I have is, would they be making such a big deal over it if the kid was WHITE? That's the real race problem. (22 September 2010)

As we shall see in the second data section, this simultaneous rejection and recognition of race was also evident in benevolent liberal race talk regarding school equity issues.

Next, racist hate speech was framed as 'free speech' and tied to identities of 'we real Americans'. For example, a local county resident posted: 'FEAR ME, for I am an AMERICAN and I have the RIGHT to say whatever the hell I want!!!!' Commentators on the *IJ* online system routinely complained about having their comments deleted by *IJ* editors and asserted their rights to free speech. This was also true regarding Facebook responses to a controversy about police officers 'liking' criticisms of the mayor's purported behavior in supporting the 'other side': 'I cannot believe that Ithaca has become a city that no longer allows free speech to their citizens—police officers included'. Another local resident commented, 'Last time I looked we live in America isn't this a free Country and we have freedom of speech—especially on our own time—and when we are supporting one of our own—the HELL with them!' In the context of this string of comments, the words 'one of our *own*' and 'the HELL with *them*' indexed racialized us/them binary identities and relationships, including those of the law enforcement community and non-law enforcement, Sgt. Banks supporters and Mr. Greenwood supporters, real Americans and non-real Americans, patriots and non-patriots, and Whites versus racialized Others. In the education context, free speech also translates to freedom of association as justification for tracked and segregated classrooms.

In addition, Facebook members used the online medium to mobilize and encourage members to contact reporters and investigative radio and television shows about what they perceived as the real injustice. This is reminiscent of how elite parents mobilize to secure advantages and address perceived injustices to their children (see Brantlinger, 2003; Hurd, 2008; Oakes & Lipton, 2002). Though the Facebook group membership may or may not have been of predominantly middle-class status, they nonetheless drew upon the rightness of their cause, their abilities to access resources and knowledge, and the privilege that their white 'American' identities afforded them. From this perspective, as it was articulated, reverse racism and non-Americanism was not just a local problem, it was a greater systemic problem that affected 'all of us', meaning all of us White Americans. Cross-racial coalitions of community leaders working to address the Kearney case of racial harassment could not call upon the privilege of 'we' White Americans in order to garner national empathy and attention.

In a progressive community, racist hate speech and color-blind racism may be viewed as isolated talk on the part of a few irrational people (Leonardo, 2009). However, overtly hostile racist hate speech and indirect color-blind racism were articulated side by side in online forums, and on the Facebook page as members worked to constitute a *community* of speakers. Following van Dijk (1993), it is imperative to understand the production of and interpretive frameworks for their conversations as largely shaped by elites who command institutions of education, law enforcement and media among others. As Vaught writes: 'The individuals exercising racist hate speech are ... not speaking as individuals, but instead leveraging the power of a collective, dominant Whiteness' (2011, p. 149). This power is mutually constituted across institutions.

Race-conscious talk (seemingly) at the center

The language of racial equity, opportunities, and healing of race relations constituted the sanctioned form of race talk in the two local newspapers. Speakers of race-conscious talk certainly took the racist speech from the margins of the Greenwood case very seriously. They participated in flagging the most inappropriate comments and issued complaints about *IJ*'s online forum (Gashler, 2010). In general and over the years, *IJ*'s choices regarding coverage and representation of race-related law enforcement, equity, and schooling issues have been a subject of tension and struggle.

In the shooting's immediate aftermath, comments on the *IJ* online forum and included in the more prominent news stories voiced anger and frustration (see Drumsta, 2010d, 2010a). Calls for justice and for collective action for civil rights were also noted. In the weeks that followed, the *IJ* ran news articles which emphasized the softening of personal accusations, the continuing discussion of systemic racism as it relates to law enforcement, and unanswered questions about the tragedy (Drumsta, 2010a; Gashler, 2010). Reporting on a community forum, Gashler (2010) noted leaders' 'hopes that Greenwood's death could act as a catalyst to spur progress toward better employment opportunities, especially for people of color and people re-entering the workforce after release from prison'. This article served as one of the first public introductions of the CLOC, a coalition that had been meeting since the shooting death took place. As we have seen, all of these more prominently placed stories in turn sparked virulent and color-blind racist talk in the margins of the online forum and in the few opinion pieces. This strong contrast in racial storylines illustrates how community members lived, understood, and articulated their lives in racial terms; it also illustrated the types of race talk that are sanctioned in a progressive community.

Immediately following the Grand Jury's finding that Sgt. Bangs was justified in his use of lethal force, the *IJ* published voices expressing concern for all involved while calling for continued focus on racial equity and healing. A few words from CLOC's statement featured in a news story read as follows:

> This tragedy has been painful and difficult for the people of Ithaca, and our wishes for peace and healing go out especially to the Greenwood family, Sgt Bangs and his family, the Ithaca Police Department, and all who have been deeply affected by the events that occurred that night ... We also think it is critical to see this terrible event as an opportunity to address, once and for all, some of the underlying problems facing this community with respect to racism and racial equity. (Gashler, 2010)

Similarly, in the aftermath of the fire that burned down Sgt. Bangs' home, two of the *IJ* news stories included a statement from CLOC expressing sadness about the incident, condemning the violence and urging the community to 'engage in calm, thoughtful conversation and peaceful work for improvements in police community relations' (see http://ithacacloc.blogspot.com/). There was also a focus on healing with stories on the faith community (see Lawyer, 2011). On the other hand, the race-conscious talk of the Shawn Greenwood Working Group was given very little attention in the media. This group formed to share ways of acting as empowered agents against institutional racism, police violence, and the US system of mass incarceration. In public forums and educational workshops on the history and politics of the disproportionate incarceration of and violence against men of color, this group reframed the shooting as an 'illegal killing'. Notwithstanding, race-conscious speakers of all stripes continued to hone their discursive strategies, and in the process to build relationships to more effectively address institutional racism in all domains, including in education.

Racist hate speech (both the vitriolic kind and less hostile color-blind speech) and race-conscious talk were thus actively constituted in Ithaca's print media. The racial 'divide' and the different 'sides' were discursively produced and reproduced in the *IJ*'s front pages, viewpoint sections, online forums, and on Facebook pages on which *IJ* pieces were posted. Seemingly isolated, racist hate speech operated from the margins of the online forum and the related Facebook page as an expression of larger social and cultural practices and policies of white racial power (see Vaught, 2011). Racist hate speech operated as a source of tension by signaling degrading messages about the inferiority of people of color, and by its non-recognition of the legacy of racism. It potentially detracted from and tempered the power and the message of race-conscious discourse, for example, in the media's lack of attention to the Shawn Greenwood Working Group. As we will examine in the next data section, racist hate speech contributes to whiteness' flexibility by legitimizing other kinds of more benevolent yet nonetheless color-blind forms of race talk in education.

Special education and racial disparities: benevolent liberal race talk, excellence-for-*all*, and race-conscious talk on school equity

In this section, we discuss an example of everyday conversation on race and school equity to parse out the discursive work done by benevolent liberal race talk in relation to a range of different kinds of equity and race-conscious talk. In general, the voices and language of equity, cultural competency, and diversity were evident across news print coverage of school board candidate forums and the yearly equity report card. As a former superintendent acknowledged on the local community radio show, 'All Things Equal' on WHCU (16 June 2009), equity-minded and race-conscious community members kept people's feet to the fire and the conversations on the table.

This next example concerns several *Ithaca Times* publications regarding the district's disproportionate classification of students of color as having disabilities and the ensuing conversation about special education reform. The news stories include 'Ithaca schools: Minorities more likely to be labeled as students with disabilities' (Leone, 2011b) and a more in-depth story with interviews, 'ICSD data "tells a difficult story" about race poverty, gender and disability" (Leone, 2011c). These articles report that one-third or 35.1% of African American students are classified as having disabilities, more than double the number for white students (16.6%). African American female students are three times (20.9%) more likely to be classified as such than white female students (Leone, 2011b, 2011c). For students of color who also qualify for free lunch, the number jumps to 63% among African American students, with 94.1% of Hispanic male students classified as having a disability (Leone, 2011c). Once classified, these students have a slim chance of being declassified, and only a 50% chance of graduating (Leone, 2011c).

In the news article 'Ithaca data tells a difficult story', the author pointed out the two views at stake: 'Some are calling these facts evidence of "structural racism" in public school. Others explain that the numbers are in line with national trends and not unique to Ithaca' (Leone, 2011c). The selected quotes in the article moved from comments pointing to structural racism to comments by the district's Special Education director that normalized the racial disparities as part of a national trend. As an example of the former, a community leader and educator who also worked with CLOC is quoted as saying that for a long time many people have been 'unwilling to address the reality of structural racism and structural poverty'. He points to the problem of cultural racist explanations in his remark that ICSD is a good school district for about 75% of the students, and for the other 25%, the families are blamed. 'They say it's about the families, not the school district', and that therefore it is not the ICSD's problem to solve. There is fear, says the community leader, of siphoning off resources to address these kids' needs: 'That is a narrative that has been a big part of this community'. This article allots more space to the community leader's explanation than to the words of the Special Education director, who was quoted as saying that although the data is cause for concern, it is not news to her as it mirrors similar statistics presented to the board in the past, and that she does not have a theory for the racial disparities. 'I don't have a theory, I think it's a question we have to find the answer to' (Leone, 2011c). This statement was about recognizing racial disparities, but not publicly naming the role of systemic racism in educational practices and outcomes. This message by a person in a position of power, as quoted in the article, served to reinforce the normalization of benevolent and color-blind explanations with its neutral-sounding and fact-finding language, despite the print space also allotted to the community leader's race-conscious explanations.

The above articles were followed by opinion pieces and online forum conversations in both the daily *IJ* and the weekly *Ithaca Times*. The following opinion piece mirrors the 'de-raced' quote by the Special Education director above. In a different way, it explicitly offers a theory of racial disparities that echoes benevolent liberal race perspectives. In a very long opinion piece, 'Open letter to ICSD parents, district residents' (*Ithaca Times*, 4 January 2012), the Special Education PTA (Parent Teacher Association) president positioned himself in relation to race-conscious talk, referring to the continuing conversation of structural racism as potentially becoming toxic. He continued:

> The fact that the data shows that children of color and females are disproportionately represented in the 'classified' category is a fact, not an indictment of the ICSD educational system. We have no evidence of bias or a flawed assessment process. There simply is no data to support the article's undertones of racial or gender animus.

He then proceeded to locate the problem with youths and their families by arguing that children of color are disproportionately of low socioeconomic status, that the 'educational level of the parents within the economically disadvantaged group resulting from past discrimination' may be low, and that, for some parents, there may be flawed cultural beliefs about educational expectations for girls 'resulting in less early developmental activities for females and/or a non-academic focus during the early years'. The author ends his letter with a plea to the public that is reminiscent of the race-card argument in color-blind and racist hate speech; that is, that to consider racism is to be racist. He writes: 'Please do not let the discussion turn to racial or gender bias without a sound basis for such ugly allegations. In Ithaca, we are on the side of the angels in helping children with disabilities …'. As an example of Gotanda's (1991) idea of the technique of non-recognition, race is noticed or recognized, but not considered. It is recognized in terms of 'past discrimination', but not in terms of current issues of subordination. Instead of turning to the role of race in labeling and categorization, this statement turns to cultural deficiency (i.e., educational level of the parents). It also equates 'non-academic' home preparation with disability, rather than with a consideration of how home language and literacy practices may be different from those sanctioned by the institution of schooling. Though well meaning, this talk is not very different from the language of deservedness in the racist hate speech about Mr. Greenwood. It moves to the center of public discourse precisely by virtue of its being dis-identified with racist hate speech. The ideas are positioned as objective, fact-based, non-impassioned examples of reason and benevolent care. Whiteness powerfully operates in its appeals to objective fact, rather than as a message articulated by a messenger whose race and worldviews are privileged in society (Vaught, 2011). This message relies on naturalized labels of intelligence and merit and blames the children and families.

In addition to race-conscious and benevolent liberal race talk, there were other voices included in the *IJ* and *Ithaca Times*, in particular a progressive school voice promoting inclusion and the leveraging of diversity for engaging and developing the whole child. Overall, the district categorizes one-third more children (16%) with a disability than the state average (Leone, 2011c). Thus, a sizeable group of caregivers across race and class share concerns about instruction and diversity, inclusion in school life, and educational outcomes. In response to a new Special Education improvement plan, two guest viewpoints published in the *Ithaca Times* and *IJ* asked questions about how to change the learning environment, measure students' success in different ways, provide support for teachers, and facilitate caregiver participation. For example, in her guest viewpoint, 'Conversation begins about students with special needs' (*IJ*, 24 March 2012), one author says that the plan is but a 'first step in the development of a more robust approach'. She then proceeds to ask what she called the overarching question in moving forward: 'What can we do to change the learning environment so that all children will be more successful?' Other questions included: How do we use diversity to 'build learning communities that respect the strengths and needs of all learners'? What pedagogical approaches will 'optimize student engagement and achievement'? and how do we 'encourage teachers to introduce best practices'? She concludes: 'As we create a plan to improve the educational experience of children with disabilities, we need to be thinking about systemic changes that will improve the education of all students'.

In a school district striving for excellence, these are the questions regarding inclusion and systemic change that have recently been serving as points of discussion for reforming current school policies and practices. It is a critical approach different from the Special Education PTA president's benevolent liberal race talk insofar as it addresses racial disparities in education (i.e., the disproportionate categorization of students of color in special education) as requiring excellent educational practices that will benefit *all* students. Rather than starting from cultural deficit perspectives, this excellence-for-*all* approach takes into account and honors diverse learners and diverse cultural practices and focuses on student engagement (Kugelmass, 2004). This approach also has a history in the community and is supported in race-conscious perspectives. Yet, there is a tension when the political and racial contexts for Black and Latino/a students' learning are not explicitly acknowledged and addressed the way they are in the community leader's race-conscious talk in the above article, 'Ithaca data tells a difficult story' (see also Perry, Steele, and Hilliard, 2004). In one sense, the ways in which excellence-for-*all* talk is taken up may be viewed in terms of interest convergence (Bell, 1995): Whites will support racial minority rights only when it is in their interest to do so. This tension is evident when educational responses to the needs of students of color need to be articulated as directly benefiting White and economically privileged students. Excellence-for-*all* makes sense in its inclusiveness, but when the enduring ideologies supporting racial disparities are not part of the conversation, it is not long before convergent interests wear thin. Reformers are then caught ill-prepared to deal with elite parents' organizing against reform and their underlying color-blind liberal racism, which may bear only the smallest guise of benevolence (see Oakes & Lipton, 2002). This is a big part of the story of the ways in which deeply entrenched institutionalized policies and practices have been protected at the community level in Ithaca (see Eversley Bradwell, 2009).

In this section, we have presented one example of many conversations that took place in and through Ithaca's print media that concern race and educational equity. We see how media is a stage for many different kinds of race talk – benevolent liberal racism, race-conscious, excellence-for-*all*, and for the continuing racist hate speech in the margins of online forums (though not specifically addressed here). Across the different kinds of race talk in print media, we found that while race-conscious and excellence-for-*all* perspectives were privileged in some news stories and by inclusion in the guest viewpoint and opinion sections of the *IJ* and *Ithaca Times*, benevolent liberal racism often served as a default position that was routinely articulated by people in leadership positions. For example, in response to the district's math achievement gap along racial lines, a school board member was quoted as saying, 'It's about class, not race' (Leone, 2011a). No doubt, socioeconomic class distinctions in educational equity need critical attention, including greater focus on racialized, gendered, class experiences. But embodied racial differences cannot be left out of the picture and flattened out into other differences. To be sure, speakers of benevolent liberal race perspectives often spoke from a position of commitment and caring for the district's students. Vaught (2008) reminds us that color-blind racism is not about a bad person or even an individual person's racism; it is about speech that is complicit with and supported by school policies and practices, and by a larger societal structure of racism. In this vein, benevolent liberal race talk also serves as racist hate speech in the messages sent to students of color when they are disproportionately tracked into non-honors courses and special education, when they are suspended in higher numbers, when they do not graduate, and when they do not see teachers of color nor curriculum that represents their histories and cultural lives (see Lawrence, 1990; and Vaught, 2011).

Conclusion: toward the promise of race-conscious talk

In a liberal-progressive community in which race-conscious talk has a public forum in local print media, we have asked questions about how whiteness functions through everyday talk by highlighting the links between race talk surrounding a police shooting tragedy and concerning educational equity. We asked how racist hate speech and benevolent liberal race talk serve to normalize and mystify white dominance when race-conscious talk presents a challenge and creates a context for its crisis. How and to what extent does whiteness flex? We have argued for whiteness' elasticity in the face of race-conscious talk. Race-conscious perspectives certainly held sway, and its speakers/actors worked hard to shape the discursive public arena. However, whiteness' flexibility was undergirded by the force of benevolent liberal race talk, which worked in tandem with racist hate speech on the margins. It echoed racist hate speech's language of deservedness, merit, and color-blindness, and participated in the identity-making of 'we (middle class) White Americans' as culturally superior. It benefited from the perceived exceptionality of racist hate speech and low-grade racism, which kept the community on edge, thus allowing benevolent liberal racism to move closer to the center as normative race talk. Benevolent liberal race talk accommodated the language of race-conscious talk in its caring for racial minority youths, but it decontextualized racial disparities to individual deficits. It turned to class over race and to individualized notions of success. It naturalized and normalized the educational disparities faced by students of color with the language of 'it's always been like this', or 'these are national trends'. The more progressive excellence-for-*all* talk ran the risk of suppressing race by not addressing the particular racial and political contexts of youths' lives and schooling (see Perry et al., 2004; Pollock, 2004). Attention to structural racism and racially embodied difference was the tipping point or point of tension in equity discussions, and such tensions were at play in Ithaca's print media across issues of education and law enforcement. Whiteness' flexibility thus depended on the more blatant and vitriolic race talk of racially polarizing events, such as the police shooting, to reinforce benevolent liberal race talk in school equity discussions. Put another way, van Dijk (1993) argues that elites who are the shapers of talk and text take advantage of spontaneous, popular racial resentments in order to develop their own racial and ethnic policies with which to maintain white dominance.

But just as whiteness flexes, so does race-conscious talk. Social movements around the world respond to new globalizing forms of capital and new forms of oppression with differing and flexible strategies, organizing methods, coalition-building efforts, and discourses about justice. In Ithaca, race-conscious speakers have been enacting the methodologies of the oppressed (Sandoval, 2000). They engaged in effectively reading and deconstructing power, re-signifying pivotal terms, such as 'community', and introducing new 'old' terms, such as 'human rights' and 'beloved community' (Dwyer, 2011). They created new opportunities for dialogues on race with community-wide 'Talking Circles on Race', sponsored by the Multicultural Resource Center, a local and non-profit community organization, and with a community reading of Martin Luther King Jr.'s book, *Where do we go from here: Chaos or community?* (see Montana, 2010). Members of the Shawn Greenwood Working group, who also received the Rere Sojourner Hassett Social Justice Award (see Hart, 2012), have called attention to the deep roots of structural racism undergirding police violence and the US prison system through informational workshops, forums, marches, print material, and letters/essays in alternative print media. Importantly race-conscious actors were developing mobile, flexible subjectivities as they worked to build relationships and form coalitions across difference. They have sought to strategize their race talk while not forsaking the goals of racial justice and school equity. As we saw, media was an important arena for this work. In the weekly *Ithaca Times*, race-conscious speech was mobilized to call out the racism articulated in the '$175K is too much' opinion piece, but also to redirect the newspaper itself and the institution of Ithaca media in general. CLOC members inserted a critical narrative in print media that called attention and demanded a response to structural forms of racial disparities in law enforcement, the economy and education. Race-conscious actors were thus well aware of the connection between race talk and race-conscious efforts across issues, and their consequences for the lives and futures of youth of color. This story is to be continued.

References

Bakhtin, M. M. (1981). *The dialogic imagination: Four essays* (C. Emerson and M. Holquist, Trans.). Austin: University of Texas Press.

Bell, D. A. (1995). *Brown vs Board of Education* and the interest convergence dilemma. In K. Crenshaw, N. Gotanda, G. Peller, & K. Thomas (Eds.), *Critical race theory: The key writings that formed the movement* (pp. 20–28). New York, NY: The New Press.

Bell, D. A. (2005). Racial realism. In R. Delgado & J. Stefancic (Eds.), *The Derrick Bell reader* (pp. 73–77). New York, NY: New York University Press.

Blas, N. (2012, January). Shawn Greenwood. *Occupied Ithaca Journal*. Retrieved from http://occupiedithacajournal.files.wordpress.com/2012/02/oij-2-small-1.pdf

Bonilla-Silva, E. (2006). *Racism without racists: Color-blind racism and the persistence of racial inequality in the United States*. Lanham, MD: Rowman & Littlefield.

Brantlinger, E. A. (2003). *Dividing classes: How the middle class negotiates and rationalizes school advantage*. New York, NY: RoutledgeFalmer.

Bush, G. (2010, August 14). Greenwood shooting is just history's latest injustice. *Ithaca Journal*. Retrieved from http://www.ithacajournal.com

Castagno, A. E. (2009). Commonsense understandings of equality and social change: A critical race theory analysis of liberalism at Spruce Middle School. *International Journal of Qualitative Studies in Education, 22*(6), 755–768. doi:10.1080/09518390903333905

Chang, R. S. (2002). Critiquing 'race' and its uses: Critical race theory's uncompleted argument. In F. Valdes, J. McCristal Culp, & A. P. Harris (Eds.), *Crossroads, directions, and a new critical race theory* (pp. 87–96). Philadelphia, PA: Temple University Press.

Chapman, T. K. (2007). The power of contexts: Teaching and learning in recently desegregated schools. *Anthropology & Education Quarterly, 38*(3), 297–315. doi:10.1525/aeq.2007.38.3.297

Community Leaders of Color. (2010, July 10). Community group issues statement on fire at Ithaca police sergeant's home. *Ithaca Journal*. Retrieved from http://www.ithacajournal.com

Delgado, R., & Stefancic, J. (2004). *Understanding words that wound*. Boulder, CO: Westview Press.

Drumsta, R. (2010a, April 31). Angry words that followed Greenwood shooting, now soften. *Ithaca Journal*. Retrieved from http://www.ithacajournal.com

Drumsta, R. (2010b, March 9). Forum on Greenwood shooting brings out crowd, emotions, racism charges. *Ithaca Journal*. Retrieved from http://www.ithacajournal.com

Drumsta, R. (2010c, April 30). Loss still fresh for family, friends of Shawn Greenwood: Ithacan was turning around his life, they say. *Ithaca Journal*. Retrieved from http://www.theithacajournal.com/article/20100430/NEWS01/4300358/Loss-still-fresh-for-family-friends-of-Shawn-Greenwood

Drumsta, R. (2010d, March 2). Mourners of police shooting victim Shawn Greenwood fill Ithaca church: Fond memories mixed with frustration, anger. *Ithaca Journal*. Retrieved from http://www.theithacajournal.com/article/20100302/NEWS01/3020374/Mourners-of-police-shooting-victim-Shawn-Greenwood-fill-Ithaca-church

Drumsta, R. (2010e, July 10). Update: Fire damages house of IPD officer involved in Greenwood shooting; mayor pledges full investigation. *Ithaca Journal*. Retrieved from http://www.ithacajournal.com

Dwyer, D. (2011, October 13). Speakeasy: Kirby Edmonds bring human rights education to Ithaca schools. *Ithaca Times*. Retrieved from http://www.ithaca.com

Eversley Bradwell, S. W. (2009). *Always room at the top: Black students and educational policy in Ithaca, NY* (Unpublished PhD diss.). Cornell University, Ithaca.

Fairclough, N. (1995). *Media discourse*. London: Edward Arnold.

Gashler, K. (2010, June 3). Greenwood death may lead to progress, forum organizers hope. *Ithaca Journal*. Retrieved from http://www.ithacajournal.com

Gillborn, D. (2008). *Racism and education: Coincidence or conspiracy?* New York, NY: Routledge.

Gotanda, N. (1991). A critique of 'our constitution is color-blind'. *Stanford Law Review, 44*(1), 1–68. doi:10.2307/1228940

Gumprecht, B. (2003). The American college town. *Geographical Review, 19*(1), 51–80. Retrieved from http://www.jstor.org/stable/30033889

Hamann, E. T., & Reeves, J. (2012). Ice raids, children, media and making sense of Latino newcomers in flyover country. *Anthropology & Education Quarterly, 43*(1), 24–40. doi:10.1111/j.1548-1492.2011.01155.x

Harris, C. I. (1995). Whiteness as property. In K. Crenshaw, N. Gotanda, G. Peller, & K. Thomas (Eds.), *Critical race theory: The key writings that formed the movement* (pp. 276–291). New York, NY: The New Press.

Hart, G. (2012, May 25). *Ithaca Times* editor among Multicultural Resource Center, GIAC community award honorees. *Ithaca Times*. Retrieved from http://www.ithaca.com

Hurd, C. A. (2008). Cinco de mayo, normative whiteness, and the marginalization of Mexican-descent students. *Anthropology & Education Quarterly, 39*(3), 293–313. doi:10.1111/j.1548-1492.2008.00023.x

Kailin, J. (1999). How White teachers perceive the problem of racism in their schools: A case study in "liberal" Lakeview. *Teachers College Record, 100*(4), 724–750. doi:10.1111/0161-4681.00014

Kugelmass, J. W. (2004). *Inclusive school: Sustaining equity and standards.* New York, NY: Teachers College Press.

Ladson-Billings, G. (1999). Just what is critical race theory, and what's it doing in a nice field like education? In L. Parker, D. Deyhle, & S. Villenas (Eds.), *Race is … race isn't: Critical race theory and qualitative studies in education* (pp. 7–30). Boulder, CO: Westview Press.

Ladson-Billings, G., & Tate, W. F., IV (1995). Toward a critical race theory of education. *Teachers College Record, 97*(1), 47–68.

Lawrence, C. R., III (1990). If he hollers let him go: Regulating racist speech on campus. *Duke Law Journal, 1990*(3), 431–483. doi:10.2307/1372554

Lawyer, L. (2011, February 16). Healing Ithaca helps build bridges through prayer. *Ithaca Journal.* Retrieved from http://www.ithacajournal.com

Leonardo, Z. (2009). *Race, whiteness, and education.* New York, NY: Routledge.

Leone, S. P. (2011a, November 17). ICSD tries to pinpoint culprits for minority student math achievement. *Ithaca Times.* Retrieved from http://www.ithaca.com

Leone, S. P. (2011b, December 7). Ithaca schools: Minorities more likely to be labeled as students with disabilities. *Ithaca Times.* Retrieved from http://www.ithaca.com

Leone, S. P. (2011c, December 20). ICSD data 'tells a difficult story' about race, poverty, gender and disability. *Ithaca Times.* Retrieved from http://www.ithaca.com/news/article_e11f072c-2b4a-11e1-90c6-001871e3ce6c.html?mode=print

López, G. R., & Parker, L. (2003). Conclusion. In G. R. López & L. Parker (Eds.), *Interrogating racism in qualitative research methodology* (pp. 203–212). New York, NY: Peter Lang.

Matsuda, M. J. (1989). Public response to racist speech: Considering the victim's story. *Michigan Law Review, 87*(8), 2320–2381. doi:10.2307/1289306

Montana, R. (2010, September 30). Ithaca's MLK build preparing book distribution. *Ithaca Times.* Retrieved from http://www.ithaca.com

Oakes, J., & Lipton, M. (2002). Struggling for educational equity in diverse communities: School reform as social movement. *Journal of Educational Change, 3*(3–4), 383–406. doi:10.1023/A:1021225728762

Olsen, L. (2008). *Made in America: Immigrant students in our public schools.* New York, NY: New Press.

Peller, G. (1995). Race consciousness. In K. Crenshaw, N. Gotanda, G. Peller, & K. Thomas (Eds.), *Critical race theory: The key writings that formed the movement* (pp. 127–158). New York, NY: The New Press.

Perry, T., Steele, C., & Hilliard, A., III (2004). *Young, gifted, and black: Promoting high achievement among African-American students.* Boston, MA: Beacon Press.

Pollock, M. (2004). *Colormute: Race talk dilemmas in an American school.* Princeton, NJ: Princeton University Press.

Richardson, J. E. (2007). *Analysing newspapers: An approach from critical discourse analysis.* New York, NY: Palgrave Macmillan.

Rousseau, C. K. (2006). Keeping it real: Race and education in Memphis. In A. D. Dixson & C. K. Rousseau (Eds.), *Critical race theory in education: All god's children got a song* (pp. 113–128). New York, NY: Routledge Taylor and Francis Group.

Sanders, T. (2007, December 19). Contentious discrimination case reaches public hearing stage today. *Ithaca Journal.* Retrieved from http://www.ithacajournal.com

Sandoval, C. (2000). *Methodology of the oppressed.* Minneapolis, MN: University of Minnesota Press.

Spayde, J. (1997, May/June). Ithaca, New York: Our kind of town. *Utne Reader,* Retrieved from http://www.utne.com/Politics/Americas-Most-Enlightened-Towns-Ithaca-New-York.aspx

Stern, P. (2012, June 12). NY appeals court rules in favor of Ithaca school district in Kearney case. *Ithaca Journal.* Retrieved from http://www.ithacajournal.com

van Dijk, T. A. (1993). *Elite discourse and racism.* Newbury Park, CA: Sage.

Vaught, S. E. (2008). Writing against racism: Telling white lies and reclaiming culture. *Qualitative Inquiry, 14*(4), 566–589. doi:10.1177/1077800408314355

Vaught, S. E. (2011). *Racism, public schooling, and the entrenchment of White supremacy: A critical race ethnography.* Albany, NY: State University of New York Press.

Villenas, S. A. (2002). Reinventing educación in new Latino Communities: Pedagogies of change and continuity in North Carolina. In S. Wortham, E. Murillo Jr., & E. T. Hamann (Eds.), *Education in the new Latino diaspora: Policy and the politics of identity* (pp. 17–35). Westport, CT: Ablex.

Wortham, S. (2001). *Narratives in action: A strategy for research and analysis.* New York, NY: Teachers College, Columbia University.

Zamudio, M. M., Russell, C., Rios, F. A., & Bridgeman, J. L. (2011). *Critical race theory matters: Education and ideology.* New York, NY: Routledge.

'Waiting for Superman' to save black people: racial representation and the official antiracism of neoliberal school reform

Michael J. Dumas

Department of Administration, Leadership and Technology, Steinhardt School of Culture, Education and Human Development, New York University, New York, NY, USA

The author argues that the documentary, *Waiting for Superman*, effectively employs bodies and texts in ways that reproduce hegemonic constructions of race, and more specifically, offers an image and imagination of black engagement in education that reinforces neoliberal-multicultural narratives about black disinterest in, and responsibility for their own lack of educational attainment. Black subjects are understood as sympathetic primarily because, and only to the extent that they accept individual 'responsibility' and move toward neoliberal school 'choices' as a corrective for their own past cultural and educational shortcomings. The author also uses his analysis to encourage a (re-)commitment to critical cultural analysis of racial signification in educational policy discourse.

In this paper, I argue that the representation of black subjects in *Waiting for Superman* must be viewed in the context of a global cultural-political shift toward what Jodi Melamed (2009) has called neoliberal multiculturalism, a period in which we no longer have to consider race or pursue racial equality in any direct way, because neoliberal policies and subjectivities are seen as the guarantors of multiculturalism. Neoliberal multiculturalism is able to account for continued racial disparities by insisting that racialized subjects who still suffer are either unable to access race-transcending neoliberal opportunities, or more damning, are *unwilling* to surrender their racial allegiances in favor of neoliberal ones. I contend that *Waiting for Superman* and similar cultural products sentimentalize the lives of people of color, and thereby offer white consumers a kind of racial redemption, available for purchase largely through reading of the text and softening of the heart. However, I also suggest that the sentimentality that used to be readily available now exists in tension with a more recently intensified antipathy toward black bodies, identities, and cultural politics, all of which are increasingly viewed as impediments to a more advanced postracial, but (neoliberal-), multicultural nation and world (Sexton, 2008).

I interrogate black representation in *Waiting for Superman* not only to highlight the power of antiblack neoliberal-multicultural ideological and cultural practices, but also to make a broader case for a (re-)commitment to cultural analysis of *racial signifying practices* (Hall, 1992; Omi & Winant, 1994) in educational discourse, particularly related to urban school reform. Racial *signs* are any bit of text – including words, images, sounds, even gestures – that, when situated in relation to other signs, come to hold meanings or represent race in specific ways. That is, the sign itself is no longer merely innocent or a thing-in-itself, but can be 'read' as communicating something about race. *Racial signification*, then, denotes the systematic organization of *signs* through which we generate, transmit and reproduce cultural meanings of race. Through the politics of racial representation, on the terrain of the *discursive*, we (collectively) construct what race means and does in education, and from this, how we then explain the causes of, and remedies for racially disparate educational experiences and outcomes.

Beyond this, my analysis here offers insight into the role of cultural products such as *Waiting for Superman* in solidifying the state's relationship to the management of race in an increasingly diverse society. As David Goldberg (2009) contends in his discussion of racial neoliberalism, 'modern state and regional arrangements have come to form, fashion, make and mold – in short … manage – their heterogeneous populations' (p. 328) under shifting conditions in the political economy and the cultural politics of racial representation. What we see in *Waiting for Superman* is the celebration of the privatization of schools and the pursuit of market-based education reforms as means to either save black people (for use by the state) or, save the nation *from* black people, and particularly their claims to redress for persistent racial inequities in education. Neoliberal multiculturalism or racial neoliberalism is, from this ideological position, the end of racism (and if we are lucky, race along with it).

I begin by providing an explanation of the US state's efforts to situate itself *against* racism, beginning after World War II and continuing through the ascendance of neoliberalism beginning in the 1980s. I rely primarily on Melamed's (2009) analysis of official state antiracisms, because she is concerned specifically with how *black* people are imagined and explained (away) within these political-ideological formations. While I do not mean to naturalize a black-white racial binary, I do aim to focus on the *specificity* of antiblack racism, not only because 'black' operates as a racial signifier in very precise ways, but also as a way to push back against multiculturalist tendencies to think about racism only in globalizing or universalizing ways (Nakagawa, 2013; Sexton, 2008). I then situate *Waiting for Superman* as an important cultural product in the rightist project to discredit public education and institute neoliberal school reforms. Next, I interrogate the representation of black children and adults in *Waiting for Superman*, emphasizing throughout the specific ways in which the film not only reinforces an antiblack imagination, but also – and this is the central point of this paper – exploits black subjects in order to claim for neoliberal educational policies a privileged place in the struggle for (multicultural) racial justice and educational opportunity. Finally, I conclude with some broad implications for research on race and representation in education.

Official antiracisms in the USA

In her recent book, *Represent and Destroy*, Jodi Melamed (2009) argues that, after World War II, the US adopted a formal, state-supported antiracism in response to critiques from around the globe, and particularly from the Soviet Union. This was done to blunt the ascendancy of communism and solidify the legitimacy of the United States as an imperial power, and as the global leader in capitalist expansion. Whereas white supremacy has formed the dominant governmental and ideological regime prior to World War II, after the war, the USA formally adopted the liberal stance that resolving the 'Negro problem' would both facilitate, and serve as evidence of the nation's democratic ideals, and therefore, its right to lead the (free) world. Melamed explains that the US government, assisted by corporate entities, advanced cultural representations of black life in an effort to change the hearts and minds of white citizens, but more, to secure a sense of certainty about the moral rightness of global capitalism. 'Full African American citizenship', Melamed contends, 'would demonstrate that liberal freedoms were antithetical to racial exploitation, and African American economic success would prove capitalism to be neutral to race rather than structured by it' (p. x).

One of the most prominent means of disseminating stories of black experience were protest novels, such as Richard Wright's (1940) *Native Son*, in which black protagonists both experienced racism, but also sought to be saved from it. Unfortunately, in the view of critics, including James Baldwin (cited in Melamed, 2009), protest novels presented racism as merely a moral flaw, and black people as tragic figures whose salvation required their integration into the very system that terrorized them in the first place. As Baldwin recounts in his essay, 'Everybody's Protest Novel', a white liberal once remarked to him, 'As long as such books are being published ... everything will be alright' (quoted in Melamed, 2009, p. xiii). In this view – and central to Baldwin's critique – the very existence of the protest novel was seen to guarantee 'everybody's' redemption, rescuing whites from white supremacy, and black people from the burden of their own blackness. As a result, Melamed explains:

> Rather than a challenge to normal orders, protest novel discourse came across as thoroughly normative, in the sense that it generated precisely the knowledges about race that contemporary epistemological and political forms of postwar American modernity required. (p. xiii)

Thus, these kinds of Black representations destroyed a full sense of *black* humanity (since white racial salvation necessitated that black people also give up racial claims), and more materially, justified continued racial violence globally in the name of advancing a capitalist and colonialist US state that was now presumably antiracist.

The protest novel appeared during the period of *racial liberalism*, which Melamed identifies as the first era of official antiracism, spanning from the mid-1930s through the 1950s. During the early part of this period, the focus was primarily on correcting the attitudes of white Southerners. The latter part of this period centered more on addressing white prejudices more generally, and opening up opportunities for black people to pursue their own social and economic mobility as American citizens. The primary – and ultimately destructive – limitation of racial liberalism is that it never required white citizens to take responsibility for their own complicity in, and benefit from, structural forms of racial inequality. Instead, racial liberalism invited black people to pursue mobility as individuals, as Americans, without acknowledging the intransigence of antiblack racism both in the market, and in state policies intended to 'free' that market for exploitation by individual capitalist-citizens. Of course, it is also during this period that the US pursued the decidedly *non*-liberal racial policy of physically removing and incarcerating thousands of Japanese Americans, so it is important to understand that the trajectory of racial liberalism identified by Melamed is applicable specifically to black people. As such, the preoccupation here is in addressing the divide between black and white citizens, and again, primarily in the South, which is imagined in this formation as the region with the most egregious (and perhaps only truly damaging) racial problem.

By the early 1960s, racial liberalism gave way to what Melamed calls *liberal multiculturalism*, as a number of new social movements offered materialist antiracisms arguing convincingly that white goodwill was insufficient to create genuine opportunities for black advancement, and as the black-white racial paradigm itself collapsed in the face of similar demands from other marginalized peoples of color. Even so, Melamed contends, these challenges to liberalism were co-opted, or in Omi and Winant's (1994) term, 'absorbed', into a new liberal multiculturalism, which appropriated radical calls to recognize cultural difference in ways that made difference marketable as a value and skill to be taught in the university, and as a principle that could be used to serve the interests of the market, all the while further extending citizenship to a broad range of marginalized racial groups. If liberal multiculturalism invited all citizens to celebrate cultural pluralism on (and perhaps as) the pathway to economic mobility, it also insisted that persistent social reproduction of poverty along certain lines of racial difference was due to specific groups' own failures to take advantage of the opportunities being provided by the *multicultural* antiracist state. Important for my analysis here, it is during this period that a greater number of affluent and middle-class whites gained access to multiculturalism through consumption of multicultural texts offered in the university classroom. As Hazel Carby (1992) has lamented:

> For white suburbia, as well as for white students in universities, these texts are becoming a way of gaining knowledge of the 'other': a knowledge that appears to satisfy and replace the desire to challenge existing frameworks of segregation. (p. 17)

Characteristic of this period, and perhaps due to increased confidence (or arrogance perhaps) afforded by greater (textual) familiarity with things multicultural, it became easier for all citizens to offer – without racial guilt – bold assessments of the relative worth of different groups' claims of racial injustice. Melamed explains:

> Within racialized communities and according to the dictates of liberal multiculturalism, responsible and representative community members were identified as good over and against those identified as bad, while relational judgments were made about minoritized communities as a whole, with model minorities – primarily Asian racial formations – being elevated over and against African American racial formations that came to signify intractability in the face of liberal-multicultural mores. (2009, p. 38)

As I will demonstrate in my analysis of *Waiting for Superman*, black families become subject to the patronizing liberal-multicultural gaze; racial representations powerfully signify their status as moral citizens and as deserving (or not) of educational opportunity.

The rise of neoliberalism in the 1980s and 1990s shifted the relationship between governmentality and race; while in earlier periods, the state positioned itself as the leader in advancing antiracism, under *neoliberal multiculturalism*, it is neoliberal economic policies and ideological formations that are seen to resolve the problem of racism. The market, in this hegemonic frame, knows neither race nor racism, and is therefore regarded as best suited to facilitate racial equality. Neoliberal multiculturalism promises to usher in the post-racial period, by nurturing a new global citizenship centered around economic participation. 'In short', Melamed contends, 'neoliberal multiculturalism has portrayed an ethic of multiculturalism to be the spirit of neoliberalism' (p. 42). In doing so, neoliberal multiculturalism abandons any explicit mention of race. While liberal multiculturalism employed discourses of equity, diversity and freedom, 'now *open societies* and *economic freedoms ... and consumerist diversity* signify multicultural rights for individuals and for corporations' (p. 43; italics in original).

Neoliberal multiculturalism is still attentive to racial difference and recognizes inequitable outcomes, but explains these differences as essentially not about race or (in) justice, but individual and group choices. As Melamed explains:

> Neoliberal-multicultural racialization has made this disparity appear fair by ascribing racialized privilege to neoliberalism's beneficiaries and racialized stigma to its dispossessed. In particular, it has valued its beneficiaries as multicultural, reasonable, law-abiding, and good global citizens and devalued the dispossessed as monocultural, backward, weak, and irrational – unfit for global citizenship because they lack the proper neoliberal subjectivity. (2009, p. 44)

In contrast to black stigmatization under liberal multiculturalism, here the focus is on the distance between black subjects and the market. Through the neoliberal-multicultural lens, we can still feel sympathy to the extent that these subjects are perceived as being *prevented* from participating in the market. However, if they *reject* opportunities to participate in the market, no matter how rigged that system may be, then our sympathies can be justifiably withheld. Any argument that the economic sphere is already regulated by racial privilege will fall on deaf ears, as the market is already presumed to be multicultural and racially ethical (i.e. *post*-racial) on its face.

I want to suggest that, even in a neoliberal-multicultural period, we can still identify elements of racial liberalism and liberal multiculturalism. History is never erased or transcended; dimensions of the previous periods are evident in our national-racial imagination and in the racial representations that inform and are informed by that imagination.

Waiting for Superman as a cultural and political product

Near the beginning of *Waiting for Superman* (Guggenheim, 2010), Harlem Children's Zone founder and so-called education 'reformer', Geoffrey Canada, recalls his childhood disappointment in learning that Superman is not real. 'Even in the depth of the ghetto', he explains to the off-camera interviewer, 'you thought, he's coming. I just don't know when, because he always shows up and he saves all the good people'. As he speaks, images of a young Canada fade to black, interspersed with images of George Reeves as the hero in tights in the 1950s TV series, *Adventures of Superman*:

> I asked my mom, do you think Superman is – she said, Superman is not real ... and I said, what do you mean, he's not real? And she thought I was crying because it's like, Santa Claus is not real, and I was crying because there was no one coming with enough power to save us.

In inspiring the title of the controversial documentary, Canada presents an image of a poor urban black community without a sense of hope, innocent but helpless in the face of social, economic and spatial marginalization. A people in need of a savior, the young black boy reckons, would do well to appeal for help to the ultimate all-American (white) superhero. Here, his city neighborhood becomes constructed as an uninhabitable jungle (Leonardo & Hunter, 2007). Unlike in some rightist interpretations, the black residents of Canada's ghetto are not to blame for their condition, but instead are victims of something unnamed, a tragic historical accident. Blameless, they earn our sympathies; however, they clearly do not have enough agencies to help themselves. Or as Canada suggests, poor African Americans are so far gone, their salvation may require someone with superhuman powers. The producers of *Waiting for Superman* use Canada's childhood memory to frame the film's heartbreaking, liberal racial narrative, in which racial inequities are bemoaned without any acknowledgment of racism, (good) people of color eschew collectivist racial politics, and black subjects in particular are quick to point out their own personal moral and emotional failures as the cause of their own low educational aspirations and attainment.

Waiting for Superman is significant as a cultural and political product, because it has been largely embraced by corporate education reformers like wealthy philanthropists Bill Gates and Eli Broad, and because of its harsh critique of teacher unions and uncritical praise for private educational-entrepreneurial ventures like KIPP and Teach for America. Although the film generated a massive critical response from academics and progressive education advocates (see, for example, http://www.notwaitingforsuperman.org), it enjoyed a generally sympathetic and often enthusiastic response everywhere else, from glowing newspaper and magazine stories, to favorable coverage by influential media personalities like Oprah Winfrey and Katie Couric.

Waiting for Superman is also important, because it is perhaps the most influential popular-discursive effort to advance a new managerialism in education reform. Managerialism, as Michael Apple (2006) explains is led by an emerging group of middle-class professionals committed to using business models of profit, competition and efficiency to 'reform' education (and other public institutions and functions). This entails privatizing some schools, and financially and politically undermining remaining public institutions, which are then forced to compete with these marketized schools. Ultimately, then, the argument can be made that private entities can more effectively deliver services that have previously been understood as public, as part of our collective responsibility for the public good. Managerialism is 'an ideal project', Apple contends, 'merging the language of empowerment, rational choice, efficient organization, and new roles for managers all at the same time' (p. 25). *Waiting for Superman* is, in effect, a managerialist manifesto for education in the United States. What we learn in examining racial representations in the film is exactly how mangerialism aims to win for the rightist project a certain innocence vis à vis racism, and more, a sense that racial progress *depends* on adopting conservative ideology and reform policies.

The story arc of *Waiting for Superman*, its primary suspense, centers on a competitive public lottery system in which children and their families vie for a severely limited number of student spots in highly-regarded charter schools. It is *The Hunger Games* in reverse; here, those *not* selected are presumed to be the unfortunate ones, condemned to suffering and abuse, while the masses watch. And like that blockbuster motion picture, *Waiting for Superman* is a cultural product, not simply a documentation of truth, or policy, or everyday life. The filmmakers construct a dramatic plot, with messages embedded in the images and also made explicit in the text. We meet the families, hear them share their struggles and dreams, and explain what they believe accounts for their own educational and/or social marginality. The filmmakers intend to evoke enough sympathy that as the film comes to its dramatic final scenes, we are emotionally invested in the outcome, anxious to discover if the students will be offered admission, as the number of still available seats becomes smaller and smaller. In most cases, the families experience crushing disappointment, which allows opportunities for wrenching close-ups of terrified eyes, tear-stained cheeks, and hands still clenching strips of paper with losing numbers. To a great degree, the filmmakers need, perhaps the audience too needs, or at least desires, to see suffering. Not only does it help the filmmakers make their argument about the state of public education, but it is also better theater, more compelling entertainment. Ultimately, our own humanity is affirmed, because we care so much about these strangers on the screen.

In one particularly moving scene, we see a Latina mother, Maria, touring a Harlem charter school where she hopes her first-grade son, Francisco, will win a spot, to escape his low-resourced school in the South Bronx. Maria is clearly impressed with the resources of the charter school, and looks longingly at the warm, inviting classrooms. 'I don't care if we have to wake up at 5 o'clock in the morning in order to get there at 7:45', she says, almost plaintively. 'That's what we will do'.

But, as the *New York Times* later reported (Otterman, 2010), when this scene was filmed, Maria *already* knew that Francisco would *not* get to attend this school. The scene was staged after the lottery, in order to 'see her reaction to the school, and her genuine emotion', according to director Davis Guggenheim. For him, the scene was 'real' because the pain and longing in her eyes revealed her excitement about the possibility of having her son attend the charter school, although it might also be argued that they exploited her pain for their own purposes. It is certainly not uncommon for documentary filmmakers to re-enact and re-order scenes; my point here is to underscore that *Waiting for Superman* is *produced*, and produced in ways which evoke not only specific emotions, but produce and reproduce certain cultural discourses and ideological formations.

As a *racial* cultural product, the film provides images of racialized bodies and differences that seem natural largely because they draw upon the familiar or the popular, that which we already accept about race, and more specifically here, blackness. As Herman Gray (2005) explains, 'the movement of black images and representation is never free of cultural and social traces of the condition of their production, circulation, and use' (p. 21). Hence, what I want to highlight in my analysis of the film is the ways in which black social actors take their (expected) place within the broader ideological conditions of official antiracisms – speaking, gazing and even moving on screen in support of that grander narrative.

As I have hinted, if not said explicitly thus far, neoliberal multiculturalism, in conjunction with managerialism, brings an inherent effort to move beyond the black-white racial paradigm. This is more than an acknowledgment of a fuller plane of racial diversity, but an ideological position in which 'black' is understood as anachronistic, passé and a threat to national progress. Jared Sexton (2008) is worth quoting at length:

> Modernizing the nation – at least the segment of the nation with the potential to be 'more than black' or simply to move 'beyond black' – and liberating it from the deadening weight of the past requires that the signature of its persistence ... be effaced. In this light, multiracialism can be read ... as an element of the ascendant ideology of colorblindness, but it is not thereby identical to it. Its target is not race per se, since multiracialism is still very much a politics of racial identity ... but rather the categorical sprawl of blackness in particular and the insatiable political demand it presents to a nominally postemancipation society. (2008, p. 6)

Neoliberal multiculturalism, or what Sexton calls multiracialism, seeks to rescue racial identity from blackness, which is seen as largely responsible for giving race its offensive and oppositional signification. The neoliberal-multicultural cultural product, then, finds effective ways to situate blackness and black bodies as absent of rationality or agency, and black racial politics an ineffective explanation of, or solution to persistent racial inequity.

I am not suggesting that there is a direct line between racial representation and racial intent. That is, my aim is not to provide evidence that the film is racist, or that the filmmakers were motivated by racism. Rather, my argument is that the film was produced, and enters a field of already existing cultural productions, in which race and blackness have already been and continue to be imagined discursively, and in which black bodies are situated materially, disproportionately among the poorest and least regarded. What becomes important and potentially destructive about *Waiting for Superman* is the extent to which its representations reproduce and reify antiblack imaginations, ideologies and sentiments, even as the filmmakers claim to have offered a cultural product – an officially antiracist cultural product – that advocates for poor black people and other marginalized racial groups.

Saving black people, one story at a time

In this section, I explore black racial representation in *Waiting for Superman* by highlighting a number of scenes in the film, beginning with the introduction of the white narrator and continuing until the final frames, when we learn the fate of Anthony, the black boy whose story provides the bookends of the film. Throughout, I demonstrate how the stories are constructed in ways that provide support for neoliberal multiculturalism, and display elements of earlier official antiracisms as well.

The filmmaker: 'Betraying the ideals I thought I lived by'

Early in the film, we meet the narrator, who is also the film's director, Davis Guggenheim. His face is never fully shown, but we see images of him driving his child to school, as he explains his unease about the state of public education in the US. 'No matter who we are', he says, 'or what neighborhood we live in, each morning, wanting to believe that our schools will take a leap of faith'. Here, he evokes a universal desire that educators believe in our children as much as parents do. 'Neighborhood', and his reference to different kinds of neighborhoods, signifies race and class without doing so overtly. If race and class have ever mattered, and Guggenheim seems to implicitly acknowledge that differences have structured opportunities, he proffers a vision in which they should not, and an ideal in which all parents, regardless of differences in status, identity or geography, share the same interests. Of course, Guggenheim effectively acknowledges spatial differences without explicitly connecting space to systematic racism and maldistribution of economic resources, thus setting the stage for the rest of the film, which, while offering a detailed history of public education, fails to include any discussion of how our history with race and class might help explain the current unequal state of schooling in the nation.

For Guggenheim, it is all a matter of luck and choice, albeit wracked with liberal guilt. 'Every morning, betraying the ideals I thought I lived by, I drive past three public schools as I take my kids to a private school', he laments. 'But I'm lucky – I have a choice'. At this moment, we see a white child leap eagerly from the car, and run toward a clean, brightly-colored playground. On the one hand, Guggenheim is merely expressing the difficult decision any parents might have in choosing the best educational options for their children. However, the underlying racial narrative is that poor Blacks and Latinos, because of their unluckiness, do not get to attend schools with white children, or perhaps that they do not get to attend schools as good as the ones (affluent and middle class) white children attend. What motivates him in making the film is a desire to extend that opportunity to these unlucky souls. While the emphasis on 'choice' is clearly consistent with neoliberal multiculturalism, Guggenheim's anguish about 'betraying' his own ideals reveals a concern about values more reminiscent of racial liberalism. Although he does not frame his 'betrayal' in terms of race or racial prejudice – one could read this more narrowly as his conflicted commitment to public education – I would suggest that his words enter a larger discursive field in which liberal whites wrestle with their own privilege relative to people of color, even as they continue to make education-related decisions that benefit their children at the expense of children of color. Similar to Baldwin's critique of the popularity of protest novels, whites can take comfort in their own awareness of, and bad feelings about racial injustice in schools (for a similar case, see Dumas, 2009). Here, then, Guggenheim's confessional musings secure for *Waiting for Superman* its (official) antiracist credentials without ever addressing structural racism or the material effects of his own white racial advantage.

Anthony: 'no TV, no games, no nothin'

When we first meet Anthony, he is sitting on his bed talking with Guggenheim, who is off-camera, asking him a question: If he had four cookies and ate two, what percentage would he have left? We see Anthony thinking aloud, cross-multiplying and finally, with a grin, offering the correct answer. After a few other scenes, including Canada's desire for Superman to come to the ghetto, and Guggenheim's lament about betraying his own ideals, we return to Anthony's bedroom.

'School, like at first, I was having difficulties, but that's because I wasn't coming home and studying', Anthony explains to Guggenheim.

'And then I started to pass ... and I stayed back one grade, and that was in the second grade'.

'Why?' we hear softly from off-camera.

'Huh? That's because my father had passed ... He just *died*'. Anthony pauses. 'He took drugs'. He looks away, tearfully, and the screen fades to a photo of a younger, happier Anthony with his father at an amusement park.

We then see Anthony's grandmother, a plainly-dressed, heavy-set middle-aged woman with sad eyes. She is pouring Anthony a glass of orange juice and stares at him, straightfaced, while he drinks it. 'Be careful', she yells after him as he leaves the house on his way to school.

Next, we see her sitting at her kitchen table. From off-camera: 'What was your choice in taking him in?'

Anthony's grandmother looks incredulous. 'There *wasn't* no choice. I wouldn't have had it any other way'. We see Anthony walking past a chain-link fence, seemingly a signifier of haunting urban realness, but here, it appears to be surrounding a church parking lot.

'I made a lot of mistakes when I was younger with my kids', his grandmother is explaining mournfully. 'I don't know what I would do without him at this point'.

'But he needs you', Guggenheim asks, again, the white voice out of view. 'Why do *you* need him?'

Anthony's grandmother looks taken aback at the question. 'I-I don't know. I think we need each other. And there's nothin' I won't do for him. *Nothin'*.' She smiles sadly, but resolved.

After a number of other scenes, and immediately after a scene focused on Black men in prison, we return to the same kitchen table. 'I'm just so afraid for him. I just cries for him sometimes, because I am so afraid', she says to the interviewer'. I am. I pray all the time, because I know he could be easily influenced to do things he shouldn't do. And it scares me'.

Again, we see Anthony walking through a drab urban scene, with empty lots and worn-looking homes. 'He never knew his mom', his grandmother explains. 'I think his mom had other kids but Anthony doesn't know those kids. My mom left me when I was probably about 8, so my grandparents raised me'. We see Anthony walking across a patchy, yellowing lawn to enter his school, a low brick building with rusty steel grates over all the windows.

'Was school important to you?' Guggenheim asks Anthony's grandmother.

'No', she says, shaking her head. 'It wasn't. It probably wasn't because I never had nobody to push me, to talk to me about stuff. So, it wasn't. It wasn't'.

Once again, we see the photo of Anthony with his father. 'And your son?'

'Mmm, he didn't think school was important either. No …' She furrows her eyebrows. 'He didn't. He did his thing, I guess'.

The scene closes with Anthony in class, pledging allegiance to the flag.

Later, we are there when Anthony visits a charter school that operates as an urban boarding school; students share cramped rooms, study and live together, away from their families, under the supervision of residential staff and teachers. We see a group of Black students touring the rather drab facility, as a Black female staffer explains, 'Because it's like a boarding school, when it comes time to go to college, you will already know what it's going to be like'.

Anthony is now back in his room, discussing the school with the filmmaker, off camera. 'You have 7 classes, you have to wake up early, usually in there you have to wear ties and stuff. No TV, no games, no nothin'.'

'So are you hoping to get in or hoping that you *don't* get in?'

'Uh, it's bittersweet', Anthony replies slowly. 'If I get in, that'll just give me a better chance in life, but if I don't, I just – just be with my friends'.

We then see Anthony enthusiastically playing a violent video game, while his grandmother, seemingly oblivious, is interviewed in the kitchen. 'In a way, I want him to get in, but then another part of me don't want him to get in'.

'Why?'

'Because he'll be gone all that time. But I want him to go'. We now see Anthony outside, alone, bouncing a basketball in a local court, almost as if he might be seduced by the urban streets, avoiding the academic work he should be doing. 'A part of me wants him to go', his grandmother says. 'I – hmm – I uh, I don't know …' Her voice trails off.

During the lottery for admission to the boarding school, Anthony is offered a spot on the waitlist. Toward the end of the film, we are there to witness the (undoubtedly staged) phone call when Anthony receives 'good news' – a spot has opened up for him at the school! We see Anthony, his grandmother and what appears to be his grandfather (who never speaks) dropping Anthony off at the school. Choosing an upper bunk in his new room, he tapes the photograph of he and his father to the cinder-block wall. The last we see of Anthony, he is laying there staring at the image on the wall.

Anthony's story, as told here, could be an exhibit from Daniel Moynihan's infamous 1965 report, *The Negro Family: The Case for National Action*, in which the sociologist and US senator argued that the most significant barrier to economic and social mobility for African Americans was not racial discrimination or unemployment, but the absence of traditional patriarchal, two-parent families. The result, according to Moynihan, was a culture of pathology in which women led, and black culture suffered a loss of values and direction (Dance, 2004). The problem in Anthony's family, in this narrative, begins with his grandmother, who, by her own account, failed to take education seriously. Although we see her with a man at the end of the film, we never hear from him, nor receive any explanation of who he is. Therefore, we are left with the sense that she raised her son, and passed along her lack of aspiration to him. Naturally, he then fathers a child with a morally questionable woman, and becomes a drug addict. Once his father dies, Anthony is left to be raised by his grandmother, a woman who seems repentant and devoted, but limited in her abilities as a parent, and ultimately, still noncommittal about a rigorous educational path for Anthony.

Anthony is offered rescue (his Superman) in the opportunity to attend the boarding school. His ineffectual grandmother, loving and doting though she may be, allows him to play violent video games and fritter away his life on a local basketball court, while expressing ambivalence about the lottery, because she would miss him should he be admitted. Anthony is at risk of succumbing to his grandmother's weakness. In the context of the narrative offered here, his complaints about long school days, strict rules, and being away from his friends read less as a young teen's reasonable anxieties and more as signs of personal moral failure, and the transmission of flawed cultural values. We are to be relieved when Anthony's grandmother relinquishes control to the charter school; here, at least, he can have the opportunity to be more than his father ever was.

The absence of a structural analysis is striking, and in accord with the neoliberal-multicultural project. When pressed by Guggenheim, Anthony's grandmother suggests that the reason she was not interested in school was because her own family did not encourage her to succeed. However, even if one wanted to argue that Anthony *now* has access to educational options and good reason to be hopeful – a dubious contention, to be sure – there should be general consensus that his grandmother likely did not, as a black child attending school in the 1950s and 1960s. Here, Guggenheim unwrites that historical context, and with it, any consideration of the material and emotional impact of racially discriminatory policies in education, housing and employment. By relying on, and even pressuring Anthony's grandmother to explain her own lack of educational attainment, Guggenheim fetishizes individual choice, while subtly providing a nod to Moynihan's thesis of cultural disintegration, which would have been ascendant during early periods of official antiracism. Anthony's family's blackness, in the representation offered here is of the counterproductive, anachronistic sort that Moynihan warned about; the boarding school, with its all-black and mostly male staff is presented as a necessary cultural corrective. The state, in offering Anthony's family this choice, positions itself as providing post-black black subjects the opportunity to transcend their destructive racial selves and adopt new, historic and market-friendly racial and educational identities.

Nakia: neoliberal redemption for the 'Bad Black Mother'

Nakia heaves her heavy frame up the several flights of stairs to her apartment, breathing hard as her young daughter, Bianca, follows quickly behind. We hear her sighing loudly as she fans herself. The camera pans to her feet as she struggles to make it to her floor; her front door creaks loudly as she opens it. 'I never did envision having children', she tells the off-camera interviewer, sitting in front of her window, which has a metal security grate obscuring the view of the Harlem street. 'It's – it's something, because they grow so fast, and you just see so many different things with them'. We see Bianca unpacking books in the sparsely furnished apartment, and then a scene of Nakia reviewing her daughter's homework.

'I don't care what I have to do. I don't care how many jobs I have to obtain. But she will go to college. It's just – no second-guessing that one'. She shakes her head, somber. The apartment is dark around her.

Later in the film, Nakia explains that she attended public schools, and remembers a teacher talking about getting paid whether or not students learn. 'It sticks with you', she says, 'and that's something that no parent wants their child to bear witness to when they're going to school'. So Nakia decided to enroll Bianca in a parochial school that happens to be across the street from her apartment. Each month, she must pay $500 to cover the cost of tuition and fees. We see a close-up of her brown hands as she sits at her dining table, writing a check. 'It's a struggle. It's a struggle. But it's a choice that I made. It's my responsibility to my child'.

From off-camera: 'Do you ever think that if you sent Bianca to a public school, that there would be less pressure with money?'

'I have given that some thought', she says, and then smiles, shaking her head, 'But I just revert back to the same thing. I'll just have to find a way'.

Several scenes later, we return to the apartment, just in time to see little Bianca staring longingly out a grate-covered window at the school across the street. 'Mom, everybody's going to school now', she says plaintively.

'I know'.

'I'm not graduating'.

'No, you're graduating. You just won't be at the ceremony'. Nakia is tearful as she explains that she has been unable to keep up the tuition payments, as her hours have been cut at work. 'Today is, uh, her graduation, and she's not allowed to go because I do owe some tuition, and they would not allow her to go to the ceremonies. It's enough that I have to explain it to her. Why penalize her for my responsibilities?'

We now see Nakia boarding the subway alone, as she continues to tell the story. 'I said, "Mommy wanted you to stay in your school" and she [Bianca] finished my sentence; she said, "I know, but you didn't have enough money". And I said, "That's right, but that was Mommy's choice to put you in that school, and it's gonna be Mommy's job to get you in a school that's better"'. Standing alone on the train, Nakia rhythmically rocks back and forth. And now, we see her sitting alone in her apartment, in the dark, with a lone light on, apparently filling out charter school applications in the dead of night.

We later see Nakia and Bianca at the lottery, as the winning numbers are called, ever so slowly. Nakia's worried face reflects utter defeat as the last number is called and the announcer says, 'Thank you to all of you. Thank you for being here'. As people begin to file out of the auditorium, Bianca begins to cry as she sees her mother tearing up. 'Don't cry', Nakia says softly. 'You're gonna make Mommy cry'. In their final scene, we see Nakia and Bianca on the bus ride home from the lottery, both sitting sullen, silent.

In some sense, Nakia is presented as a noble figure. We witness her sacrifice and commitment to her daughter's education, and her heartbreak when she cannot give Bianca everything she has promised. However, she is also what Patricia Hill Collins (2004) has called the 'Bad Black Mother', that single, young, poor mother, who has failed to have a child within the confines of the traditional family and 'pass[es] on [her] bad values to [her] children who in turn are more likely to become criminals and unwed teenaged mothers' (p. 131).

While it might be argued that Nakia offers a counternarrative to that discursive formation, I contend that she is still a Bad Black Mother, only redeemed through her suffering and her tireless faith in private educational options. 'Mommy's choice', here, is to eschew all public education in favor of a parochial school that she can ill afford. However, this follows her 'bad' choice to have a child out of wedlock in the first place. One of the first things we hear Bianca say on camera is that she 'never did envision having children'. By including this piece of arguably unnecessary narrative – why couldn't we have been allowed to imagine that Nakia intended to have a child? – the filmmaker positions Bianca as a Bad Black Mother, and then offers her redemption in presenting a sympathetic portrayal in which she doggedly seeks a charter school for Bianca.

Her efforts may earn her some reprieve in the eyes of the viewers; however, in the end, Bianca loses, and we are left with Nakia, perhaps not quite the Bad Black Mother, but certainly having shown it is inevitable, even natural that some should be trapped in poverty. Consistent with Melamed's (2009) formulation, Nakia's failure to take advantage of market-based reforms has little to do with racism or lack of economic fairness, but with her (chosen) subjectivity as a poor, black, single mother. We can feel good for rooting for Nakia – we are merciful, after all – but when her daughter does not earn a spot in the charter school, it becomes clear that it was Nakia who made that initial ill-advised *choice* to have a child that even an antiracist nation couldn't fix.

Michelle Rhee and the model minority vs Negro problem

'Just in case there was any confusion', Michelle Rhee says, smiling broadly at the podium, 'I am 37, and no, I have never run a school district before'. The camera pans the mostly black audience, sitting stone-faced, some with their arms crossed, clearly suspicious of, if not hostile to the 'reformer', this young, crisply-dressed, Korean-American woman brought in to clean house in one of the poorest and blackest school districts in the nation. To underscore that metaphor, the next image is of the now-famous *Time* magazine cover, showing a dour-faced Rhee in a sharp black pantsuit and heels, in a classroom, holding a broom.

When Rhee was appointed chancellor of public schools for the District of Columbia in 2007, she was heralded as a reformer, one of a new, entrepreneurial breed of professionals with little patience for ignorance, excuses and laziness (again, characteristic of Apple's explanation of managerialism). Yes, there are specific policies advocated by the so-called reformers – increased high-stakes testing, numbers-driven teacher evaluation, breaking the power of the unions, handing over control of public schools to private entities, including venture capitalists. However, it is the celebration of Rhee as a no-nonsense heroine in the fight against ignorance, excuses and laziness that most powerfully informs how *Waiting for Superman* situates her over and against the predominantly black communities and teaching force of the 'Chocolate City' that is the nation's capital. A narrative of *black* ignorance, *black* excuses, *black* laziness is consistent with, and only reinforces the popular-cultural imagination of black people.

We see Rhee effortlessly multitasking, being driven around the District of Columbia, on her phone and laptop at the same time, as the narrator laments the tenures of her predecessors, whose black faces are shown on the screen, failures all. Now Rhee is walking briskly through her suite of offices. We see office after office of black employees, none moving as quickly as she is, most looking slightly dazed and confused. The camera follows her as she points out inefficiencies and just plain clutter, and expresses her care for the district's children.

Later in the film, after we learn more about Anthony's and Bianca's troubles, we return to Rhee, who is still moving quickly, texting on her phone. Now, she is sitting tight-lipped, in front of another auditorium full of black people, and what may be dark-skinned Latino/as, who are all yelling, fists raised and brows furrowed. They are holding placards: 'Get up, stand up for your rights'; and in all caps, 'MICHELLE RHEE, DID YOU KNOWINGLY SIGN UP TO BE A HATCHET LADY?!!' The camera pans, almost frenetically, to capture dark-skinned DC residents pointing their fingers, rolling their heads, apparently angry about the reforms Rhee has instituted. Even black people in suits – men and women – are screaming and waving their hands, although we cannot hear what they are saying. Not once in the film, in fact, do we genuinely *hear* the black people we see in these angry scenes – none are interviewed, none asked to explain their grievances against Rhee. Meanwhile, the white narrator, in a calm voice, details Rhee's (reasonable) closure of schools and righteous firing of administrators and teachers who couldn't or wouldn't get on board with her reform agenda.

Rhee is now standing in front of the group, again in the sharp black pantsuit, arms folded, with a slight smile on her face, silent. We then hear her offer a calm explanation for her actions, and explain that she doesn't have to worry about the repercussions, because she is not a career superintendent and is only interested in what is right for the kids. We then see another black woman, yelling loudly, 'We will not be moved! We will *not* be moved!'

When we return to Rhee later, it seems that perhaps some black people have warmed to her, as we see her surrounded by a smiling crowd, apparently pleased with her reforms. However, now she is speaking to a room of teachers, mostly black, offering higher salaries as merit pay – that is, more money for higher test scores. They shake their heads, disapprovingly, as if they are reflexively opposed to hard work. This assumes, of course, that they are not objecting to Rhee's policies on pedagogical or even ideological grounds, but rather, because they are characteristically lazy, overly sentimental, and, much like the black parents and caregivers in the film, just a bit ambivalent about education. When the vote is taken, the teachers reject Rhee's proposal. We then see her alone in the back of a sedan, somber, being driven through the dark streets of DC, the Capitol in the rearview mirror.

Waiting for Superman situates Rhee not only against teachers unions and bad educational policy, but also against a recalcitrant black city mired in a problem of its own making – A problem of its own *blackness*. Here we see black teachers reluctant to work harder and black parents so ill-informed and perhaps unsupportive of education that they would oppose Rhee's reasonable reforms – reforms intended for their own good. The black subjects express their opposition to Rhee through familiar forms of protest – rallies, chants, signs – but here they are denied claim to a righteous legacy of black freedom protest. Instead, the film gives us permission to chastise them for privileging tired racial allegiance over the simultaneously post- and multiracial progress offered by Rhee.

That Rhee is Korean American only contributes to the neoliberal-multicultural discourse on 'good' and 'bad' racialized groups, of Asian Americans as 'model minorities' prepared to take advantage of the new global economy versus those other racialized groups who will be understandably left behind. As Tamara Nopper (2010) explains:

> Koreans are … associated with an important figure in US history – the pioneer – and thus are becoming incorporated into the 'American dream' narrative that centralizes the white immigrant trajectory … [T]he pioneer is depicted as oriented toward the future; risk-taking is

therefore understood to be in the service of a larger vision of prosperity and success for future generations. (p. 77)

Although the filmmaker never makes reference to Rhee's Koreanness, or for that matter, the blackness of the District of Columbia, the representation of the 'pioneer', Rhee, in contrast to the foolishly resistant city and its people culturally reproduces this alignment of Koreans and Asian Americans with whiteness, and signifies DC's black residents, and indeed, their blackness, as standing in the way of true multicultural advancement.

In this sense, *Waiting for Superman* problematically defends a position of Asian Americans 'in the racial middle', as Mari Matsuda (2010) has described it – a place between white and black in the nation's racial hierarchy. In this configuration of the racist model minority myth, Asian Americans are celebrated as a kind of 'racial bourgeoisie' (Matsuda, 2010, p. 558) whose presumed overwhelming success in the marketplace – overstated and overly generalized as it is – serves witness to the market's racial fairness, indeed its antiracism. Thus, when Rhee faces resistance in this predominantly black school district, it can be understood as a kind of unjustified resentment against Asian Americans for being successful, where black people have failed (Omi & Takagi, 2010). In presenting a sympathetic portrayal of Rhee and highlighting black opposition (but without giving it a clear voice) the film effectively chastises black people for refusing to learn from, and *refusing to become* model minorities themselves.

Privatizing (anti)racism in education and education policy discourse

While *Waiting for Superman* highlights racial disparities in educational outcomes and claims to offer a corrective, it offers no historical or political-economic context to explain the production and reproduction of racial inequities, and it seems to eschew any remedy that takes account of persistent racism, or the significance of racial identities and homeplaces (Fullilove, 2005; Haymes, 1995) Thus, on-screen, race is both highly visible and powerfully invisible. Here, race is lamented as a regrettable difference that makes a difference, or more accurately, *used to* make a difference. Race is transcended: even as racial signs fill nearly every frame of the film, we are instructed not to read the signs racially. In the end, if racial inequality in urban education was ever about race, urban school *reform*, from the perspective of *Waiting for Superman*, demands that we not only move beyond (that is, *post-*) race, but more devastatingly, imagine ourselves that much more forward-thinking and benevolent because of our insistence on doing so.

This is what Goldberg has termed 'born again racism' (2009, p. 23), in which self-conscious, urgent racial progress quickly gives way to formal state policies intended to achieve equality without attention to race. The state is thus 'born again' in two senses: First, it is washed clean – *white* as snow? – of all racial transgressions; second, it is a new creature, absent of any history or relations of power. Born again racism, Goldberg explains, is 'racism without race, racism gone private, racism without the categories to name it as such' (p. 23). Although racism may still exist, it is the stuff of individual moral failure to empathize, not state actions, not the power of capital, not ideological formations or maldistribution of economic resources along racial lines.

'Superman', as invoked here, need not be interested in racial justice in order to save black people. *He* just needs to save the 'good' people, which can best be accomplished by not attending to race, through erasure of racial context and racial explanation of inequality. Racism is privatized: A discourse of racism as a legitimate grievance against the state is removed from the public sphere, since any 'lingering' racism is a matter of the heart. Hence, (consuming) stories of black suffering in *Waiting for Superman* allows us to keep race and racism in their proper, private, emotional place. But *anti*racism is also privatized, as the state cedes that role to market forces, which are understood as better equipped to more efficiently manage the pursuit of opportunity for all. The officially antiracist state takes credit for facilitating the end of inequality, yet assumes none of the responsibility for the inequitable outcomes.

'Born again racism', Goldberg warns, 'reappears whenever called upon to do the dirty work of racist politics but purged of its categorical stiffness ... [R]aceless racism operates in denial, anywhere and anytime' (p. 25). In *Waiting for Superman*, the 'categorical stiffness' of race and race-conscious explanation of educational inequities are rejected in favor of neoliberal school reforms, even as the film repeatedly employs representations of black people and other people of color to do the dirty work of denying the validity of claims of persistent, structural racism.

Conclusion

What I have attempted to do here is: (1) offer an analysis of how the officially antiracist stance of neoliberal education reforms helps secure for these reforms moral rightness and cultural-political hegemony; (2) reveal how racial representations powerfully inform our understanding of educational policy; and (3), explain how, in newly ascendant multiculturalisms or racial neoliberalisms, blackness increasingly occupies a marginal location, and signifies not only an obstacle to social and economic progress, but to *racial* progress as well. The aim is not to cast *Waiting for Superman* as 'racist' or even racially insensitive. Rather, what I aim to show is that the filmmakers made choices in production, editing and narration that reinforce already existing racial representations, and confirm our imaginations of black people and their tentative relationship to education. In doing so, the filmmakers enhance the appeal of the film, since the text and images are familiar to us (i.e. do not challenge hegemonic constructions of race or blackness), and, as with the racial protest novels, allow us to believe we have gained new insight into black pain and suffering, and that we are better people – *antiracist* people – just for watching. More than this, the film provides a policy solution that promises an end to racial educational inequality, for those who *choose* it.

Finally, I want to encourage more critical policy researchers to attend to the politics of racial representation. When *Waiting for Superman* was released in 2010, the critical response centered almost entirely on analysis of the film's advocacy of neoliberal policies (Au, 2012; Goldstein, 2010; Ravitch, 2010). Troublingly, the lack of deep analysis of racial representations – and the politics of those representations – signals that even among critical scholars, it is proving difficult to find a space to take account of the construction of *racial meanings*. It is perhaps more apparently urgent – and more in the tradition of education scholarship – to explore race in education through inquiry about disproportionate opportunities and outcomes. That is to say, the predominant aim of education scholarship on race is to explain how social and educational policies and practices impact identifiable racial/ethnic groups. Here, then, 'black' becomes invoked primarily in reporting that black students are (most often) positioned on the racial bottom of whatever measure of educational opportunity or attainment. What I want to instigate is interrogation of how *imaginations* of those on the 'racial bottom' of education are produced, disseminated, and consumed, a task made all the more important as cultural products like *Waiting for Superman* (and the more recent studio release, *Won't Back*

Down) invite an even broader audience to participate in a popular-discursive form of education policy analysis.

References

Apple, M. W. (2006). *Educating the 'right' way: Markets, standards, God and inequality.* New York, NY: Routledge.

Au, W. (2012). Learning to read: Charter schools, public education and the politics of educational research. *Seattle Education.* Retrieved from http://seattleeducation2010.wordpress.com/

Carby, H. V. (1992). The multicultural wars. In G. Dent (Ed.), *Black popular culture* (pp. 187–199). Seattle: The New Press.

Collins, P. H. (2004). *Black sexual politics: African Americans, gender, and the new racism.* New York, NY: Routledge.

Dance, L. J. (2004). *Tough fronts: The impact of street culture on schooling.* New York, NY: Routledge.

Dumas, M. J. (2009). Redistribution and recognition in educational research: How do we get dictionaries at Cleveland? In J. Anyon (Ed.), *Theory and educational research: Toward critical social explanation* (pp. 81–102). New York, NY: Routledge.

Fullilove, M. T. (2005). *Root shock: How tearing up city neighborhoods hurts America, and what we can do about it.* New York, NY: One World.

Goldberg, D. T. (2009). *The threat of race: Reflections on racial neoliberalism.* Malden, MA: Blackwell.

Goldstein, D. (2010, May 21). Grading 'Waiting for Superman'. *The Nation.* Retrieved from http://www.thenation.com

Gray, H. (2005). *Cultural moves: African Americans and the politics of representation.* Berkeley: University of California.

Guggenheim, D. (Director). (2010). *Waiting for Superman* [Motion picture]. Retrieved from http://www.waitingforsuperman.com

Hall, S. (1992). Encoding, decoding. In S. During (Ed.), *The cultural studies reader* (pp. 90–103). New York, NY: Routledge.

Haymes, S. N. (1995). *Race, culture and the city: A pedagogy for black urban struggle.* Albany: State University of New York.

Leonardo, Z., & Hunter, M. (2007). Imagining the urban: The politics of race, class, and schooling. In W. Pink & G. Noblit (Eds.), *International handbook of urban education* (pp. 779–802). Dordrecht: Springer.

Matsuda, M. (2010). We will not be used: Are Asian Americans the racial bourgeoisie? In J. Y. S. Wu & T. C. Chen (Eds.), *Asian American studies now: A critical reader* (pp. 558–564). New Brunswick, NJ: Rutgers University.

Melamed, J. (2009). *Represent and destroy: Rationalizing violence in the new racial capitalism.* Minneapolis: University of Minnesota.

Moynihan, D. P. (1965). *The Negro family: The case for national action.* Washington, DC: Office of Policy Planning and Research, United States Department of Labor.

Nakagawa, S. (2013, March 1). *Revising blackness is the fulcrum [blog post].* Retrieved from http://www.changelabinfo.com/2013/03/01/revisiting-blackness-is-the-fulcrum/#.UV8AnatEStW

Nopper, T. K. (2010). Colorblind racism and institutional actors' explanations of Korean immigrant entrepreneurship. *Critical Sociology, 36*(1), 65–85. doi:10.1177/0896920509347141

Omi, M., & Takagi, D. (2010). Situating Asian Americans in the political discourse on affirmative action. In J. Y. S. Wu, & T. C. Chen (Eds.), *Asian American studies now: A critical reader* (pp. 118–125). New Brunswick, NJ: Rutgers University.

Omi, M., & Winant, H. (1994). *Racial formation in the United States.* New York, NY: Routledge.

Otterman, S. (2010, May 21). In 'Waiting for Superman,' a scene isn't what it seems. *New York Times.* Retrieved from http://www.nytimes.com

Ravitch, D. (2010). *The death and life of the great American school system: How testing and choice are undermining education.* New York, NY: Basic.

Sexton, J. (2008). *Amalgamation schemes: Antiblackness and the critique of multiculturalism.* Minneapolis: University of Minnesota.

Wright, R. (1940). *Native son.* New York, NY: Grosset & Dunlap.

From model minorities to disposable models: the de-legitimisation of educational success through discourses of authenticity

Alice Bradbury

Institute of Education, University of London, London, UK

This article explores teachers' use of discourses of authenticity in relation to minoritised students, with a focus on the relationship between these discourses and 'model minority' status. The paper aims to advance the critical thinking about 'model minorities' in the education system in England by examining the diversity of identity positions and minoritised groups that can be constituted as belonging to this category in different contexts. It is argued that in England there is 'intelligible space' for some students from the Afghan and Kosovan communities to be constituted as 'model minorities', alongside the Chinese and Indian communities usually identified with this term, with similar links made between the home lives of students and their educational attainment. However, this status carries with it racist assumptions about students' motivation, and the perception of high attainment as inauthentic and therefore illegitimate. Building on Archer and Francis' discussions of Chinese students' success as being achieved in the 'wrong way', it is argued that the idea of authenticity/inauthenticity can be used to delegitimise educational success in multiple ways. A theoretical framework influenced by Critical Race Theory is used to discuss the role of this partial and precarious recognition of some minoritised groups' high attainment in the continuation of White dominance in education.

Introduction

This article aims to develop two related discussions in the field of race and education concerning the constitution of some groups as 'model minorities' and the use of discourses of authenticity to dismiss minoritised students' attainment. This discussion is motivated by the need to examine in more detail the limits of 'model minority' status and to emphasise the multiplicity of ways in which the attainment of minoritised students can be rendered illegitimate. This is a combination of effects which, it is argued, allows for the continued idealisation of White students and their successes and the maintenance of the status quo in terms of disparities in educational attainment. Data from qualitative research based in Primary (age 5–11) and Secondary (age 11–16) schools in London is used to illustrate the widening groups of students who may be intelligibly understood as 'model minorities', and the range of ways in which their educational successes are rendered inauthentic. The analysis is informed by tools offered by Critical Race Theory (CRT), which illuminate how changing classroom discourses can work at a systematic level to maintain long-standing racial disparities.

The article begins with a discussion of 'model minority' discourses and the related issue of authenticity based on research in the UK and international educational contexts.

A second section examines the theoretical tools offered by CRT and their use in this discussion, before a description of the research studies which gave rise to the data used. The following sections are organised around the two main arguments proposed: first, that 'model minority' status is fluid and has, in the English context, expanded to include smaller minoritised groups identified as having a good 'education ethic'; and second, that all forms of 'model minority' status are accompanied by multiple concurrent dismissals of educational success in the form of discourses of inauthenticity. A final section examines the role of this partial and precarious recognition of some minoritised groups' high attainment in the continuation of White dominance in education, and the lessons for those who wish to challenge this state of affairs.

'Model minorities'

The discussion of 'model minorities' in this paper builds on David Gillborn's (2008) examination of this concept, which has origins in the United States, in the UK context in his book 'Racism and Education: Coincidence or conspiracy?' Of particular relevance is his argument that there is 'a disposable character to model minorities' (2008, p. 146); a fluidity in which groups of pupils can be intelligible as 'model'. Gillborn argues that some groups may no longer be seen as 'model' when they 'no longer serve the interests of powerholders'; following this argument, this paper considers as to who may be added to the list of model minorities when this serves some purpose.

The term 'model minority' has a longer history in the US than the UK, and is usually applied there to 'Asian Americans', particularly the Chinese and Japanese communities.[1] According to Li and Wang's history of the term, the first use dates back to a 1966 *New York Times* article on Japanese Americans (2008, p. 3). This was followed by a US *News and World* Report on the success of Chinese Americans (cited in Pang & Palmer, 2012, p. 1518), and a 1971 article in *Newsweek* discussing how some minority groups were 'outwitting the whites' (Li & Wang, 2008, p. 3). The emergence of this stereotype has to be seen within the changing racial dynamics of the Civil Rights era, and the historic and continued constitution of Asian-Americans as Other; as a *New York Times* commentator reminds us in a reflective piece on 30 years since the racist murder of Vincent Chin, 'history … teaches us that before Asian-Americans were seen as model minorities, we were also perpetual foreigners' (Wu, 2012).

Within the 'model minority' discourse, which has remained persistent into the twenty-first century, Asian Americans are stereotyped as displaying 'proper behaviours and attitudes (e.g. uncomplaining and docile) and proper work ethics (e.g. hardworking, persistent, diligent, and self-abnegating)' (Li, 2008, p. 216); students from this community are essentialised as 'whiz kids' (Lee, 2008, p. ix). Chang and Au list the characteristics of the 'model minority' student as 'devoted, obedient to authority, respectful of teachers, smart, good at math and science, diligent, hard workers, cooperative, well behaved, docile, college-bound, quiet and opportunistic' (2007, p. 15). This is an infantilising discourse, which positions Asian-Americans – in school and beyond – as dependent on their parents and lacking in agency. The stereotype had been fuelled, Min (2004) argues, by statistics showing that Asian Americans have a higher median family income than White Americans, although this is a flawed measure skewed by higher average family sizes (Chang & Au, 2007).

Although some Asian Americans have accepted and explored this 'model' status (see discussion in Li and Wang) many scholars have rejected the term as 'complimentary on its face' but 'disingenuous at its heart' (Wu, 2002, cited in Li & Wang, 2008, p. 2). The term is a 'bomb cloaked in sugar', as it positions Asian Americans as 'perpetual foreigners and/or honorary whites' (Li & Wang, 2008, p. 5). Extensive scholarship in this area has shown that there are multiple negative consequences of being positioned as a 'model minority', including the invisibility of racism against Asian Americans and a dismissal of claims of prejudice. Yamada (1981, cited in Chang, 2000, p. 359) gives an example of how university students reacted angrily to an anthology of 'outspoken Asian American writers', whom they saw as militant although they had been sympathetic to literature from other minoritised groups; for Asian Americans to complain of racism, it seemed, was going too far. The stereotype disguises structural inequalities suffered by Asian Americans; Min (2004) points out that although Asian Americans have higher levels of attainment overall, they do not receive equal rewards for their educational investments; their success in school does not necessarily translate into higher incomes or more rewarding careers.

At the same time, the status of Asian Americans as 'model' can cause resentment from other minority communities and from the White majority, concerned that Asian Americans 'crowd out places for Whites in the classroom and workplace' by winning scholarships and increasing grade averages (Li, 2008, p. 219). The consequences of this discourse can also be significant for those students who do not fit the stereotype, including those having special educational needs, whose barriers to learning may be not be recognised (Li, 2008; Lo, 2008); as Guofang Li argues 'If we blindly measure students against the stereotypes, we run the risk of ignoring their needs and overlooking their strengths' (2008, p. 228).

Furthermore, beyond the impact of the community under discussion, there is also an impact on wider discussions of racism and other minoritised groups, a topic which is discussed in more detail later on in this paper. The construction of successful Asian Americans, Min argues 'legitimates the supposed openness of American society' (2004, p. 334), with consequences for other groups. Moreover, as Stacey Lee argues, there can be 'no "model minority" without the concomitant stereotype of the lazy and unintelligent Black or Brown other' (Lee, 2008, p. ix). 'Model minorities' thus function as a discursive tool to deny accusations of racism and divert attention from continuing racial inequities.

In the UK, and more specifically England, the term 'model minority' has more recently been applied to different communities, namely the Indian and Chinese communities (Gillborn, 2008), due to their high levels of attainment in standardised national tests through the 1990s and 2000s. However, it would be wrong to suggest that the emergence of this discourse is due only to availability of statistics; it is based on far more complex understandings of the place of the Indian and Chinese communities within the multiplicity of migrant groups in the UK. In the case of Indian students, educational success has been linked to the supposedly middle-class occupations of many migrants from India in the post-war period, through perceptions of an appropriate 'education ethic'. There is certainly an important class dimension to this discourse – the proportion of students from these groups in receipt of free school meals are similar to the White British majority – although this is sometimes denied by those who seek to compare the Indian and Chinese students' success with other minoritised students' levels of attainment (Gillborn, 2008, p. 147). This class-based analysis of differential attainment is also recognisable in the academic literature; for example, the argument of Chang and Au that differences within the wide Asian-American group can be explained by 'the first rule of educational inequality ... Class matters' (2007, p. 16).

In England, pervasive discourses which link parental attitudes and students' home lives to inevitable paths of educational attainment or failure, both linked to and separate from class explanations, are powerful in the operation of the 'model minority' discourse. Qualitative research on British Chinese students' experiences by Archer and Francis (2007) found that they were understood by teachers as hardworking and successful in education, but were also subject to racist discourses of 'Chinese geeks'. British Chinese families were seen as too 'pushy' and students were homogenised through 'oppressive expectation' and pathologised as too focused on school at the expense of other activities. Despite their successful learner identities, British Chinese students' stereotyped subservience and passivity were criticised by teachers, leading to a 'negative positive', where teachers had high expectations based on racist assumptions (Archer & Francis, 2007). As in research in the US, there were consequences for the British Chinese students' experiences of education.

Other than Gillborn's CRT-informed analysis, there has been little academic discussion of the 'model minority' discourse in education in England, despite its prevalence in discussions of racism in schools (Archer and Francis do not use the term in their research on British Chinese students). As Gillborn argues, the fact that Indian and Chinese students attain higher scores in exams at age 16 than White British students (the government's term) is frequently cited as evidence that the education system is not institutionally racist. This argument is predicated on the idea that *a system must be racist to all minority groups, or none at all*; it denies the fact that racist assumptions may work in contradictory ways, and may have different effects on different groups. It also suggests that if a system (or indeed an individual) is racist, then they must be so equally to all groups, when this is patently not the case. A system may discriminate against one minority group, while leaving another apparently unaffected. Underlying this 'racist to all or none' argument, I would argue, is a persistent conception of racism as individual prejudice manifested in explicitly racist actions, which refuses to accept the impact of unwitting actions on minoritised groups' experiences and attainment. This denial of the idea that racism can be systematic without intention and indeed institutional is a major barrier to progress in anti-racist work in the UK. This paper seeks to open up discussion of the discourse of model minorities, by exploring the fluidity of who is constructed as 'model' and emphasising the negative elements of this status, particularly the denial of authenticity. In doing so, this aim is to further reduce the impact of the 'racist to all or none' argument as a denial of institutional racism in education.

The research studies

The data used in this article arose from two studies, both conducted in London in the period 2009–2011. First, I use data from an ESRC-funded research project involving long-term ethnographic studies of two Reception classrooms (children aged 4–5) in inner London. The schools, which I call Gatehouse and St Mary's primary schools, were located in an economically deprived area of London and the majority of the children in these two classes were from minoritised communities. The study involved classroom observation over the course of a year and regular interviews with the Reception teachers; the overall findings are discussed in detail elsewhere (Bradbury, 2011, 2013a, 2013b). The second study, funded by the London Educational Research Unit at the Institute of

Education, was a small pilot project exploring the experiences and attainment of students from the Afghan community in London. This involved background research on the community and semi-structured interviews with a primary school teacher (children aged 5–11) and a secondary teacher (ages 11–16) in schools with high number of Afghan pupils. These schools were located in a different area of London.

Data from both of these studies were coded using NVivo and analysed using a theoretical framework influenced by CRT, and also by post-structural theory, including Foucault's conception of discourse and Butler's use of performative identities (Butler, 1993, 2004). In particular, Butler's theories of recognisable identities are used to examine as to which discourses need to be deployed to allow particular groups of children to be intelligible as students, and in this case the 'intelligible space' required for these students to be constituted as 'model minorities'. Davies (2006), using Butler's work, argues that 'Subjects, and this includes school students, who are constituted as lying outside intelligibility are faced with the constitutive force of a language that grants them no intelligible space' (p. 434). This lack of intelligibility is a significant theme in the discussion of authenticity in the later section of this article. Drawing on CRT, I use the principle of interest convergence (Bell, 2003) to examine the purpose of 'model minorities' in the continuance of white dominance. Simply put, this principle suggests that gains are only made when they serve white interests; this is a useful starting point for the consideration of why some groups become constituted as 'model'. I also build upon on Gillborn's (2008) CRT-inspired discussion of 'disposable minorities', who may only be temporarily constituted positively, but serve some purpose.

The fluidity of 'model minorities'

One, the central ideas of CRT and much other literature on 'race' is the historicity of the social construct of race – that racisms and racial terms are flexible and serve the political interests of the time. Omi and Winant's (2004) 'racial formation' approach, which takes neither a 'race as illusionary' nor a 'racial objectivist' position, takes into account 'the importance of historical context and contingency in the framing of racial categories and the social construction of racially defined experiences' (p. 11). Thus the relative positions of different groups within popular discourse are dependent on the expediencies of a particular time and place; the movement of different communities into and out of 'model minority' status (a status which is entirely constructed rather than an actual phenomenon, I should emphasise) is further indication of the fluidity with which race-based stereotypes can operate to maintain the status quo. I argue, using data from London schools, how students from a number of smaller Muslim communities from Afghanistan, Iraq, Kosovo, and elsewhere have access to 'model minority' status alongside their Indian and Chinese counterparts. I comment here only on the situation in the UK, and only speculatively, given the scale of the data used; nonetheless, this data raises questions regarding the overall assumption that 'Muslim' students are constituted negatively in schools in England (Shain, 2010), and the idea that 'model minority' status is fixed.

Previous discussion of 'model minorities' in England has included discussion of groups of students who temporarily move into 'model' status, as mentioned. Gillborn's (2008) examination of the positioning of students from Montserrat, who arrived in the UK after being evacuated following a volcanic explosion found these students were initially lauded in the national press as part of criticism of the school system. However, in using the work of Gertrude Shotte, a Montserratian headteacher who researched the experiences of the students, Gillborn argues that in the long term, the educational experiences and attainment of the Montserratian students were low and a disproportionate number were excluded from school (2008, p. 159). Gillborn's discussion of these 'disposable models' also reminds us of the subjectivity of 'model minority' status; his discussion is based on one *Mail on Sunday* newspaper article, which had an alternative agenda, and unfortunately there is little research on how the Montserratian students were received in schools initially. It may be that these students were never 'model' to the schools involved and experienced racism from the very start of their time in the UK education system. Nonetheless, what this discussion emphasises is the way in which the use of discourses of 'model' students, however temporary, serves some interest other than that of the group itself. In this case, this interest is the denigration of the school system, but in wider terms, 'model minorities' provide evidence of a supposed meritocratic system in which any student can achieve.

Model minorities in reception

The flexibility of 'model minorities' was evident in the Reception classrooms of young children I researched in inner London. In these classrooms, some minoritised children, and girls in particular, were held up as 'model' students and in turn their families and communities were positioned as 'model minorities' (see also Bradbury, 2013b).[2] At one school, which I call Gatehouse, five students from the Afghan and Kosovan communities were the highest attaining girls in the teacher's assessment,[3] alongside a White working-class girl.[4] They were also held up as examples for the other students, and chosen for special tasks requiring sensible behaviour. These students were constituted as hard-working, well-behaved, and conscientious. Their teacher described one Afghan girl, Khadija, as 'amazing, kind of, just funny and "how do you know that?" kind of girl'. As with the research on Chinese students, this 'model' status was linked explicitly and implicitly to their families' attitudes and aspirations. In this fieldnote, the staff are discussing a new student, Farah, who would go on to become the highest attaining pupil in the class:

> The teachers are discussing a new pupil after a home visit: the new girl is described as 'quite bright, quite a bit of English'. They hope the new girl will be good model of English for the other children. She is described as Afghan and Pashto speaking. They discuss if there are any other Afghan children. The class teacher mentions that older children in the family have gone to university and says 'obviously they have high aspirations'. The family is also described as very 'with it'; Dad took time off work to meet Farah's new teacher. (Fieldnotes, Gatehouse)

From the very beginning of her first year in school, before she even enters the classroom, Farah's nascent 'model' identity and the link with her family are established. Similarly, discussions of Khadija, the student mentioned above as 'amazing' included references to her father's job at a broadcasting organisation, such as 'obviously [he] talks about stuff at home'. This link with children's families' attitudes toward education was also mentioned in the other Reception classroom, where the teacher commented on what he saw as a hierarchy of different groups in terms of their 'education ethic':

> In my last school it was a lot of Kurdish children, who'd come from villages, whose parents didn't know what ... They really weren't that interested in education to be honest, and so they did no work with them at home ... Those children seriously didn't move the way that some of our Arab-speaking children from Baghdad, whose parents have fled the country but

are very highly educated, who can't speak much English, but they've got high education ethic. (Class teacher, St Mary's)

In this teacher's view, the children who had left the city of Baghdad during conflict were preferable to the Kurdish children from villages, because of the two communities' different parental attitudes; this is similar to the way in which the justification of Indian students' success is often the assumed middle-class origins of their families.

The data from the second project on Afghan pupils suggests that this model status and the connection with family attitudes is present in relation to this specific group more widely: the primary teacher interviewed made the following comments:

> The pupils themselves are very keen, behaviour is never really an issue. They're kind of wide-eyed and very respectful and very well behaved. They respond to the opportunities of school very well. We assume that ... if they've managed to get out of a war-torn area like Afghanistan they must have the means and the wherewithal ... They are aspirational for their children, they understand that education is going to be the key way out. (Primary Teacher)

As in the Reception classrooms in the first study, the Afghan students are constituted as 'model', well-behaved, keen to learn and eager to make the most of 'the opportunities of school'. This last phrase is also indicative of a neoliberal discourse of individual responsibility for success which, as much of the US literature on model minorities points out, locates responsibility for differential success firmly with the student and family and not with the school system. Like the Reception teacher's comments on Iraqi families above, these children's assumed escape from a conflict zone is taken as an indication of both middle-classness and aspiration; their refugee status is seen as a barrier to be overcome through education, and the wider structural inequalities faced by these communities are ignored. The secondary teacher interviewed also commented positively on her teenage Afghan students' attitudes toward school, saying they were 'Pretty motivated, they all have that in common'. She made explicit comparisons with the British Indian community in the school and commented that 'that kind of cultural aspirational desire to achieve well academically is something throughout the school'. Both teachers made comments that identified the Afghan students as (relatively) middle class. The primary teacher said 'They are probably middle class, whatever that means for the Afghan community', while the secondary teacher explained how an Afghan student had told her that it was 'people with money, not necessarily the wealthiest in society, but you know people with access to money, could afford to escape the country'.

As I have explained, it is not clear whether students from the Afghan, Kosovan and Iraqi communities are more widely constituted as 'model' and the lack of available data on the attainment levels of these students[5] (and more detailed qualitative research) makes such a claim only tentative. However, there is some purpose in considering how these students are intelligible as 'model' to these teachers, and what this means for the operation of 'model minority' discourses more widely. Using Butler's ideas of intelligible subjects who are constituted through discourse (Butler, 1993, 2004), and following Youdell's (2006) work on intelligible student-subjecthood, we can explore how some students can become recognisable as successful learners, albeit temporarily. I would argue that these students from smaller Muslim minority communities that had originated in countries, which have experienced recent conflicts are constituted as 'model' through a web of discourses relating to good/bad migrants, assimilation, class and religious moderation. Their assumed 'middle classness' (not equivalent to White middle classness, however, as I discuss below) resonates with wider discourses relating to the connection between income levels and attainment, middle-class parenting styles and a positive 'education ethic'. At the same time, neoliberal individualist discourses of responsibility with an emphasis for on 'upward mobility' applied in the past and present to working-class children (Walkerdine, 2003), make the discourse of aspiration among minoritised communities more potent. Assimilationist discourses of 'good migrants' who have aspirations and are hardworking and keen to adopt 'Western' values, which are present in a policy context of 'contemporary assimilationism' (Gillborn, 2008), position these families as acceptable minorities in general.

More specifically for the girls, discourses of 'Asian' pupils as passive and obedient (Connolly, 1998; Shain, 2003) and girls' success in the education system overall, make their high attainment and good behaviour intelligible within educational discourse. Furthermore, in a context of increased Islamophobia and the regular connection of Iraq and Afghanistan in particular with Muslim extremist violence in popular discourse, these families who have come to the UK are positioned as models of a kind of submissive, assimilating, liberal and Westernised Islam, which is acceptable and welcomed. This is an important final point, given the tendency in the UK to use a binary notion of 'Asian' communities (a term which may or may not include some of the communities under discussion here) divided into 'good' Indian/Hindu and 'bad' Pakistani/Bangladeshi/ Muslim (Archer & Francis, 2007, p. 42). Within the Muslim communities there is a wide variety of different groups (including those not included within an 'Asian' category) and there is a danger that discussion of 'Muslim students' homogenises a wide array of students into a singular, negative identity. Thus it is important to emphasise that not all Muslim students are understood negatively in schools. In fact, through this complex set of discourses, some Muslim children are intelligible as 'model' minoritised students.

A key element of the 'model minority' discourse is the constitution of an *entire* community as successful, not just individuals within that perceived racial group. Although some of the data here do suggest this is the case, this is an argument requiring further research and exploration. Furthermore, some of these schools may be atypical in terms of the absence or small numbers of White students. However, these data suggest that there is some 'intelligible space' for other groups of students to be constituted as 'model minorities' in the current context in England. This is particularly the case where these groups provide a contrast to other minorities, who are seen to have less positive attitudes toward education or lower attainment. As I discuss further below, the fluidity of 'model minority' status, although it may offer some benefit to some students who have access to high expectations and positions of success (however temporarily) principally serves to maintain the status quo in terms of White dominance in education. I now turn to what I see as the sharper side of the double-edged sword of 'model minority' status, the dismissal of high attainment as inauthentic.

Multiple discourses of (in)authenticity

As in the US literature on Asian Americans in schools, the research on British Chinese students has identified the notions of 'pushy parents', overwork and unnecessary pressure in teachers' perceptions. In Archer and Francis' (2007) study, British Chinese students' success was seen as having been 'achieved in the wrong way' and their parents' enthusiasm for learning was described by teachers as 'aggressive, producing the "wrong sort" of learning, being too "enclosed" and denying children individuality' (p. 42). This discourse of inappropriate parental pressure among Chinese communities is familiar in the public domain, and has more recently been discussed explicitly with the debate surrounding the publication of 'Battle Hymn of the Tiger Mother' by Amy Chua, a guide to 'ultra-strict' parenting (2011).

In the US, the model minority myth has led to the marketing of books revealing the 'secrets' of Asian American parenting (Chang & Au, 2007). There are parallels between the discussion of British Chinese students and Youdell's research findings that Indian students were constituted as diligent and successful 'but not intrinsically gifted' (Youdell, 2006, p. 143). In schools, I would argue, this discourse of success through mere hard work and as a result of parental pressure can be applied to a wider range of students, and works powerfully to render these young people's successes *inauthentic*. The idea that high attainment among some minoritised students is caused by 'overwork' or external parental pressure has as its counterpoint, the idea that White students' successes are caused by something innate and internal; a White normative ideal is implicit, I would argue, in this dismissal of some students' success as inauthentic.

I use the term authenticity as shorthand for this complex discourse, as it arises both in Archer and Francis' analysis and independently in the data I collected in Reception classrooms (see the quote below). This discussion builds upon previous work on teachers' descriptions of girls' learning styles, particularly in masculine subjects, as not the 'proper way' (Walkerdine, 2003), although two decades on the associations of gender and success are perhaps altered (Renold & Allan, 2006). With regard to authenticity, Archer and Francis conclude:

> The 'ideal learner' is an inherently embodied discourse which always excludes minority ethnic pupils and denies them from inhabiting positions or identities of 'success' with any sense of permanency or authenticity. (2007, p. 170)

For the British Chinese students in their study, the association of their success with overwork and parental pressure meant that although they were constituted as 'model', they could not be positioned as ideal *authentic* learners. A similar analysis applies to the successful children from range of minoritised communities in the Reception classes I observed. In both classrooms, discourses of authenticity were used to delegitimise the attainment of minoritised students; here, the class teacher at St Mary's is discussing 'thinking skills':

> They all, there are some children who are very good at repeating, and memorising, but in terms of real thinking skills: not really there … So you get what I mean, there are a lot of children who have learned a lot, but they haven't intellectually got that thinking skills and problem solving … There are too many children coming out that are able to repeat things, like a parrot, or follow a writing frame … they'll do that but ask them to really truly do something authentic and they can't do it and I think that's a major problem. (Class teacher, St Mary's)

For this teacher, there is a clear distinction to be made (which he can identify) between repetition, memorising or following a writing frame, and something 'authentic'. This discourse, which places the responsibility for assessing authenticity with the teacher, can work as a refusal to recognise educational success in various forms, for any student. In the other Reception classroom I studied, the same discourse of skills which were 'not really there' was used to question the attainment of one of the 'model' Afghan girls discussed earlier in this paper, Khadija. Although her class teacher had described her as 'amazing' earlier in the year, when it came to placing the children in groups based on 'ability', Khadija was placed in the second group of five. When I discussed the groups with the class teacher, he explained that 'She's very vocal, but she's there for consolidation. I'm not sure it's all there'. As I have discussed in more detail elsewhere (Bradbury, 2013b), this was part of a wider shift in Khadija's learner identity, a central part of which was the rendering of her success as inauthentic. She was not the only student to be dismissed in this way: another Afghan girl, Bilqis, was initially praised by the staff as the only child in the class who could read all the required 'high frequency words', a list of words which the curriculum requires Reception children to recognise instantly. However, she remained in a lower 'ability' group for reading because, her class teacher explained, 'Her mum has been working flat out since she joined Reception' to teach her these words. This achievement, just like that of the British Chinese students, was deemed to be entirely due to parental pressure rather than an inherent skill.

This discourse of authenticity has its roots in a model of an ideal student, a subject which has occupied a range of literature (Becker, 1952; Gillborn, 1990; Youdell, 2006). The idea that some learning is *not* authentic cannot exist without the idea that some *is* authentic. The problem is that the authentic ideal appears to be possible and intelligible only for the White student, leaving the successes of minoritised students unrecognised. Furthermore, authenticity is not simply about academic achievement; it can be used to dismiss a wider range of 'good student' characteristics. In the Reception classes I observed, discourses of authenticity also applied to behaviour and attitudes: some children were seen as being naturally well behaved and others as putting on a show of good behaviour. Others were seen as taking part in activities, because their enthusiasm for learning was a natural trait, while other children were seen as merely trying to please the teacher. Thus, perceptions of a 'performance' of good learning could be used to demean students' wider attributes, beyond their academic attainment.

Authenticity discourses also have a complex relationship with ideas about innate intelligence and the organisation of education on the basis of 'ability'. On many occasions, as in the quote about repetition and memory above, authenticity is linked to innate intelligence and contrasted with a lack of inherited 'ability'. But it is important to note that some students from minoritised communities *are* constituted as inherently 'able' or intelligent; some teachers in Archer and Francis' study described their Chinese students as 'clever', for example. But this intelligence is often described as being linked to the racial group; thus it becomes another essentialising characteristic based on biological notions of 'race', while simultaneously demeaning the achievement of the individual. At the same time, notions of achieving in the 'right way' can continue to delegitimise attainment, even if students are seen as intelligent.

Thus far, this discussion has focused on discourses of authenticity based on parental pressure and attainment which is 'not all there'. In this final section I want to consider another facet of authenticity, which was deployed in discussions of teenage Afghan children's attainment. In an interview with a teacher in a London secondary school with a number of Afghan students, clear distinctions were made between the motivations of successful Indian students and successful Afghan students. Although, as mentioned, motivation was seen as something that all the students had in common, the teacher explained that for the Afghan students, 'motivation comes more from within themselves than from parental expectations'. She went on to say:

> I think that kind of psychological impact of having to flee your country, essentially as a refugee, has kind of affected their identity in a way that for another student it may not have the same effect. (Secondary teacher)

Several of this teacher's Afghan students had come from Afghanistan without their families and/or in traumatic circumstances; this was linked, it appeared, to her sense of their motivation. I would argue that this explanation is another form of dismissal through inauthenticity. These students' motivation and success is attributed to being refugees and needing to use education as a 'way out' (like the Afghan parents' views mentioned by the primary teacher). It is based on a kind of 'refugee mentality' and not, implicitly, due to their intelligence. These students' success is delegitimised through a slightly romanticised notion of a lone teenage refugee struggling against the odds, which resonates with wider ideas about 'good migrants' and their aspirations. I would argue, albeit tentatively given the limits of these data that, this is an alternative form of the authenticity discourse, which instead of linking success to parental pressure, bases inauthenticity on a need for escape. Authenticity, being in the eye of the beholder is a flexible concept, which can be re-deployed in multiple forms. This difference between the data from Reception and Primary classrooms and the Secondary teacher in relation to Afghan students, this 'model Muslim' minority, is perhaps due to the age of the students involved. Nonetheless, what it does point to is the multiplicity and complexity of discourses of authenticity and how they can be deployed to dismiss minoritised attainment.

Discussion

A central argument of this paper is that, in the education system in England, discourses of 'model minorities' and 'authenticity' are flexible, and can be used to delegitimise the academic successes of minoritised communities. These two discourses are intertwined, and one works to resolve the other: model minorities are useful in denying claims of institutional racism based on 'racist to all or none' assumptions, but their success is achieved in the 'wrong way'. If a wider range of minoritised groups including Afghan, Iraqi and Kosovan students begin to be constituted as 'model' (and again, I reiterate this is certainly not a universal or widely used discourse yet), discourses of inauthenticity based on parental pressure and a 'refugee mentality' can be used to dismiss this. Furthermore, assumptions that certain minoritised families are 'pushy' linked to inauthenticity are the basis for 'model minority' status, which leads to the argument that the system cannot be racist. Together, these ideas work powerfully to maintain a White idealised norm and deflect attention from race disparities in attainment.

What this discussion has not considered is the wider picture, which includes the significant problem of the lower attainment of many minoritised groups. Using a CRT framework, I want to explore as to what purpose model minorities serve in the wider maintenance of White dominance in education. A well-used theoretical tool in CRT is Bell's principle of interest convergence (Bell, 2003), which argues that gains made by the Black community in the US are only those which serve White interests. Bell argues that the *Brown versus Board of Education* decision to desegregate schools was motivated by foreign policy interests; there was a convergence of interests, not a desire to reduce racial inequality. Although the issue of model minorities and authenticity discussed here is not an example of interest convergence, some of the ideas have some resonance with the concept. There is a sense with model minorities of having given something up (White groups at the top of attainment statistics) for the continuation of the wider project of White dominance. But while something is lost, the fundamentals are maintained through dismissals based on authenticity; Whiteness is still idealised, associated with authentic intelligence and educational success. As in interest convergence, what is gained is only partial and only occurs when it serves White interests.

Based on this argument, why would additional groups gain access to 'model' status? The concept of interest convergence suggests that the minimum is only ever conceded. Furthermore, as Gillborn notes, 'it does not matter who provides the model as long as there is a model to point to' (2008, p. 157), and Chinese and Indian high attainment in England continues to provide this model. Even if their positions are not as prominent as these two communities (and are limited by the statistics available), why would other groups be intelligible as 'model'? Perhaps there is some purpose in positioning some smaller Muslim minorities as model, while the majority Pakistani and Bangladeshi Muslim minorities continue to be pathologised in what Youdell (2003) in a different context has called a 'hierarchy of the Other'.

In a context of concern over Islamophobia, perhaps a version of the usual 'model minority' argument, a 'racist to all Muslim groups or none' position is useful in denying accusations of racism. There is a need for a good/bad binary in discussions of all groups: perhaps what we see in the positive descriptions of Afghan, Iraqi and Kosovan students is the emergence of a 'good Muslim'/'bad Muslim' division, similar to the division of British Asians into good/Indian/Hindu and bad/Pakistani/Bangladeshi/Muslim in the 1990s and 2000s. Research from the US on Asian Americans has provided examples of a similar binary within the 'model' Asian-American group: Lee has argued that in some contexts Asian-Americans are discursively divided into passive high-achieving 'good kids' and 'bad kids', who were 'Americanised' among students who adopted a 'hip hop style associated with urban youth of colour' (Lee, 2005, cited in Li & Wang, 2008, p. 7), for example. What remains potent in all these possibilities, both in the UK and US, is the centrality of the White ideal, as the measure against which all groups will be compared. It is also important not to overstate the planned or intentional nature of shifting boundaries of 'model' status, and to reiterate the difference between this case and examples of interest convergence from legal studies. However, there is some utility, I would argue, in considering how changing patterns of how to adapt Gillborn's phrase, 'racism plays favourites' (Gillborn, 2008, p. 153) and to what ends, this serves.

The roles played by 'model minorities' and discourses of authenticity serve as useful reminders of continued White dominance. For all minoritised students, 'model' or not, these discourses continue to locate the source of disparities with students and families, not with the education system. 'Model minorities' deflect attention from continued educational difference in the UK and elsewhere, while students from these communities continued to be subject to racist assumptions of inauthentic learning. One of the tensions in discussions of 'model minorities' lies between the need to reduce the idea to the status of myth, and recognising the very real impact of this myth on the lived experiences of both people from that minority and those from other minoritised groups. Although it may have its advantages, as Chang (2000) argues, to accept that some minorites are 'model' is to be 'complicitous in the oppression of other racial minorities and poor whites' (p. 361). But while it exists and becomes established—and the US is a cautionary tale for the UK in this respect—it must be challenged and questioned.

Acknowledgements

The research studies discussed in this paper were funded by the UK Economic and Social Research Council (Grant number ES/G018987/1) and the London Education Research Unit at the Institute of Education, University of London.

Notes

1. To clarify, I use the term Asian-American (sometimes referred to Asian Pacific American) in the sense that it is used in the US; the term 'Asian' in the UK is usually used to refer to the Indian, Pakistani and Bangladeshi communities, not the Chinese community. In reference to the UK, I avoid the term, except when citing research which uses this terminology.
2. These classes included only two or three White students, and few or no students from the Chinese or Indian communities, which may be relevant here.
3. This teacher assessment, which is a standardised system across Reception classrooms in England, is conducted through observation and, as I have argued elsewhere is not a true measure of what children can or cannot do. It is, however, a measure of what a teacher expects a child to be able to do (within the constrictions of a performative accountability system), and therefore is an indication of these students' 'model' status.
4. It is worth noting that some of the literature on Asian American students makes use of the concept of 'honorary Whites'; which I do not use but may be relevant here. In particular, there is scope for further exploration (which I do not have space for here) of the status of Kosovan children, who are listed in official document as White European, but are nonetheless a minoritised group in contrast to the White British majority.
5. The UK Department of Education publishes data by 'ethnic group', but not in a form that allows the consideration of the attainment of these smaller groups.

References

Archer, L., & Francis, B. (2007). *Understanding minority ethnic achievement: Debating race, gender, class and 'success'*. London: Routledge.
Becker, H. S. (1952). Social-class variation in the teacher–pupil relationship. *Journal of Educational Sociology, 25*(8), 451–465. doi:10.2307/2263957
Bell, D. (2003). *The Derrick Bell reader*. New York: New York University Press.
Bradbury, A. (2011). Rethinking assessment and inequality: The production of disparities in attainment in early years education. *Journal of Education Policy, 26*(5), 655–676. doi:10.1080/02680939.2011.569572
Bradbury, A. (2013a). Education policy and the 'ideal learner': Producing recognisable learner-subjects through assessment in the early years. *British Journal of Sociology of Education, 34*(1), 1–19. doi:10.1080/01425692.2012.692049
Bradbury, A. (2013b). *Understanding early years inequality: Policy, assessment and young children's identities*. London: Routledge.
Butler, J. P. (1993). *Bodies that matter: On the discursive limits of 'sex'*. London: Routledge.
Butler, J. P. (2004). *Undoing gender*. New York, NY: Routledge.
Chang, R. (2000). Towards an Asian American legal scholarship: CRT, post-structuralism and narrative space. In R. Delgado & J. Stefancic (Eds.), *Critical race theory: The cutting edge* (2nd ed., pp. 354–368). Philadelphia, PA: Temple University Press.
Chang, B., & Au, W. (2007). You're Asian, how could you fail math? Unmasking the myth of the model minority. *Rethinking Schools, 22*(2), 15–19.
Chua, A. (2011). *Battle hymn of the Tiger Mother*. London: Bloomsbury.
Connolly, P. (1998). *Racism, gender identities and young children: Social relations in a multi-ethnic, inner-city primary school*. London: Routledge.
Davies, B. (2006). Subjectification: The relevance of Butler's analysis for education. *British Journal of Sociology of Education, 27*(4), 425–438. doi:10.1080/01425690600802907
Gillborn, D. (1990). *'Race', ethnicity and education: Teaching and learning in multi-ethnic schools*. London: Unwin Hyman. doi:10.4324/9780203400265
Gillborn, D. (2008). *Racism and education: Coincidence or conspiracy?* London: Routledge.
Lee, S. (2008). Foreword. In G. Li & L. Wang (Eds.), *Model minority myth revisited: An interdisciplinary approach to demystifying Asian American educational experiences* (pp. ix–xi). Charlotte, NC: Information Age.
Li, G. (2008). Other people's success: Impact of the 'model minority' myth on underachieving Asian students in North America. In G. Li & L. Wang (Eds.), *Model minority myth revisited: An interdisciplinary approach to demystifying Asian American educational experiences* (pp. 213–231). Charlotte, NC: Information Age.

Li, G., & Wang, L. (Eds.). (2008). *Model minority myth revisited: An interdisciplinary approach to demystifying Asian American educational experiences*. Charlotte, NC: Information Age.

Lo, L. (2008). Interactions between Chinese parents and special education professionals in IEP meetings: Implications for the education of Chinese immigrant children with disabilities. In G. Li & L. Wang (Eds.), *Model minority myth revisited: An interdisciplinary approach to demystifying Asian American educational experiences* (pp. 195–212). Charlotte, NC: Information Age.

Min, P. G. (2004). Social science research on Asian Americans. In J. Banks & C. Banks (Eds.), *Handbook of research on multicultural education* (2nd ed., pp. 332–348). San Francisco, CA: Jossey-Bass.

Omi, M., & Winant, H. (2004). On the theoretical status of the concept of race. In G. Ladson-Billings & D. Gillborn (Eds.), *The RoutledgeFalmer reader in multicultural education: Critical perspectives on race, racism and education* (pp. 7–15). London: RoutledgeFalmer.

Pang, V., & Palmer, J. (2012). Model minorities and the model minority myth. In J. Banks (Ed.), *Encyclopedia of diversity in education* (p. 1518). London: Sage.

Renold, E., & Allan, A. (2006). Bright and beautiful: High achieving girls, ambivalent femininities, and the feminisation of success in the primary school. *Discourse: Studies in the Cultural Politics of Education*, *27*(4), 457–473. doi:10.1080/01596300600988606

Shain, F. (2003). *The schooling and identity of Asian girls*. Stoke-on-Trent: Trentham Books.

Shain, F. (2010). *The new folk devils: Muslim boys and education in England*. Stoke-on-Trent: Trentham.

Walkerdine, V. (2003). Reclassifying upward mobility: Femininity and the neo-liberal subject. *Gender and Education*, *15*(3), 237–248. doi:10.1080/09540250303864

Wu, H. (2012, June 22). Why Vincent Chin matters. *New York Times*. Retrieved from http://www.nytimes.com/2012/06/23/opinion/why-vincent-chin-matters.html?_r=0

Youdell, D. C. (2003). Identity traps or how black students fail: The interactions between biographical, sub-cultural and learner identities. *British Journal of Sociology of Education*, *24*(1), 3–20. doi:10.1080/01425690301912

Youdell, D. C. (2006). *Impossible bodies, impossible selves: Exclusions and student subjectivities*. Dordrecht: Springer.

14 souls, 19 days and 1600 dreams: engaging critical race praxis while living on the 'edge' of race

David Stovall[a,b]

[a]Educational Policy Studies, College of Education, University of Illinois, Chicago, IL, USA;
[b]African-American Studies, College of Liberal Arts and Sciences, University of Illinois, Chicago, IL, USA

Because the dynamics of race are wrongly ignored in a current shroud of post-racialism (i.e. re-election of Barack Obama as president of the USA, shifting racial demographics in the USA, etc.), there are still communities in the USA and throughout the world that experience the damaging effects of racism entangled with the realities of class. Many still do not live in a post-racial utopia where 'things are getting better'. Instead, for some, things are getting worse. In light of these realities, this article is an account of a community's attempt to interrupt the popularly shared notion that low-income/working-class communities of color do not deserve quality education. The title has particular significance in that the 14 is reflective of the 14 community members that endured a 19-day hunger strike to secure a school for 1600 students. It should be considered on the 'edge' of race in that it recognizes that race is often placed on the periphery of urban education, allowing policies to continually marginalize communities of color.

The first day

Like most first days of school in Chicago, it was a hot day after the Labor Day holiday. Spirits were high as students descended on the brand new high school campus, ready to go to class for the first time in a brand-new, seventy-three million dollar building equipped with an Olympic-sized swimming pool, two professional quality gymnasiums, computer corridors, and a collegiate style library with bay windows and artistic steel structures adorning the entrance. Using the service entrance to enter the building, I was amazed the structure was finally finished, with all the politics that go into the development of new schools in Chicago. Even though minor construction was still taking place as students were entering the building, the structure itself was testament to something much deeper – a process where lives were placed in harm's way for an equitable education for students in the neighborhoods of Little Village and North Lawndale.

I was surprised as I approached the building in that I saw a couple of the former hunger strikers holding placards and signs. At the original planning of the opening of the high school, there was supposed to be a grandiose ceremony, attended by the mayor of the city and the CEO of Chicago Public Schools (CPS). Because they decided to attend an event at another school in the city, they first day at the building was without the fanfare of many 'dog-and-pony' photo opportunities public officials are known for when anything is considered 'new' or 'innovative'. Nevertheless, there stood the community activists/residents holding the signs and passing out pamphlets. Because I had a meeting with a teacher,

I wasn't able to read the signs or read the pamphlets. As the school day continued, I checked to see if the community residents were still around after the first period of classes.
It's always interesting how the rumor mill works. I asked what the 'protest' was about, and no one seemed to really know. Because the vast majority of the people was familiar with the school and the process that made it a reality, many expressed surprise at the sight of the placards and pamphlets. Because the original plan was to have a ribbon-cutting ceremony with the hunger-strikers in tow, it didn't make too much sense that community members would be staging a protest. As Rito (principal of the Social Justice High School) shrugged shoulders in the hallway about what was going on, we went about the day. However, I couldn't get it out of my mind: Why the signs and placards?

Like many experiences in teaching, the process of reflection can offer tangible solutions. Later in the day, while standing in a corridor of vending machines at the university where I teach, I ran into one of the hunger strikers. She and I were having small talk about the first day at the high school. 'Oh, so you were there too?', she asked. When I replied yes, I also mentioned that I saw two of the hunger strikers in the service drive holding a sign and passing out pamphlets. Before I could ask a question about what I perceived to be a protest, she informed me that 'we just wanted to greet families and remind them of why the school was built and our availability to them if they had questions for us'. She also told me of how they wanted to develop a parent center that would be accessible to the parents of the students and the community at large. In my mind I was puzzled for about twenty seconds, and then it dawned on me: what I thought to be a protest was actually the hunger strikers welcoming students and parents to the high school! By this time, while wallowing in my own ignorance, the importance of the work I originally set out to do would smack me in the face. Before assuming, one must listen. Only from these spaces will we gain understanding.

Because the dynamics of race are wrongly ignored in a current shroud of post-racialism (i.e. re-election of Barack Obama as president of the USA, shifting racial demographics in the USA, etc.), there are still communities in the USA and throughout the world that experience the damaging effects of racism entangled with the realities of class. Many still do not live in a post-racial utopia where 'things are getting better'. Instead, for some, things are getting worse. In light of these realities, this article is an account of a community's attempt to interrupt the popularly shared notion that low-income/working-class communities of color do not deserve quality education. The title has particular significance in that the 14 is reflective of the 14 community members that endured a 19-day hunger strike to secure a school for 1600 students. It should be considered on the 'edge' of race in that it recognizes that race is often placed on the periphery of urban education, allowing policies to continually marginalize communities of color.

By engaging in this task, this account is divided into five sections. First is the articulation of CRT and its utilization in this project by way of critical race praxis. The second section articulates the current educational landscape of Chicago, which currently serves as the laboratory for local, state, federal, and international neoliberal school reform. Third is my involvement in an outgrowth of a community-driven initiative for equitable education in two communities ignored for decades by the establishment. Included is my own positioning as a researcher/educator in a design-team process where I participated in the development of mission, vision, school culture, and curriculum for an urban high school with the blessings of community members. Section four provides the duties and responsibilities of the design team into the beginnings of the school. The last section revisits the initial community-driven initiative through the current struggle to keep the school's doors open.

More than solely a research project, the process challenged me to place my own understanding theory into action. To those that would argue that I am 'too close' to my research, I offer an alternate interpretation: because we are traditionally trained to distance ourselves from our research, we fall victim to a false sense of 'objectivity'. In the attempt to create 'objective' research, we move further away from grasping with the 'messiness' of human life. Fortunately and unfortunately for us, our lives are not perfect, clean, and ordered spaces – they are not objective. These murky, contested, difficult, and affirming spaces pose unique challenges at any given moment in time. Such contradictions remind us why the struggle for justice is so critical. If we do not honor and articulate the messy imperfections of community-engaged research, we do ourselves a disservice. For it is from these spaces that we get the lessons so drastically needed to improve our condition.

The word: narrative, counterstory, and critical race theory

Critical race theory (CRT), as a theoretical construct in education, 'seeks to inform theory, research, pedagogy, curriculum and policy' (Solorzano & Yosso, in Yosso, 2006). Operating on theoretical and practical level, CRT in education should be included as making a contribution to praxis, in that it supports 'action and reflection in the world in order to change it' (Freire, 1969/2003). In the ensuing pages, I use CRT to frame the struggles and success in my experience as a researcher, concerned citizen, and members of the design team in the creation of the Lawndale Little Village School for Social Justice (SOJO) in Chicago, Illinois.

In doing so, I must embrace a level of subjectivity. Referenced as 'the Word' by Charles Laurence III, our stories, by nature of the subject matter (in this case, racism and hegemony), are 'subjective, consciously historical, and revisionist' (Laurence III, in Crenshaw, Gotanda, Peller, & Thomas, 1995, p. 337). Where some may consider Professor Laurence's statements as conflicting, CRT locates the stories of people of color in the USA and the larger world as historically relevant and valid. I agree with Laurence that our stories (in conjunction with the historical record) are key to 'praxis … in the ongoing work of the scholar as teacher (and activist)' (1995, p. 337). Through our subjectivity, we are able to acknowledge and validate the myriad of experiences and perspectives. Ours is not the only viewpoint, but a perspective that is often excluded. Due to these omissions, it is critical for the activist/scholar to intentionally engage the political exercise of claiming space to tell our story.

Referenced as by Yosso (2006) as 'counternarrative', the ensuing document 'seek(s) to document the persistence of racism from the perspectives of those injured and victimized by its legacy' (p. 60). As counternarrative, my involvement on the SOJO design team operated under the premise of a community commitment to challenge white supremacy/ racism by gaining access to quality education.

By infusing CRT, this article claims solidarity with the likes of Duncan (2005) in that the stories of people of color are 'necessary to disrupt the allochronic discourses that inform racial inequality in schools and society' (Duncan, 2005, p. 113). Narrative, as a conduit by which to communicate issues and concerns, encourages us to engage practical means by which to address issues brought forward by racism. As scholarship committed to social justice, the responsibility is to move beyond our rhetoric and push toward developing models of praxis.

For this article, I use a composite of the tenets developed by Solorzano in education (1997) and Yamamoto (1997) in legal theory. Although CRT has its grounding in legal theory, it has been adopted by scholars in education to address issues faced by urban youth of color in schools. The following tenets, with specificity to education, were instrumental in developing the framework for this account. Where the italicized tenets are directly from the Solorzano text, the following sentences are how I used the tenet to frame the article:

The intercentricity of race and racism: Race and racism are not monolithic concepts. Instead, they are complex, dynamic, and malleable social constructions endemic to life in the US. Due to their shifting contexts, definitions of race can include and exclude groups depending on the historical moment. For example, as immigrating and native-born Latinoa/s in the US were once categorized as 'White', they have now been largely vilified as the culprits responsible for taking jobs from US citizens. By recognizing the historical and social evolutions of race, CRT seeks to problematize the paradigm.

Challenge to dominant ideology: The master narrative on African-American and Latino/a students in public education is engulfed in theories of deficit. CRT challenges the master narrative on the inability of students of color to excel in academic settings.

Commitment to social justice: CRT offers itself as a theoretical and methodological paradigm aimed at the elimination of race, class and gender oppression.

Centrality of experiential knowledge: The knowledge of people of color in the fight against hegemonic forces in education is legitimate, valid, and necessary in creating spaces for said communities to engage justice work.

Interdisciplinary perspective: CRT borrows from legal theory, ethnic studies, women's studies, sociology, history, philosophy, economics, and other fields to argue for a comprehensive analysis of the functions of race and racism in education. (Solorzano, in Yosso, 2006, pp. 7–8)

From these tenets, two questions emerge that guide the remainder of the document.

- What are tangible strategies for researchers and community members to negotiate the immanent tensions between hegemonic educational systems and community self-determination to create an urban high school?
- How can CRT make real its connection to the material conditions of people's lives?

Key to the questions was Yamamoto's Critical Race Praxis. His analysis encourages scholars to enhance 'attention to theory translation and frontline action' (Yamamoto, 1999, p. 129). Where his suggestions for race praxis are directed toward attorneys and law professors, I incorporate his suggestions to entail the work of educational researchers who are concerned with social justice. As method, Yamamoto suggests that race praxis is characterized by reflective action. Such reflection is based on the application of theoretical concepts to the work done in solidarity with communities, and the recasting of said concepts in relation to our on-the-ground experiences. In my work on the design team, this entailed reflection on the 'nuts and bolts' work (developing the proposal for the school, interviewing teachers, presenting in community forums, etc.) and recasting it through a CRT lens. By using this process, I was able to frame communication between myself, members of the design team, community organizations, CPS, and the respective Latino/a and African-American communities of Little Village and North Lawndale.

Chicago in context: breadth, depth, and scope

In the larger context of working on the design team, the city of Chicago is a key component in understanding the socio-political context in which SOJO becomes a reality. As SOJO was developed under the community initiative to secure quality education, it also occurs in a political moment unique in the history of public education in the USA. Documented extensively in the works of Lipman (2003, 2004, 2011), Saltman (2007, 2010), and Fine and Fabricant (2012), Chicago has been a hotbed for educational 'reforms'. I am particularly parenthesizing 'reform' because the changes have been touted as positive changes, but they have largely resulted in the further marginalization of low-income, working-class communities of color (i.e. language used in Chicago Public Schools, Office of New Schools). Instead of considering the following analysis of policy as justice-minded reforms, an accurate description of said policies and their implementation is neoliberal policy reform. Largely rooted in the belief that free market economies provide solution to the vast majority of social concerns, neoliberal reform is centered in the rights of the individual. The market is understood as correct and without fault, resulting in the rationale for privatization of public goods for the purpose of cost-effectiveness and the maximizing of profits. For low-income families of color, this often results in a rhetorical charge that the market can solve the vast majority of political, economic, and social issues. Because these resources are falsely positioned as available to all, low-income, working-class families of color are often blamed for not accessing the resources.

This manifestation has been most evident in Chicago over the last 17 years. Centered in the 1995 educational policy shift resulting in mayoral control of Chicago Public Schools (CPS), the mayor currently has the sole authority in appointing the school board, which is responsible for final approval of school-related issues (e.g. financial matters, curricular shifts, contract procurement, approval of new schools, hiring of school principals, etc). In addition to the mayor's ability to appoint members of the school board, s/he has the ability to overturn any decision made by the board. Facilitated under the 22-year mayoral tenure of Richard M. Daley, the city has laid a blueprint for numerous cities in the USA desiring to centralize control of its school system. In that time frame, the number of educators on the school board has decreased significantly. Currently, the board membership consists largely of people from business, legal, and philanthropic sectors. This fosters a reciprocal relationship between the board and the mayor's office as board members are usually individuals or employees of entities that have contributed significantly to the mayor's re-election campaign.

Fast-forward 41 years to the present from the city planning initiative known as the Chicago 21 Plan (targeting 21 specific geographic areas for redevelopment) and actions by the mayor and other state actors to secure corporate contributions via free market strategies has become the norm locally, nationally, and internationally (Smith & Stovall, 2008). Further strengthening ties among the business community, the mayor's office, and public schools, the collaborative of business interests known as the Commercial Club of Chicago commissioned its Civic Committee to develop a 2003 report known as 'Left Behind'. Included in this report was the notion that students in the USA are falling behind internationally in reading, math, and science. Their suggested solution was to re-tool the public educational landscape by infusing 'innovation' from the business sector. These innovations would be for the purposes of strengthening the US workforce, and return the US economy to supremacy in the global marketplace. The people best suited for this direction were those who possessed an intimate knowledge of free market strategies to boost competition amongst education providers (Civic Committee of the Commercial Club of Chicago, 2003). Key to this strategy is the idea that competition is best to boost academic performance. Under free-market capitalism, the belief is if one school is performing well, it will push others to improve due to the interests of both institutions for students. Contrary to this understanding is the fact that each school serves a different set of students requiring a unique set of resources germane to that particular population. The competition strategy becomes ridiculous and absurd when accounting for the unique needs of students in a particular school.

Nevertheless, the city moved forward with the policy and rolled out a plan in the summer of 2004 called Renaissance 2010. SOJO, in opening its doors in the Fall of 2005, wrongly became engulfed in this initiative due to the timing of the building of the school. The idea promoted to the public was to implement the suggestions of the Civic Committee. By 2010, CPS proposed to target up to 70 'chronically underperforming' schools for 'transformation' into 100 schools with the distinction of either charter, contract, or performance school. Where charters are granted by the state, contract schools have a different distinction in that they are a designation for individuals or groups that have secured individual contracts with the city to create schools. Where contract schools are a close cousin to charters with regard to funding formulas, the distinct difference lies in the direct partnership with the city, as charters are traditionally granted by the state. Schools in the performance category were another manifestation of schools, aimed at giving principals and teachers some levels of autonomy regarding curriculum and schedule. Simultaneously, the internal understanding was to lessen the city's financial commitment to education through the use of partners that could in turn use their contributions to education as tax subsidies (through the federal tax code's provision for charitable donations). Returning to the public sphere, the manifestations were posited to community residents as Chicago Public Schools moving to provide 'choice' and 'options' in the 'education marketplace' (www.cps.edu/NewSchools/Pages/ONS.aspx). Schools, as the final frontier, provide the necessary push for buyers to take the final step in securing life in the city. Fortunately, for the families that are experiencing the brunt of the policies, a collective of community organizations have been able to develop strategies to contest the efforts of CPS.

The residual effects of the convergence of Renaissance 2010 have been devastating for a growing number of African-American and Latino/a communities in Chicago. According to the 2010 US Census, Chicago lost 200,000 residents from 2000 to 2010 (Glanton, Mullen, & Olivio, 2011). Since the initial rollout of 'Ren 2010', 101 schools have been permanently closed, phased out (when students are no longer admitted), and labeled as turnaround (when the existing staff is fired and an Educational Management Organization (EMO) is hired to re-staff the school, usually with a new curricular focus). Ninety-nine of the 101 schools in these categories were predominantly African-American or Latino/a (Lipman, Smith, Gutstein, & Dallacqua, 2012). Coupled with the destruction of over 80% of public housing stock (whose population was 95% African-American), many schools became depopulated while others were converted to 'receiver schools'. Institutions in this category would conduct an intake of students from the depopulated or closed schools. Massive over-crowding in historically under-funded and under-resourced African-American and Latino/a schools on the South and West sides of the city resulted from this strategy while populations in affluent regions of the city actually grew (Lipman et al., 2012).

As neoliberal educational reform, Renaissance 2010 has since morphed into numerous entities, securing private interests through organizations such as the Renaissance Schools Fund (a private philanthropic entity), the Chicago Public Education Fund (a philanthropic entity specifically for securing resources for charter and turnaround schools), and the

Office of New Schools (an internal office to CPS). Coupled with new policy initiatives from the federal government (e.g. Race to the Top, No Child Left Behind re-authorization, etc.), this particular form of school reform has been touted as a replicable model over the last 17 years. In addition to CPS having five CEOs over the last seven years (2005–2012), the rotating door of administration has created a central office structure with minimal transparency for communities that are demanding fair and equitable education for students of color in low-income working-class areas of the city.

As some would cite the convergence of Renaissance 2010 and the Plan for Transformation as conspiratorial, I offer to take it a step further in that there is no longer a clandestine conversation surrounding policy aims. Instead, we should understand these policy machinations as public, where state actors and interested parties are supporting rhetorical rationales while materially implementing strategies to permanently remove particular residents from urban areas. Coupled with the neoliberal push for privatization of the public sector, schools become the conduit for an illusion of progress, placing students and families of color in the affected areas on the periphery.

SOJO beginnings: into the hunger strike

Where the context of Chicago lays an important framework to understand the development of sites of resistance, the predominantly Mexican and Mexican-American neighborhood of Little Village on Chicago's Southwest Side has been steeped in community organizing. From the struggle to develop bilingual education programs in public schools in the early 1980s to assisting in the election of Chicago's first African-American mayor (Harold Washington), the community of Little Village has a rich history of community activism. The events leading to the hunger strike beginning on 13 May 2001 should be included in the same trajectory.

Through political and grassroots organizing, members of the Little Village community began to place pressure on the City of Chicago and Chicago Public Schools (CPS) to create a high school for their neighborhood. Currently, Little Village is one of the youngest communities in the city, with 4000 children of high school age and one public high school with a capacity for 1800 students. Twenty-five percent of the residents have incomes below $15,000. Only 17% of all high school residents have a high school diploma and 5.5% have college degrees. Adding to the concerns is the fact that the overcrowded high school has a 55% graduation rate and a dropout rate of 17% (2004, p. 5). Moreover, the grade schools that serve as feeder schools for the one high school are also overcrowded.

Culminating in the mayoral campaign of 1997, $30 million was set aside by the city to build a high school in Little Village. Despite the city designating a site for the school and holding a press conference to announce the decision to build the school, no construction took place from 1998 to 2001. Instead, the city of Chicago moved forward with a plan to create four selective-enrollment high schools in gentrifying and affluent areas of the city.

As selective enrollment high schools were given first priority, plans to build the high school in Little Village were placed on the backburner. Community members, with the assistance of elected officials for the neighborhood, sought to address the problem through the protocols of CPS. Outraged at the decision to build the selective enrollment schools, Little Village residents approached CPS. They were given the response that the funds originally allocated to build their high school had been spent. Echoing the sentiments of Kozol (2012), CPS understands the selective enrollment system as:

> ... highly attractive to the more sophisticated parent, disproportionately white and middle class, who have the ingenuity and, now and then, political connections to obtain admission for their children. It is also viewed by some of its defenders as an ideal way to hold white people in the public schools by offering them 'choices' that resemble what they'd find in private education. (Kozol, 2012, pp. 59–60)

Selective-enrollment schools, created to attract high-achieving students, require applicants to have a particular composite test score upon entry. Prospective applicants are not allowed to take the entrance exam if they do not have the required composite score. These institutions are important politically and physically to a city like Chicago, whose re-vitalization efforts in housing, commerce, and education are geared toward attracting middle-class residents from the suburbs back into the city. Schools, as the primary conduit in attracting middle-class and affluent residents to a neighborhood, are critical to the city's effort to establish itself as a global city free of blight and despair. Although viewed positively by many, others, like the residents of North Lawndale and Little Village, understand these new developments as part of a larger effort to displace poor and working-class African-American and Latino/a residents.

In the case of Little Village, because the funds were non-renewable, high school construction was postponed indefinitely. From the indefinite postponement, community members in Little Village were subsequently informed that CPS had come to a final decision not to build a high school. Fortunately, community members refused to take the CPS decision lying down. Recognizing the community's desire to attain a school, a community organizer and Little Village resident, named Tomas Gaete, began to gather community opinions block by block. Because Little Village has a highly organized network of Block Club associations, Mr Gaete was able to field the opinions of community members on what should be done to protest CPS and the building of the school. From the concerned community members fielded by Mr Gaete, Little Village residents took it upon themselves to attend a leadership training institute organized by Mr Gaete's employer, the Little Village Community Development Corporation (LVCDC). In these workshops, community members were trained on the basics of community organizing and effective strategies to achieve goals.

After the trainings, community members decided one of their first targets for action would be the CPS board meetings. One of the first approaches was to register for the speaker's list at each board meeting and to express their displeasure on not getting their school. When these tactics did not yield results, more direct, high-profile approaches were employed. One action even brought a Mariachi band to the board member to sing a song about the high school that was promised to Little Village. In addition, a sit-in was staged in CPS headquarters. Despite the determination of the community in presenting pubic disgust at CPS's decision, Little Village still did not have a second high school. Upon regrouping, members of the Little Village community decided to take drastic measures. The decision was to stage a hunger strike, beginning on 13 May 2001, ending on 2 June of the same year. This form of protest was chosen due to its ability to demonstrate the seriousness of the community. To the contrary, it was not a decision couched in desperation. Instead, it was an intensely planned strategy to alert CPS of the community's ability to organize and amass power. The hunger strike took place on the site originally planned for the school. Renamed 'Camp Cesear Chavez' after the leader of the United

Farm Workers, medical staff remained on site in case of emergency. Because some of the hunger strikers were senior citizens, careful attention was given to the hunger strikers as the days progressed. Although there were only 14 hunger-strikers that went the 19 days, community support surpassed the participants' expectation. During the 19 days, the community staged community theater events, community rallies, and prayer vigils. All were key in keeping the hunger-strikers in good spirits.

Of the 14 hunger-strikers, two were under the age of 20 years. One was a high school senior at the time, while the other was a college student at a local university. Recognizing the importance of young people to the development of the community-led initiative, it was agreed by the hunger-strikers that all events following the hunger-strike in the planning of the school would include the community at large. From getting the school built to having the power to name the curricular foci of each school is a testament to what communities can do with concerted efforts to self-determine and name their own realities. Education, as a human need, is one of the most salient spaces to engage on such a project. For this reason, the members of the Little Village community who decided to engage on such a project will be remembered in the historical record as the people who took initiative and put their thoughts into action.

As the process moved forward, CPS informed the original planning committee for the high school that African-American residents from the neighboring community of North Lawndale would have to be included in the process. This posed a challenge in that they were brought into the process after the initial organizing by community members in Little Village. As the force of the hunger strike originated in Little Village, African-American residents of North Lawndale were included in the school formation process by CPS' interpretation of a consent decree to desegregate. Operating under the decree since 1982, Chicago Public Schools (CPS) has been required by the federal government to engage in a concerted effort to desegregate its public schools. Critical to the decree, however, is the idea that desegregation initially implied the inclusion of students of color in 'White' schools. The fact that there aren't enough White students in CPS to 'desegregate' in this mode has created a process where CPS is allowed to interpret what constitutes compliance with the decree. In the attempt to operate in compliance with the mandate, CPS interprets 'desegregation' as integrating the four high schools with the neighboring African-American community of North Lawndale. Under the consent decree, each high school is required to maintain a population that is no less than 30% African-American and no more that 70% Latino/a. As a loose interpretation of the desegregation mandate, CPS is able to argue to the federal government that their attempts at new school development remain in concert with the legal statute. Throughout the design team process, this became an issue as many parents and community members in North Lawndale knew little about the strike, and initially felt as if they were being 'tokenized' for the sole purpose of acting in compliance with a federal mandate.

Correspondingly, the issues in North Lawndale have not diverged from what Kozol documented 15 years prior. Forty two percent of North Lawndale's population lives below the poverty line with a median family income of $18,000. Families with children under 18 represent 52% of the total population under the poverty line, while families with children under five years of age represent 56% of the population. Additionally, the 2000 census reported that 58% of families with one or more child under 18 indicated a grandparent as caregiver (2). In terms of school performance of K-12 students in North Lawndale, 18.6% of high school students are performing at or above the state standard.

The high school graduation rate in the community is 26.2%, with only three percent of its residents earning a bachelors degree.

Currently, the building houses four schools: (1) visual and performing arts, (2) math, science, and technology, (3) world languages, and (4) social justice. The 'school-within-a-school' concept was a design chosen by members of the community, to provide students with the ability to choose their educational paths. Since 6 September 2005, the school has opened with 400 students (100 freshmen in each high school). Currently, the multiplex's population is just shy of 1600 students for the entire (averaging around 360 students per school). Remembering the spirit of the hunger strike, the original planning committee vowed the new high school complex to be a space that reflected the core values of democracy, community ownership, self-discipline, flexibility, collaboration, lifelong learning, innovation, accountability, leadership development, cross-cultural respect, efficacy, teamwork, and empowerment. The core values were key in the inclusion of the African-American community, as students from two distinct ethnicities and cultural backgrounds converge to create effective schooling.

I engage this way because ...

For myself, the hunger strike serves as a 'necessary interruption'. Historically, the status quo of urban school policy imposes new 'innovations' on communities, ignoring the political economy that has shaped the educational experience of African-American and Latino/a students. By interrupting the status quo, community members of Little Village and North Lawndale challenged CPS to remain accountable to the communities they serve. When I was informed about the strike by one of the protesters, it reminded me of some of the tenets of community organizing in terms of 'speaking truth to power', remaining accountable to the groups you work in solidarity with, and meeting people where they're at, to dispel any notion of hierarchy in the process you're about to undertake. For these reasons, and for the remainder of this account, I operate on numerous fronts; first as a concerned citizen, second as a documentarian responsible for recording the process of creating a neighborhood school, and third as a member of the design team for SOJO. Due to the circumstances that created the school, I take my work as design team member and researcher with great responsibility. Since the inception of the design team, I continually challenge myself to engage my own theories and praxis in the hope of remaining accountable to community members, community organizations, teachers, students, and administrators, as the high school moves into its fourth year. Echoing the sentiment of Michael Apple (1994), I understand my work as raising:

> Intensely personal questions about ourselves—as raced, gendered, and classed actors—and where we fit into the relations of power, of domination and subordination, in our societies. (Apple, in Gitlin, 1994, p. x)

As an African-American teacher/researcher/professor with limited Spanish proficiency and a background in community organizing, I am closely acquainted with the relations of power between municipal bodies (in this case an urban public school system), community organizations, and community residents. Additionally, I am neither a resident of Little Village nor North Lawndale. Because I was called into the process as an education 'expert', I operate as an insider/outsider. I am 'inside' the process in that I was a member of the design team and continue to work at SOJO. In other ways, I operate as an 'outsider' due to my non-residence in either community, coupled with my limited

Spanish-speaking ability. Instead of bypassing these contradictions, I need to enter these conflicting realities to promote transparency in my struggles throughout the design team process. Following the call of Linda Tuhiwai Smith, I understand humility as key to this type of work. In recognizing the historical colonial relationship between communities and universities, I enter the process understanding that my work would be impossible without the community's blessing. I agree that 'it is not ethical to walk away, or simply to carry out projects which describe what is already known' (Tuhiwai Smith, 2012, p. 140). In this sense, the roles and relationships go beyond the ethics of traditional qualitative research and involve transparency with the people I work with who are not university professors.

Understanding the permanent, engrained, and enduring properties of racism posed many challenges for the design team. Because Chicago is a segregated city, the communities of Little Village and North Lawndale have little contact with each other. Despite brief moments in political campaigns and community organizing, African-American and Latino/a residents were forced to educate themselves about each other. As some members in both groups were reluctant at first, there were some who took the issue head-on. They reminded the group of the collective struggle of Black and Latino/a peoples, and how White supremacy (racism) has functioned in the past to divide and conquer, resulting in distrust and self-segregation. Coupled with the historical legacy of CPS and its treatment of poor Black and Latino/a youth, we continually found ourselves at a crossroads when it came between choosing accountability to the community initiative and compliance with CPS policy. It became especially difficult when the people responsible for communicating CPS policy and mandates to the design team in many cases were African-American and Latino/a. Even more troubling was the fact that many understood how hegemonic bureaucracies derail community initiatives. On numerous occasions, we were 'advised' on how not to 'ruffle the feathers' of CPS in creating the high school. In the liberal sense, they felt that they were 'doing us a favor'. In reality, it often felt like they were agents of the state with the sole intent of defeating our goal.

Nevertheless, I believe that critical race praxis should be 'reconceptualized so that it can more powerfully act on some of the most persistent and important problems of our schools, namely those surrounding issues of race, class, and gender' (Gitlin, 1994, p. ix). Education, as the process of making informed decisions to improve the human condition through critical analysis and action, is not confined to the walls of a school building. Instead, it is a political exercise with the intent of equipping marginalized communities with the ability to analyze and change systems of power. Inherent to this process is cultivating the community's capacity to utilize their own skills and expertise to address issues and concerns that threaten their existence.

Eight and a half years in ... peaks and valleys in contested space

Where an ethnographic account of the past eight and a half years at SOJO is beyond the scope of this document, there are numerous moments that are reflective of CRT's commitment to revealing the unspoken realities of race and class in education. During this time, I have team-taught classes with SOJO faculty, served on the Local School Council, and taught a college course on the SOJO campus, offering students early college credit. From my first participation on the design team to the current struggle against neoliberal education reform, our navigation of the shifts from central office to our own lives brings about a particular understanding. Highlighted in the edited volume by Hare (2008), the messiness of engaged scholarship often forces researchers/scholars to come to grips with the unevenness of life, while balancing the responsibility of remaining accountable and working in solidarity with community. Throughout SOJO history, there have been tense situations where the aforementioned political economy of the city is coupled with the local realities of regional segregation and unfamiliarity between groups. It is in these uncomfortable moments where the push by faculty and students at SOJO, combined with engaged families and community members to organize, has proven invaluable to the school's development. These relationships, no matter how strained they've become over the years, have proven critical in bringing about a working understanding of the importance of the efforts beyond the original hunger strike almost 11 years ago. The following section is emblematic of such efforts, in that it spans a period of just under one year where SOJO was thrust into the neoliberal morass of educational policy and political hubris.

There will be blood: keeping the doors open in troubling times

The ensuing section is an account of particular events occurring between October 2011 and November 2012. Where it is not a comprehensive month-to-month account of the events in question, it is reflective of the ensuing battles taking place at the school, district, and city level. As counterstory, the following italicized entry, like the opening paragraphs, is unfortunately reflective of the current situation in Chicago:

> *October 2011: During a trip to Minnesota I received a text from one of the SOJO teachers explaining that the principal called an emergency staff meeting and subsequently told everyone that he was leaving and could no longer keep working at the school. Where many of the staff knew that he was struggling in the position, it was a blow due to its sudden nature. Despite the fact that tensions had been building between staff members for the last six months, the abrupt nature of his departure sent everyone in a tailspin. Questions were abound: What will CPS do to us? Will they give us a hatchet-person as principal to shut us down? Is this the beginning of the process to close all four schools and turn it into a large comprehensive high school? Will teachers be fired? What about the students? The school year began in mid-August. This was barely the second month of school.*

> *In his defense, the principal felt the conditions at the school were untenable. Nevertheless, many of us who were involved with the school felt as if this could have been handled differently. Leaving the school mid-year had all the potential to destabilize our efforts regarding curriculum, teacher collaboration and student support. Of particular importance was the fact that we had been placed on academic probation by central office for failure to meet achievement standards (read: test score performance) set forward by the district. Currently CPS can decide who gets to be closed due to what they deem 'chronic underperformance' or 'underutilization'. Since 2004, 101 schools have been closed under said rubrics. Ninety-nine of those schools have been in African-American and Latino/a neighborhoods. What's in place to determine that we're not next? Without strong, committed leadership there will be a perpetual target on our backs. Coupled with the fact that CPS has determined small schools to be economically inefficient and too costly, we've been living under a shroud of potential consolidation. Again, we had only been in classes for two and a half months.*

At the time, CPS had a set of policies stating that a local school council could enact to secure leadership for its school. Because we were only an 'advisory' local school council (known as an ALSC – different from traditional LSCs, our recommendations could still be rejected from central office), there were a set of special provisions the council had to be in compliance with. The administrator responsible for the region that SOJO is in (known as the network chief) alerted the Local School Council that we had a couple of options. The first would be to get an 'administrator in charge' that would be responsible for leadership duties until we secured a principal. The second option would be to get an 'interim principal' that would assume leadership duties, but would also be eligible to apply for the permanent principal position. We chose the first option, due to CPS' history of placing interim principals in schools and subsequently closing the school. Our feeling was that if we chose the person (as opposed to CPS placing the principal), there would be less chance of the latter becoming a reality.

Nevertheless, there was a tight scramble for selecting a new principal. The administrator in charge brought some stability back to the campus. She was well liked by teachers, students, and families. The ALSC found her to be extremely transparent and dedicated to the lives of young people. The only problem was that because she was a retired school principal, due to the construction of her retirement pension, she could only be in the position until 1 March. If she worked beyond those dates, CPS' Department of Human Resources would cancel her retirement and list her as a full-time employee, which would jeopardize her pension.

In searching for a principal, we were in a bit of a bind. Over the last three years, the State of Illinois has changed legislation surrounding the eligibility of principal candidates. The current principal certification alone does not make you eligible for a position. In order to become completely eligible for the position, you have to go through a certain program approved by the district you're applying to. In CPS, to be eligible for a principal position, you need to complete a certification program in addition to completing a program in the Office of Principal Professional Development (OPPD). Once you complete this training, you are 'principal eligible'. In selecting candidates to be interviewed, we were only allowed to select from the eligibility list. This shortened our pool of candidates considerably. No one on our current staff was 'principal eligible'. All of our contacts in the city known to be good school leaders were either already in positions or not on the current eligibility list.

Through a series of debates on the council, we came to a vote and selected our principal candidate. It was a 5-4 vote, as some council members were concerned with the fact that the candidate was not bilingual and felt that using local and state politicians to prevent a school from closing was not the best approach. Increasing the tension was the fact that four members of our local school council were hunger-strikers. Three of the hunger strikers supported one candidate while the other supported another person. Tensions were high, in that all of us did not agree as to what type of person was needed in this particular moment to lead the school. Myself and other members of the council expressed to the larger group that because of our current probation status and in light of the current school closings, it was imperative that whomever we chose needed to have a specific plan to keep the doors open. If they didn't, SOJO would get closer to the possibility of closing within a year's time.

The candidate we chose had a specific plan. Additionally, the school she led previously had a similar racial/ethnic make-up of African-American and Latino/a students as SOJO. What also impressed us was the fact that she fought CPS on closing her school and was part of the effort to change legislation in Illinois around school closings. Again, in a contested space where many people have particular ideas around what quality education looks like, difficult decisions are made in moments of crisis.

After the selection of the new principal, there still was not an easy transition. The administrator in charge was well liked by students and staff, along with fact that some teachers had allegiances to the principal that left in the beginning of the year. This led to some teachers leaving at the end of the year and a graduation ceremony that was bittersweet due to the aforementioned transitions.

As summer ensued, teachers and students had begun their planning for the 2012–2013 school year. Students signed up for boot-camp prep courses for the Advanced Placement (AP) classes for the school year. Teachers attended professional developments on areas like the common-core standards and the college-readiness standards. Because of the departures of a few teachers, we were in the process of filling three vacated teaching positions. All of this came to an abrupt halt on 7 August 2012. On this day, the principal democratically selected by the Local School Council was summarily fired. She was not given a reason other than her services were no longer needed. The only documentation came in the form of a one-paragraph letter stating that her services as principal were no longer needed. Additionally, when CPS replaced her with an interim principal, her first decision was to cancel the current course schedule, removing students from the courses they registered for at the end of the school year. The rationale behind this was that the interim felt that the current course schedule was too 'top-heavy' with AP courses and did not address the skill deficiencies of the students. To their credit, the teachers, parents, and students did not take this lying down. This decision was made on 10 August. The first day of school was scheduled for 13 August.

From this decision, the chaos that ensued was maddening. Students were unable to get their schedules, teachers were unable to login to the automated scheduling system, while some teachers were removed from their original teaching assignments and placed in courses that had never been taught at SOJO before. Violence intervention programs were canceled and book orders were not completed. Additionally, the school didn't have paper until the third week of school, and the science team didn't get the supplies they ordered until the sixth week of school. Frustrated parents were not allowed in the school if they did not have an appointment to speak with the principal. At a school that served affluent families, this would be unthinkable. For the CPS, the aforementioned series of events were perpetually explained as 'unfortunate'.

On the 2nd day of school, over 100 students staged a sit-in demanding their original schedules. I accompanied a group of teachers and parents on the first day of school to the local city councilman's office, explaining how the decisions of the interim principal would lead to the ultimate closure of SOJO and the consolidation of the campus. On the second week of school, the area network decided to have a community forum explaining the current changes. They went on to explain that SOJO's data was trending upward, despite the new changes. I joined 200 students and parents, publicly challenging them to explain why they would move to destabilize a school despite its upward trending data. Additionally, we questioned the district on their presentation of data. If our academic achievement data indicates an upward trend, then why the move to destabilize the campus? Additionally, understanding the recent history of school closings and gentrification in Chicago, how could we not think that the current move is to close us down?

Of course, the central office representatives had no substantive answers. What they did give us, however, was eight straight weeks of meeting with central office officials. Two days after the community forum, two founding teachers were fired under the rationale of 'under-population'. Later found to be a miscalculation by central office, the two founding teachers were re-hired two weeks later. Tired of the back-and-forth with CPS, a coalition of students, teachers, families, and community members began to take matters into their own hands. On the second week of school, the aforementioned group (minus the teachers due to a school obligation) staged a community march with over 200 participants. This was a strategy to get the word out to the larger community around what was happening at the school. A number of local publications carried the story, but the major headline at the moment was the strike by the Chicago Teachers Union (CTU). This actually worked to our advantage due to the fact that SOJO has strong CTU leadership in the faculty. Throughout every event, CTU provided support for the efforts at SOJO. Their support was instrumental to the process of ensuring that the message was delivered to other bodies of teachers.

To their credit, the aforementioned coalition did not stop at the community forum and the community march. For eight straight weeks, we met with members of CPS demanding a 'rewind' to 6 August, where students had the schedules they registered for and teachers had the courses they were scheduled to teach. Despite the back-and-forth with central office, parents, students, and teachers continued their community strategy by collecting signatures door-to-door supporting the 'rewind' strategy. When a group of parents and teachers presented to the School Board of the City of Chicago explaining the last six weeks of turmoil, the CEO and the Chief Education Officer (another CEO) sounded appalled. They promised to meet with the teachers and parents immediately. When they did not call the group back, as promised, a series of phone calls were issued to the Chief Education Officer's office and we were assured to get a meeting. Both CEOs met with the group, promising the problem would be resolved.

When the teachers and parents reported back to the ALSC, two CPS officials were present at the meeting. After a series of heated discussions, both officials assured us that we would get a 'favorable' response from the district regarding our rewind strategy. Simultaneously, the Chief Executive Officer, Jean Claude Brizzard, resigned that week. Taking his place was the Chief Educational Officer, Barbara Byrd-Bennett. What ensued was a classic example of Bell's (1980) interest convergence (a foundational pillar of CRT). Because the teachers' strike called the mayor's office to task by mobilizing over 25,000 teachers and office staff, CPS found themselves in a public relations bind. The strike popularized the problematic relationship between schools and corporations, while exposing the reality of severely marginalized schools through wrongful closures and turnaround policy. If the SOJO story got to the mainstream media, it would further taint CPS' reputation as a dishonest broker, this time at the local level. As Bell cautioned in his initial coining of the term, the larger mainstream society (in this case CPS) would only advance racial/social progress to the extent that it serves its own needs. In less than a week, our fired principal was re-hired and awarded back-pay for the nine weeks lost from her unwarranted removal.

Where some may understand this victory as due to the goodwill efforts of CPS, the teachers, parents, and students of SOJO understand that if it were not for their efforts, the school would still be in the situation from 7 August to early November. Their efforts are a testament to the work needed to bring authentic community accountability to low-income/working-class families that also deserve quality education.

Conclusion: messiness and the edge of race

Returning to the tenets of CRT, we should only understand the attack on SOJO as a continuation of the racist neoliberal policies implemented by cities to further marginalize low-income African-American and Latino/a communities. As Chicago has spearheaded such efforts for the majority of cities in the USA, it becomes paramount to highlight resistance to such efforts. The struggle at SOJO, from its beginnings with the mayoral campaign in 1997 to the current 2012 struggle, is indicative of the Herculean effort needed to resist and present alternatives to the current disingenuous wave of corporate educational reforms. In the research community, if we do not engage in such efforts and/ or work in solidarity with the historically marginalized and isolated, we cannot make claims to be part of the larger justice project in education. We will remain on the 'edge' of race if we do not push these issues to the front by re-framing research as the process by which we work with communities to support their efforts in demanding justice for education. Unfortunately for some, this will not win popularity contests. Instead, it may further marginalize you in your position as an academic. Such 'occupational hazards' should not serve as deterrents to our commitment to the larger justice project in education.

In reflection, I must be cognizant of the arguments, disagreements, and misunderstandings throughout the process. Unfortunately, such imperfections can often derail any effort to mobilize. Where this is indicative to collective democratic struggle, more important is the idea that the collective of students, teachers, families, and community members agreed on what was of central importance: SOJO remaining a school that continually supports the efforts of students to make informed decisions on their lives and communities in an ever-changing world. Chicago, as microcosm for many areas through the paring of corporate neoliberal education and uneven development (gentrification), can hopefully serve as an example of the possibilities through resistance and concerted collective strategies. The road often looks long and hard, but we must remain ready.

References

Bell, D. A. (1980). Brown vs Board of Education and the interest-convergence dilemma. *Harvard Law Review*, *93*(3), 518–533. doi:10.2307/1340546

Civic Committee of the Commercial Club of Chicago. (2003). *Left behind: Student achievement in Chicago's public schools*. Chicago, IL: Commercial Club of Chicago.

Crenshaw, K., Gotanda, N., Peller, G., & Thomas, K. (1995). *Critical race theory: The key writings that formed the movement*. New York, NY: The New Press.

Duncan, G. A. (2005). Critical race ethnography in education: Narrative, inequality, and the problem of epistemology. *Race, Ethnicity and Education*, *8*(1), 93–114. doi:10.1080/1361332052000341015

Fine, M., & Fabricant, M. (2012). *Charter schools and the corporate makeover of public education: What's at stake?* New York, NY: Teachers College.

Freire, P. (1969/2003). *Education for critical consciousness*. New York, NY: Continuum.

Gitlin, A. (Ed.). (1994). *Power and method: Political activism and educational research*. New York, NY: Routledge.

Glanton, D., Mullen, W., & Olivio, A. (2011, February 18). Neighborhood population drain: Census shows central Chicago grew while outlying areas lost. *Chicago Tribune*, p. 16.

Hare, C. (2008). *Engaging contradictions: Theory, politics, and methods of activist scholarship*. Berkeley: University of California.

Kozol, J. (2012). *Savage inequalities: Children in America's schools*. New York, NY: Broadway.

Lipman, P. (2003). Chicago school policy: Regulating black and latino youth in the global city. *Race, Ethnicity, and Education*, *6*(4), 331–355. doi:10.1080/13613320320001463357

Lipman, P. (2004). *High stakes education: Inequality, globalization, and urban school reform*. New York, NY: Routledge.

Lipman, P. (2011). *The new political economy of urban education: Neoliberalism, race, and the right to the city*. New York, NY: Routledge.

Lipman, P., Smith, J., Gutstein, E., & Dallacqua, L. (2012, February). *Examining CPS' plan to close, turnaround, or phase out 17 schools*. Chicago: University of Illinois.

Saltman, K. (2007). *Capitalizing on disaster: Taking and breaking public schools*. Boulder, CO: Paradigm.

Saltman, K. (2010). *The gift of education: Public education and venture philanthropy*. New York, NY: Palgrave.

Smith, J. J., & Stovall, D. (2008). Coming home to new homes and new schools: Critical race theory and the new politics of containment. *Journal of Education Policy, 23*(2), 135–152. doi:10.1080/02680930701853062

Solorzano, D. (1997). Images and words that wound: Critical race theory, racial stereotyping, and teacher education. *Teacher Education Quarterly, 24*(3), 5–19.

Tuhiwai Smith, L. (2012). *Decolonizing methodologies: Research and indigenous peoples*. London: Zed Books. Retrieved from http://www.cps.edu/NewSchools/Pages/ONS.aspx

Yamamoto, E. K. (1997). Critical race praxis: Race theory and political lawyering practice in post-civil rights America. *Michigan Law Review, 95*(4), 821–900. doi:10.2307/1290048

Yamamoto, E. (1999). *Interracial justice: Conflict & reconciliation in post civil-rights America*. New York: New York University Press.

Yosso, T. (2006). *Critical race counterstories along the Chicana/Chicano educational pipeline*. New York, NY: Routledge.

'Too Asian?' On racism, paradox and ethno-nationalism

Roland Sintos Coloma

Ontario Institute for Studies in Education, University of Toronto, Toronto, ON, Canada

This essay examines the controversial 'Too Asian?' article published by Canada's premiere news magazine in 2010 as a case study of media and education in order to produce a sharper analytical grammar of race in liberal, multicultural societies. I argue that the article recycles racial stereotypes, perpetuates the normalization of whiteness and the mythology of meritocracy, and enacts irresponsible journalism. I situate its representation of Asians within a historical context, and delineate their paradoxical subjectivity as an un/wanted racialized minority group. Asians are desired as immigrants, workers and students when they benefit Canada's economic imperatives, but are disavowed when they challenge the sociocultural status quo. I also develop the concept of ethno-nationalism as a form of anti-racist resistance when racialized minorities identify with the White-dominant nation-state in their claim for inclusion. However, I raise concerns regarding ethno-nationalism's limitation for pan-Asian solidarity and for the advancement of a marginalized group at the expense of another.

In November 2010, Canada's premiere weekly news magazine, *Maclean's*, published an article titled 'Too Asian?' that outraged and galvanized Asian Canadians and other communities across the country (Findlay & Köhler, 2010).[1] Considered 'one of the shabbiest and laziest pieces in the history of Canadian magazine journalism' (Mallick, 2012), the article was widely reviled for depicting Asian Canadian students in racially stereotypical ways and generating a binary 'us' versus 'them' distinction between the presumptively normal Whites and the academically focused and socially insulated Asians in institutions of higher education. Concerned students and community advocates claimed that the article could end up inciting racial antipathy and division in universities and society at large, instead of fostering a constructive dialog on social diversity and cohesion (Coloma & Lee, 2010).

Consequently, many Asian Canadians demanded that *Maclean's* ought to issue a public apology and to establish anti-racist editorial and employment policies. Some called for the boycott of *Maclean's* parent company, the media conglomerate Rogers Communications, while others lobbied local and federal politicians to condemn the article and stop the $1.5 million in public funding subsidy that the magazine regularly received. Ultimately, *Maclean's* 'Too Asian?' article brought into public discourse the paradoxical position of Asians in Canada as an un/wanted racialized minority group. Simultaneously, it also marked the emergence of ethno-nationalism as a disturbing development in anti-racist resistance by Asian Canadians in response to their paradoxical subjectivity in the Canadian nation-state.

This article contributes to critical examinations of education, race and racism by focusing on Asians, who constitute the largest racialized minority group in Canada (Statistics Canada, 2010).[2] Asians in Canada are generally perceived as the model minority that has overcome racial discrimination in education and society and has integrated into the country's neo-liberal, multicultural mosaic (Maclear, 1994; Pon, 2000). Yet *Maclean's* article brought into sharp relief the paradoxical position of Asians as a racialized minority: they are needed and rejected at the same time, desired and undesirable for inclusion and integration in educational and social institutions. Such paradoxical position has historical antecedents since the mid-1800s when Asians migrated to Canada to work in the gold and coal mines, railway and road construction, and the agricultural, fishing and lumber industries (Adachi, 1976; Buchignani, Indra, & Srivastava, 1985; Lai, 1988). Asians – more specifically, the Chinese, Indians and Japanese – were welcomed for their laboring bodies in service of the economic development and prosperity of Canada, which became a confederated dominion in 1867. However, when Asians were viewed as threats to White labor and the social moral order of 'White Canada forever', their immigration was restricted and then terminated, and their civil rights were severely curtailed (Ward, 2002). In other words, Asians' economic usefulness was their key to enter Canada's racialized gates of labor, migration and eventual citizenship.

This article also addresses the edge of race within the relatively contemporary contexts of putatively race-neutral immigration and diversity-welcoming multicultural policies. Prior to the 1970s, Canada pursued and maintained a staunch white supremacist ideology in its political, economic and social policies that exalted Western Europeans, especially the British and the French, as the preferred immigrants, settlers and citizens of the nation-state (Thobani, 2007). However, the Immigration Act of 1976 moved away from national and racial origins, and instead stressed educational and occupational skills as major selection criteria for admitting immigrants (Li, 2003). The introduction of the Multi-culturalism Policy in 1971 and the passage of the Multiculturalism Act of 1988, which recognized minority groups' cultural heritages, religions and languages, have been regarded as a significant milestone in Canadian history of race and race relations and a global model for intercultural pluralism and governance (Kymlicka, 1996). With these policy changes, one might suggest that Asians as a group, overall, have benefited and thrived. Immigrants from the Asia Pacific region constituted approximately half of the total immigrants to Canada from 2007 to 2011. During the same time period, the top three source countries of immigrants to Canada were from Asia – the Philippines, China and India (Asia Pacific Foundation of Canada, 2012a, 2012c). Moreover, individuals of Asian ancestry now occupy high profile positions in Canadian government, arts, media, sports and education, such as Governor General Adrienne Clarkson, writers Joy Kogawa and Michael Ondaatje, film director Deepa Mehta, actress Sandra Oh, figure skater Patrick Chan, scientist David Suzuki and Donna Quan, director of Toronto District School Board, the largest school board in the country.

The increased immigration from Asia and the ensuing changing racial demographics in educational and social spaces serve as a crucial backdrop in the controversy over *Maclean's* 'Too Asian?' article. Many critics contended that the article was offensive and divisive by promoting anti-Asian racism and xenophobia (Coloma & Lee, 2010; Heer, 2010; Mahtani, 2010; Yu, 2010, November 16). Since the article did not depict Asians as 'real' Canadians, critics disputed such misrepresentation by asserting the subjectivity of Asian Canadians as 'real' Canadians, albeit of the hyphenated kind of a racialized minority, who rightfully belong in elite educational institutions. The assertion of Asian Canadians' genuine Canadian-ness marks what I am calling the discursive enactment of 'ethno-nationalism' by racialized minority individuals and groups. I construe ethno-nationalism as a form of identification and resistance by racialized minorities who contest and work to redress their marginalized status and conditions in White-dominant nation-states by appropriating and associating themselves with national citizenship in order to be regarded as full-fledged members of the civil society. For Asians who have been excluded from the rites and rights of White-dominant countries like Canada, a powerful strategic recourse for inclusion and integration into the nation-state has been to claim and declare their ethno-national belonging as genuine Canadians. Yet what I find troubling in the enactment of ethno-nationalism by Asian Canadians is the assertion and privileging of their Canadian-ness, while simultaneously distancing themselves from and rejecting their Asian-ness.

As a researcher, educator and activist who was involved in the political organizing related to the 'Too Asian?' controversy, I considered writing this article as an opportunity to reflect on what happened three years ago. My scholarly inclination as a historian pushed me to understand and situate the events within the broader vista of continuities and changes over time. It compelled me to document and make sense of the events as they occurred with a historical view in mind. Meanwhile, the educator and activist within me considered writing this article as a teachable moment for myself and others to self-reflexively examine our organizing praxis, its possibilities as enactments of resistance, and its limitations for social justice solidarity and coalition building. This article, consequently, will unfold as a mixture of multiple yet converging designs. The first section will examine *Maclean's* 'Too Asian?' article, and will outline the issues raised by its critics. The second section will frame the article's depiction of Asian Canadians within a broader historical context that will delineate their paradoxical subject position as an un/wanted racialized minority group. The third section will track the organizing efforts related to the 'Too Asian?' article, and will raise concerns regarding the deployment of ethno-nationalism as a form of resistance to racism.

Throughout this article, I will include the perspectives of fellow critics and activists to affirm and honor their incisive analyses of the 'Too Asian?' article and the status of Asians in Canada. I will also insert myself, hopefully appropriately, in my narration of events to dispel the usual academic stance of a disinterested scholar and locate my multiple engagements.[3] At stake are two separate yet interconnected issues: first, the production of a sharper analytical grammar of race to unpack the dynamics of social relations in liberal multicultural societies; and second, the enactment of a more inclusive political praxis for pan-Asian solidarity and for coalition building among racialized minority and immigrant communities in the context of White-dominant nation-states. My case study on media and higher education, with a focus on Asians in Canada, will aim to contribute to these intellectual, political and pedagogical endeavors.

Maclean's 'Too Asian?'

On 10 November 2010, I began receiving emails and phone calls from students, faculty colleagues and community activists about *Maclean's* 'Too Asian?' article, which appeared in its popular annual University Rankings issue. The initial online version of the article was titled 'Too Asian: Some frosh don't want to study at an Asian university'.

It was changed to 'Too Asian?' with a question mark which, according to the publisher, was:

> ... a direct quote from the title of a panel discussion at the 2006 meeting of the National Association for College Admission Counseling where experts examined the growing tendency among US university admission officers to view Asian applicants as a homogenous group. (*Maclean's*, 2010)

Then, in response to the deluge of critical comments, the final online title became 'The enrollment controversy: Worries that efforts in the US to limit enrollment of Asian students in top universities may migrate to Canada'. What is confusing and frustrating about these title changes is that the hard-copy printed version, which was published on 22 November 2010, had different titles, as well. In the magazine's table of contents, the article was called 'Asian advantage? Some frosh don't want to study at an "Asian" university', which was similar to the initial online versions with the exception of the use of the phrase 'Asian advantage?' instead of 'Too Asian' (with or without the question mark) and the use of scare quotes around the word 'Asian' in the subtitle. Yet, the article inside bore a different title:

> 'Too Asian?' A term used in the US to talk about racial imbalance at Ivy league schools is now being whispered on Canadian campuses–by everyone but the students themselves, who speak out loud and clear. (Findlay & Köhler, 2010, p. 77)

What's an 'Asian university' or a university that is 'Too Asian'? According to the article authors Stephanie Findlay and Nicholas Köhler (2010), 'an "Asian" school has come to mean one that is so academically focused that some students feel they can no longer compete or have fun' (p. 77). The term 'too Asian', Findlay and Köhler point out, is:

> ... used in some US academic circles to describe a phenomenon that's become such a cause for concern to university admissions officers and high school guidance counsellors that several elite universities to the south have faced scandals in recent years over limiting Asian applicants and keeping the numbers of white students artificially high. (p. 77)

And which Canadian universities are considered 'Too Asian'? These are 'top-tier post-secondary institutions with international profiles specializing in math, science and business: U of T [University of Toronto], UBC [University of British Columbia] and the University of Waterloo' (p. 78). According to 'Alexandra' (pseudonym), a graduate of an all-girls private school in Toronto, 'The only people from our school who went to U of T were Asian ... All the white kids go to Queen's, Western and McGill' (p. 77).

So, what's the problem with a university being 'Too Asian'? My analysis of the article reveals that there seem to be three problems. First, for many White students, like 'Alexandra' who was interviewed for the article, they believe that:

> ... competing with Asians—both Asian Canadians and international students—requires a sacrifice of time and freedom they're not willing to make. They complain that they can't compete for spots in the best schools and can't party as much as they'd like. (pp. 77–78)

Second, for institutions of higher education, their commitment to 'pure' meritocratic admissions has 'many in the education community worry that universities risk becoming too skewed one way' (p. 78). Even though the phrase 'too skewed one way' is not explained in the article, it signals what is perceived to be an overabundance of Asian Canadian and international students on campus. This problem 'puts Canadian universities in a quandary [because if] they openly address the issue of race they expose themselves to criticisms that they are profiling and committing an injustice', but if they do not address it, they are accused of being 'too Asian'.

Third, for the general populace, even though racial diversity has enriched Canadian universities, 'it has also put them at risk of being increasingly fractured along ethnic lines. It's a superficial form of multiculturalism that is expressed in the main through segregated, self-selecting, discrete communities' (p. 81). For instance, 'there is little Asian representation on student government, campus newspapers or college radio stations' (p. 80). The authors also indicate that, although Asian Canadian students may not be involved in mainstream organizations, they actively participate in ethnic cultural groups. Hence, instead of universities functioning as 'oases of dialogue, mutual understanding, and diversity' for the society at large, they 'risk becoming places of many solitudes, deserts of non-communication' (p. 78).

The vast majority of the emails, phone calls and personal conversations that I had on 10 November and afterward were overwhelmingly disapproving of the *Maclean's* article. The critiques included the *normalization of whiteness* by presuming the experiences of economically privileged and White students as the universal standard against which others' educational and social conditions are assessed; the *illusion of meritocracy* through universities' failure to account for the history and legacy of White preferential treatment, and the continuous systemic oppression of Aboriginal peoples and racialized minorities; *race baiting* through the seemingly purposeful use of a controversial title to attract public attention and boost magazine sales; and *irresponsible journalism* by not disclosing the real identities of their main interview subjects for verification and by misrepresenting the purpose of the article when discussing it with other key informants.

Other critics openly shared their concerns in mainstream and alternative media outlets. For instance, Minelle Mahtani (2010), a professor of geography and journalism at the University of Toronto, indicated that *Maclean's* article 'reveal[ed] a growing crisis in news and current affairs storytelling ... [when stories] reflect a pervasive pattern of racism and stereotyping'. To reverse this pattern, she called for 'ethical journalism' which 'honours the profession's commitment to truth, accuracy and balanced reporting. It means finding the untold stories about immigration, diversity and race and covering the undercovered'. The York University doctoral student and journalist Jeet Heer (2010) listed three key offenses of the article's 'bad aftertaste': its monolithic homogenization of 'Asians' by disregarding their diversity based on ancestral, national and economic backgrounds; its stereotypical portrayals of White students as 'privileged preppies who are more interested in partying and drinking than studying' and Asian students as 'socially dysfunctional nerds who lack any sense of fun, virtual robots who are programmed by their parents to study'; and its miscasting of the 'problem as one that is caused by the mere presence of "Asians" on campus, rather than by the social and cultural barriers that divide students'. Finally, Henry Yu (2010, November 27), a history professor at the University of British Columbia, provided a genealogy of 'yellow peril' and 'model minority' in order to claim that 'when the *Maclean's* writers and editors trafficked in this image, they invested in their article the values of a century-and-a-half of white supremacy'.

Building on the insightful commentaries offered by Mahtani, Heer, Yu and other critics, I will analyze the *Maclean's* article by drawing attention to the paradoxical position of Asians in Canada as an un/wanted racialized minority in historical and contemporary contexts. Using Yu's genealogical move as a point of departure, I will situate the racialization of Asians in Canada in relation to broader economic, political and sociocultural dynamics, and will track their status of being wanted and unwanted within a historical pattern.

Paradox of being un/wanted

From the mid- to late-1800s, Asians were actively recruited to help develop Canada's nascent agricultural, fishing, lumber, mining and transportation industries. They were considered ideal laborers by economic elites and industrial capitalists who wanted a working force that was cheap, diligent, docile and expendable (Goutor, 2007). Matthew Begbie, the first Chief Justice of British Columbia, stated, 'I do not see how people would get on here at all without Chinamen. They do, and do well, what white women cannot do, and do what white men will not do' (in Li, 1998, p. 29). The use and ubiquity of Asians in many labor-intensive industries can lead one to suggest that they were vital to the establishment and prosperity of Canada as a newly formed nation-state. However, their contributions were often minimized, if not erased altogether. For instance, the image of the 'Last Spike', considered 'possibly the best-known Canadian photograph', captures the completion of Canada's transcontinental railway in 1885 (Brown, 2007, p. 363). It shows well-dressed White men, including prominent railway financiers and officials, surrounded by a crowd of White male workers. Missing in this photograph are the Chinese workers whose labor was instrumental in the construction of the railway, which facilitated communication, trade, travel and settlement across the country. Unfortunately, the erasure of their contributions continues in recent renditions. Library and Archives Canada's (2012) video titled 'Driving the Nation: The Last Spike and the Faces of the CPR' only highlights the White men in the photograph. Not once does the video mention or show the existence and labor of Asian workers in constructing the transcontinental railway.

During periods of financial boom and stability, the presence of Asians in Canada was tolerated and drew minimal attention from the general White populace. However, their continued migration and settlement, especially during periods of economic recession, raised nativist alarm. Asians were seen as ruthless competition for jobs and dangerous threats to the social moral order (Goutor, 2007; Lai, 1988). Racial antipathy became intricately linked to labor anxiety in White-dominant countries under industrial capitalist system. White public and working laborers' sentiments against Asians were reflected and reinforced by elected politicians, who marshaled the state's institutional power to discriminate (Ward, 2002). Anti-Asian laws and regulations focused on restricting Asian immigration to Canada, such as the Immigration Act of 1885, which levied a head tax on the Chinese; the Continuous Journey Regulation of 1908, which posed a migration barrier for Indians by requiring all immigrants to travel uninterrupted from their point of origin to Canada; and the Hayashi-Lemieux Agreement of 1908, which limited Japanese immigration to 400 individuals per year. When Chinese immigration did not abate in spite of increasing head tax payments from $50 to $100 and then to $500, the Immigration Act of 1923 banned Chinese immigration to Canada, with the exception of diplomats, merchants and students.

Asians in Canada lived in an openly racist and hostile environment from the late 1800s and throughout the first half of the 1900s (Adachi, 1976; Buchignani et al., 1985; Lai, 1988; Ward, 2002). Additional legislative controls were passed in order to severely curtail their political, economic and social rights. The first bill to disenfranchise Chinese was passed in British Columbia in 1872, and was subsequently extended to Indians and Japanese. Seventy-six years later in 1948, when the last disenfranchisement statute was repealed, Asian Canadians were finally granted the right to vote. Along with losing their right of suffrage, Asian Canadians were excluded from running for political office, thereby shutting them out of political self-representation and determination. It was only in 1957 that the first Asian Canadian, Douglas Jung, was elected to a political office. Other laws prohibited Asian Canadians from owning Crown lands, getting hired in public works or underground mines and holding licenses for liquor or logging enterprises. They were also barred from white-collar professions, such as law and pharmacy, from night work in laundries and from employing White females (Li, 1998; Mar, 2010; Mawani, 2010).

Denying Asian Canadians their citizenship and civil rights was emblematic of White nativism and patriotism, and fortified the former group's status as an unwanted racialized minority. In addition to anti-Asian laws and regulations, they were subjected to frequent racial attacks and hostilities, led prominently by the Asiatic Exclusion League under the auspices of the Trades and Labour Council. For instance, Asian Canadians suffered tremendous property damage, not to mention intense psychological affliction, during the 1887 and 1907 riots in Vancouver (Ward, 2002). Anti-Asian racism culminated in the mid-1900s with the internment of 22,000 Japanese Canadians during World War II, two-thirds of whom were Canadian-born citizens (Miki, 2005; Oikawa, 2012). In the name of national safety and security, the Canadian government mobilized the War Measures Act to incarcerate, dispossess, deport and disperse Canadians of Japanese ancestry. No evidence has been found that indicates Japanese Canadians' complicity to the Pearl Harbor bombing and to speculations of sabotage or espionage, or as actual threats to Canadian national well-being.

Given these explicit anti-Asian hostilities and regulations, it is no wonder the general public would view the period from the 1970s onward as a positive transformation in Canadian racial attitudes and race relations. The legislative passage, in particular, of the Immigration Act of 1976 and the Multiculturalism Act of 1988 signaled the dawn of Canada's era of liberal multiculturalism. According to philosopher Will Kymlicka (1996), for minorities to acquire and benefit from full citizenship, 'a comprehensive theory of justice in a multicultural state will include both universal rights, assigned to individuals regardless of group membership, and certain group-differentiated rights or "special status" for minority cultures' (p. 6). Kymlicka's notion of justice is premised on a liberal-democratic theory that is 'grounded in a commitment to freedom of choice and … personal autonomy' (p. 7). Hence, on the one hand, the revised Immigration Act may be interpreted as representing a universal right since the policy no longer privileges immigrants from Europe. Instead, presumably race-neutral criteria, such as educational and employment backgrounds, have become the main filters for admitting immigrants. On the other hand, the Multiculturalism Act may be understood as forwarding a group-differentiated right since it enables minorities to preserve and celebrate their distinct cultures. Combined, these two legislations have become hallmarks of the Canadian brand of liberal multiculturalism.

The publication of the *Maclean's* 'Too Asian?' article came at a time when Canada is turning to immigrants to bolster the country's economic development. Canada set a record in 2010 when it allowed the highest number of immigrants in more than 50 years (Citizenship and Immigration Canada, 2011). Jason Kenny, minister of Citizenship, Immigration and Multiculturalism, stated:

> As we recover from the recession, increasing economic immigration will help ensure employers have the workers they need to supplement our domestic labour supply ... Canada [also] needs investor immigrants ... to keep Canadacompetitive with other countries, and keep pace with the changing economy. (Citizenship and Immigration Canada, 2010)

Economic immigrants include individuals who qualify under the federal skilled worker category of 'in-demand occupations', such as architects, dentists, medical doctors, nurses, scientists and skilled trades workers. They also include individuals who qualify under the immigrant investor program, which targets 'experienced business people' with personal net worth of at least $1.6 million who can make a minimum investment of $800,000 for economic development and job creation initiatives. These selective government priorities have generated an immigration stream from Asia that has privileged and benefited those with economic capital, white-collar professions and flexible mobility. In 2010, more than half of all immigrants to Canada from Asia were economic immigrants and their dependants. A year after, the number of economic immigrants and their dependants increased to two-thirds of all Asian immigrants (Asia Pacific Foundation of Canada, 2012b).[4]

For its future prosperity, Canada is building capacity for the 'Great Brain Race' by aiming to attract top global talent and turning to international education (Wildavsky, 2010). Right before the publication of the 'Too Asian?' article, a couple of high-profile Canadian visits to Asia were intended to build greater cooperation and partnership in education. The Council of Ministers of Education, Canada, held a consultation meeting in China in September 2010, while the Association of Universities and Colleges of Canada organized the largest delegation of Canadian university presidents to India in November 2010. Then, a couple of months after the article's release, the University of British Columbia President Stephen Toope appeared in a three-part video titled 'The Battle for Brains', where he discussed 'how international students change Canadian schools', 'why we need to assert our stake in the global brain race' and 'how universities can help Canada become a global leader' (Toope, 2011). A year later, a federal advisory panel, led by the Western University president and former University of Waterloo provost Amit Chakma, released a report titled 'International Education: A Key Driver of Canada's Future Prosperity' (Foreign Affairs and International Trade Canada, 2012). The panel's first recommendation is to double the number of international students coming to Canada to more than 450,000 by the year 2022 in order to raise the country's 'international mind share' (p. i). The report specifically identifies 'priority markets' with the 'greatest growth potential', such as China, India and Vietnam (alongside Brazil, Mexico, the Middle East and North Africa), and 'mature markets', such as South Korea (alongside the United States, France and the United Kingdom), to tap into 'innovation, trade, human capital development and the labour market' (pp. viii, xiv).

Since the 1970s, the government's immigration and multiculturalism policies have facilitated the migration and settlement of Asians in Canada and, consequently, the development of Asian Canadian families and communities. According to population projections by Statistics Canada (2010), released a few months before the *Maclean's* article, racialized minorities will double by 2031, and will be the numerical majority in urban metropolitan centers like Toronto and Vancouver, with South Asians and Chinese continuing as the largest non-White groups. Canada's political, business and educational leaders have turned to Asian immigrants, investors and international students in order to capitalize on their labor, economic and educational strengths as Canada shores up its national prosperity and global competitiveness in the twenty-first century. Similar to their counterparts in the mid- to late-1800s, today's elite have welcomed immigrants, especially from Asia, when they serve the economic imperatives of the nation-state as workers and, in recent times, as investors and students. In the era of liberal multi-culturalism, Asians from privileged economic and educational backgrounds have become Canada's preferred immigrants and desired racialized minority group.

However, traces of contemporary anti-immigration sentiments and movements are emerging. Politically conservative and nativist organizations, such as the Fraser Institute and Immigration Watch Canada, have published research reports, held conferences and community meetings, and utilized mainstream and social media to convey their alarmist message on immigration. In 2010, the Centre for Immigration Policy Reform (n.d.) was established with the following objectives:

> Immigration intake should be based on Canada's economic benefit. Immigration should be used only to complement the existing workforce in Canada and not to provide a quick source of cheap labour that discourages Canadians from entering the job market … [G]reater priority should be given to the applicants who can contribute to the economy rather than to sponsorship of extended family members … We should continue to welcome immigrants of all racial, ethnic and religious backgrounds but make it clear that newcomers are expected to have an unequivocal commitment to basic Canadian values and exclusive loyalty to Canada.

Located in Ottawa, this center is composed of prominent individuals, including ambassadors, politicians, academics and media executives, who can access and navigate the corridors of power and influence in the nation's capital in order to push forward its aims and agendas. Moreover, a public opinion poll in 2010 reveals that 'more Canadians are questioning the benefits of immigration' (AngusReid, 2010). Out of 'a representative sample' of 1007 Canadians who responded to an online survey, 46% believe that immigration has a 'negative effect in Canada', 34% indicate that it has a 'positive effect' and 20% are 'not sure' of its effect. A national poll of 2926 Canadians in 2011 indicates that:

> Canadians are somewhat conflicted about Asia and Canada's relations with the region. While the results over time show that Canadians increasingly view Asia as critically important economically and politically, we do not seem to be fully embracing Asia's rise. Indeed, the number of Canadians who perceive China and India's growing economic power as more of an opportunity than a threat has been declining over the past few years. These divergent trend lines suggest that Canadians may be growing uneasy about this historic shift and, unsure of how to engage with Asia, they seem to be reflexively turning inward. (Asia Pacific Foundation of Canada, 2011)

Canadians' uneasiness over immigration in general and over Asia's rising economic power can be gleaned in their social anxieties as they turn reflexively inward and examine the increasing presence of Asians and the consequent changes in social spaces and institutions. For instance, in the mid-1990s, long-time residents of suburban Toronto expressed tremendous concern over the construction of a large Asian-themed mall catering to the growing concentration of Asians moving to and settling in the area (Preston & Lo, 2000). The increase of immigrants in the area was 'due mainly to political events in East Asia coinciding with legislative change in Canada' including the transfer of sovereignty over Hong Kong from the United Kingdom to China; the Tiananmen Square Incident and the suppression of the student pro-democracy movement in China; and the establishment of the business immigrant program in Canada (p. 183). The residents' struggle over land use and cultural space was triggered by the influx of Asian immigrants who, in their view, were not conforming to established norms and built environments and, instead, were asserting their own identities and preferences in the local geography.

My historical delineation demonstrates that Asians occupy a paradoxical subject position as an un/wanted racialized minority population in Canada. On the one hand, they are recruited and welcomed as workers, investors and students, and become wanted as desirable immigrants and citizens when they serve the economic priorities and objectives of the nation-state. On the other hand, they become unwanted when they are perceived as threats to the normalized sociocultural order and take away positions and resources from 'rightful' Canadians. In the *Maclean's* article, an Asian Canadian student states, 'At graduation a Canadian—i.e., "white"—mother told me that I'm the reason her son didn't get a space in university and that all the immigrants in the country are taking up university spots' (Findlay & Köhler, 2010, p. 78). The White mother's anti-Asian resentment echoes the general attitude in the late 1800s and early 1900s when legislations and regulations transformed public prejudice into institutionalized forms of discrimination against Asians. In the past, political, social and capitalist elite were initially in favor of Asian immigration since they served the country's economic interests. But they ended up expressing anti-Asian rhetoric and joining the ranks of the masses when the racial tide turned. History often has a way of repeating itself, and only time will tell how the current traces of anti-immigration and anti-Asian sentiments will materialize.

Ethno-nationalism as resistance and its limits

On 15 November 2010, a few days after *Maclean's* online release of the 'Too Asian?' article, I convened a public meeting at the University of Toronto to provide a public space for collective dialog and organizing. Over 120 students, educators and community members came to share their perspectives and discuss potential plans of action.[5] Victor Wong of the Chinese Canadian National Council (CCNC) compared the *Maclean's* 'Too Asian?' article to the 1979 *W5* television episode 'Campus Giveaway' by CTV, Canada's largest private broadcaster:

> Over footage of Asian-looking faces in a pharmacy class at the University of Toronto, the show declared that 'foreign' students were invading Canadian universities, and that the federal government was subsidizing their education and denying Canadian students the opportunity of higher education. (Asia/Canada, n.d.)

Reminiscent of the *W5* program from over 30 years ago, *Maclean's* article recycled the racist and xenophobic discourse of Asian Canadians as perpetual foreigners who took educational spots away from allegedly real Canadians. Wong shared the Chinese Canadian community's successful strategy of obtaining its central goal – a public apology from CTV – by raising awareness in both ethnic and mainstream groups, outreaching and building cross-cultural coalitions and staging public protests. With key leaders from CCNC National and the CCNC Toronto Chapter, Wong met with the publisher and editors of *Maclean's* to demand an apology.

From the November 15th meeting, the idea of an open letter to *Maclean's* was hatched. Community historian and former journalist Brad Lee and I drafted the letter, with invaluable input from organizer Karen Sun, and circulated it to various individuals and groups across the country for feedback and support. The letter, titled 'A call to eliminate anti-Asian racism', generated over 100 organizational signatories from race/ethnic, labor, feminist, migrant and student sectors, including the National Anti-Racism Council of Canada, Asian Canadian Labour Alliance, CCNC Toronto, Council of Agencies Serving South Asians, National Association of Japanese Canadians (NAJC), Philippine Women Centre of Ontario, Raging Asian Women, Ontario Council of Agencies Serving

Immigrants and Canadian Federation of Students, Ontario. The letter also called for 'a comprehensive and unqualified public apology to Asian Canadians', and pressed for institutional changes including the need to 'engage in public consultation to address racial profiling and stereotyping via their media outlets', to 'implement measurable corporate and editorial anti-racism policies in consultation with relevant community constituents' and to 'implement employment equity programs to diversify their corporate and editorial boards and frontline personnel' (Coloma & Lee, 2010). Moreover, it considered the institutional contexts of higher education and demanded that universities and colleges:

> ... must develop academic programs and courses that explicitly address racism in Canada and the historical and contemporary experiences, representations, and contributions of Asian Canadians; must undertake and publish campus climate surveys of racialized students, staff, and faculty; and, must establish advocacy and support offices for racialized students, staff, and faculty. (Coloma & Lee, 2010)

From the discussions, planning and organizing that transpired in the Toronto area, the Solidarity Committee Against Anti-Asian Racism was established as a network of activists committed to racial justice, multi-sectoral collaborations and grassroots organizing.

When *Maclean's* refused to apologize and respond to the open letter demands, organizers understood the need to raise awareness and mobilize the public to obtain support and mount pressure on the media corporation. Education campaigns included holding discussion forums in universities and community gatherings; sharing views through social media, such as Facebook, Twitter and YouTube; and writing opinion pieces and letters to the editor in mainstream, ethnic and other alternative media outlets. Ken Noma of the NAJC made important historical connections at the public teach-in held at the University of Toronto. He reiterated these linkages in his own open letter to the *Maclean's* magazine in the NAJC website, where he wrote:

> ... racist stereotyping is a very disturbing reminder for Japanese Canadians of the time before and after World War II when the Government of Canada summarily condemned all Japanese Canadians living in [British Columbia] as 'enemy aliens', without a shred of evidence to support such slander ... The Maclean's article constitutes a serious setback in creating a truly free and equitable society, leaving many sadly wondering whether the media as represented by Maclean's have learned nothing about the insidious nature of racism in all its evil manifestations and effects. (Noma, 2010)

Asian Canadians enacted various forms of activism as cultural and political resistance to racism.[6] Students and community members lobbied politicians to take a public position on the issue. As a result, the city councils of Victoria and Vancouver in British Columbia, and Toronto, Richmond Hill and Markham in Ontario issued official statements condemning the 'Too Asian?' article and insisting on a formal public apology from the magazine. Member of the Parliament Olivia Chow raised the issue in the federal legislature, while Senator Vivienne Poy asked James Moore, the minister of Canadian Heritage and Official Languages, to 'consider reviewing the allocation of $1.5 million in public funding to *Maclean's*' (Poy, 2010). Poy pointed out a criterion in the Ministry's Canadian Periodical Fund indicating that periodicals with 'offensive content (defined as "material that is denigrating to an identifiable group")' can be considered ineligible for federal support. The undergraduate student council at the University of Victoria voted to boycott the sales of the *Maclean's* magazine on campus. Inspired by the student boycott, many community members canceled their magazine subscriptions and their Rogers communications services.

The educational and mobilization campaigns of Asian Canadian advocates and allies generated intense public discussions and grassroots organizing that were centered on the discursive representation and political status of Asians in Canada. I was, and continue to be, in agreement with the issues raised and strategies enacted by fellow critics and organizers. In fact, I was deeply involved in various campaigns denouncing the *Maclean's* magazine and the Rogers corporation. What I found troubling in our political analysis and organizing, however, was the enactment of what I am calling an 'ethno-nationalism' that asserted and privileged one's Canadian-ness, or rightful belonging to Canada, albeit from the vantage point of a racialized minority, while simultaneously distancing oneself from and rejecting one's Asian-ness. Put differently, my problem with those who take up the 'ethno-national' as a discourse and a subject position is their alignment and identification with the 'dominant-national' while simultaneously disavowing and rejecting the 'foreign-national'. In this configuration, the modifier 'dominant-'signifies White, while the modifiers 'ethno-' and 'foreign-'denote Asian. These modifiers are linked and related to the main word 'national' which, in this case, means Canadian. For ethno-nationals, their Asian-ness is secondary to their Canadian-ness; hence, ethno-nationals are Canadians who *happen to be* of Asian ancestry. However, for foreign-nationals, their Asian-ness primarily defines their juridical and sociocultural relationship to Canada; hence, foreign-nationals are Asians who *do not belong* to Canada due to their foreign-ness. In other words, Asian Canadians who assert ethno-nationalism are keen to claim their Canadian-ness and quick to dismiss their Asian-ness, especially when certain traits might relegate them as 'too Asian' who are'too foreign'. In my view, the move of hyphenated 'ethno-national' minorities to identify *with* the 'dominant-national' and identify *against* the 'foreign-national' is a dubious form of resistance that is based on disavowing an-other in order to assert and situate one's self in the hegemonic national order.

My theorizing of ethno-nationalism is quite different from how it has been conventionally used. It is not the same as political scientist Walker Connor's (1993) notion of ethno-nationalism, which focuses on the emotional bond or sentient identification of groups related to 'two loyalties–loyalty to the nation and loyalty to the state' (p. 81). Connor examines separatist movements during the second half of the twentieth century as instances 'when the two loyalties are seen as being in irreconcilable conflict, [and] loyalty to the state loses out'. However, for groups that are 'so dominant within a multinational state as to perceive the state as essentially their nation's state ... the two loyalties become an indistinguishable, reinforcing blur' (p. 81). My work differs from Connor's in two significant ways: first, I focus on the dynamics of racialized minorities in White-dominant nation-states, which Connor does not address; and second, I examine the strategic identification by a marginalized minority group with the nation-state, which his theory does not account for.

My work on ethno-nationalism is more akin to queer theorist Jasbir Puar's (2007) concept of homonationalism, which manifests in the convergence of three factors: 'sexual exceptionalism, queer as regulatory, and the ascendancy of whiteness' (p. 2). Puar draws from Lisa Duggan's notion of homonormativity as a 'new neo-liberal sexual politics' that 'does not contest dominant heteronormative forms but upholds and sustains them', and mobilizes homonationalism 'to mark arrangements of US sexual exceptionalism explicitly in relation to the nation' (pp. 38–39). The assertion of homonationalism by White lesbian, gay, bisexual and transgendered (LGBT) people is a 'discursive tactic' that distinguishes and distances themselves from 'racial and sexual others, foregrounding a collusion between homosexuality and American nationalism that is generated both by national rhetorics of patriotic inclusion and by queer subjects themselves' (p. 39). As an example of 'the dual movement in which certain homosexual constituencies have embraced US nationalist agendas and have also been embraced by nationalist agendas' (p. xxiv), Puar cites the post-9/11 patriotism expressed by many White LGBT individuals through their support of the war on terror, within the historical context of governmental affirmation of same-sex marriage and legal overturning of sodomy regulations. Among Puar's analytical interventions to studies of race, sexuality, nation and violence, I find two aspects particularly useful for my work: first, she reverses the conventional notion of queers as always resistant and oppositional, and instead locates their complicity as a (sexual) minority group to a hegemonic political and sociocultural order; and second, she tracks the inclusion of a marginalized community into the folds of the nation-state by rejecting and distinguishing themselves from an-other constituency.

Vestiges of ethno-nationalism can be gleaned in some of the critical writings on the *Maclean's* article. For instance, Jeet Heer, one of the book co-editors that used the 'Too Asian?' controversy to address race and representation in Canadian higher education (Gilmour, Bhandar, Heer, & Ma, 2012), states that:

> Of course, the 'Asian campus' is only a problem if you believe that Asian-Canadians are not real Canadians … [It creates a] distinction between Canadians whose presence in universities is natural and those Canadians who, even if they were born in Canada, are seen as alien intruders. (Heer, 2010)

Henry Yu (2010, November 16), a University of British Columbia professor, also asks:

> Have we not advanced enough to recognize that people with black hair who do not look like their families came from Europe can still be 'Canadian,' rather than harbouring the assumption of the writers that 'Asian' is the opposite of 'born in Canada'?

Both Heer and Yu, alongside many Asian Canadian activists and organizers whom I worked with, are making an important political point that Asian Canadians are 'real Canadians' and not opposite of Whites 'born in Canada'. Yet in their articulation to equate Asian Canadians *as Canadians*, they also indicate that Asian Canadians are *not Asians*. In short, ethno-national Asian Canadians are Canadians who happen to have Asian ancestry, but are not Asians.

The Asian Canadian ethno-national move to distance themselves from the Asian foreign-national is evident in the *Maclean's* article, as well. Describing the social dynamics at the University of Waterloo, one of the institutions considered 'too Asian', the article indicates that students call the mathematics and computer buildings on campus 'mainland China' and 'downtown China', where students 'can go for days without speaking English' (Findlay & Köhler, 2010, p. 80). The Asian Canadian students interviewed in the article highlight some of the tensions between them and Asian international students. An Asian Canadian student finds that 'The mainland China group tends to stick together', while another states that 'We can talk to them, but we don't mingle'. At various community and organizing discussions that I attended and participated in, a major point of contention for many Asian Canadians is *Maclean's* visual use of two university-aged Asian men carrying the flag of the People's Republic of China as the opening photograph for the article. They claimed that the magazine was reinforcing the stereotypes of Asian Canadians as having primary affinity and affiliation with Asia (with China, in this case) and of Asian Canadians as perpetual foreigners in Canada. Underpinning such differentiations is the growing tension between the Canadian-born or -raised Asian Canadians and the Asia-born and -raised Asians, an issue that has been openly and often heatedly discussed in social co-ethnic circles, yet has received relatively little scholarly attention.

My intellectual and political concern with ethno-nationalism derives partly from my own autobiography. As someone who was born in the Philippines, yet raised and educated in the United States, and moved to Canada a couple of years prior to the 'Too Asian?' controversy, I felt uneasy with what I perceived to be an ardent assertion of Canadian-ness by Asian Canadian friends and colleagues during the campaign. As someone who did not identify as an Asian Canadian, much less as a Canadian, I felt excluded at certain moments of our organizing, and began to wonder the limits of the political strategy in claiming Canadian-ness for pan-Asian solidarity and for coalition building among racialized minority and diasporic groups. However, given my previous experiences of anti-racist and pro-immigration advocacy in the United States, I understand and have enacted similar moves to assert allegiance and claim belonging to the dominant-national. To me, ethno-nationalism is a strategic form of identification and resistance by racialized minorities who contest and redress their marginalized conditions by appropri-ating and associating with the White-dominant nation-state to gain status and recognition as rightful citizens. Therefore, my disapproval of ethno-nationalism is an intimate and self-reflexive critique, one that is pointed toward fellow racialized minority scholars, educators and activists and toward myself who have mobilized it even in the name of social justice.

The seduction of ethno-nationalism for racialized minorities is the promise of inclusion in a hegemonic nation-state that dangles the affective rites of belonging and the juridical rights of citizenship. Its appeal can be quite considerable given the history and continuation of racist exclusion and oppression at both individual and institutional levels. Ethno-nationalism coincides with liberal multiculturalism that is premised on universal and group-differentiated rights. Ethno-national Asian Canadians can claim their universal Canadian-ness and their differentiated Asian-ness, so long as their Asian-ness remains subsumed under the dominant sociocultural order. In other words, their Asian ethnoracial background primarily functions as a modifier to their Canadian national subject position. Hence, ethno-national Asian Canadians are Canadians who happen to have Asian ancestry, but are not Asians. The ethno-national disavows the foreign-national – in this case, the Asian foreign-national – since that figure symbolizes what is deemed as too foreign, the opposite of the dominant-national or White-Canadian. The political bargain struck by the ethno-national is their strategic alignment and identification with the dominant-national, and the rejection of the foreign-national, in order to assert what they deem as their rightful place in the nation-state.

Conclusion

The educational and political organizing around the *Maclean's* 'Too Asian?' article produced a mixture of results. *Maclean's* did not apologize, thereby dismissing the central demand of the campaign. On 25 November 2010, it published an official statement to the critical public commentaries, which ended with:

> Although the phrase 'Too Asian?' was a question and, again, a quotation from an authoritative source, it upset many people. We expected that it would be provocative, but we did not intend to cause offence. (*Maclean's*, 2010)

On the following day, the Chinese Canadian National Council – Toronto Chapter – received a letter from *Maclean's* legal counsel in response to the delivered open letter, of which CCNC Toronto was one of over 100 organizational signatories. The letter from lawyer Julian Porter indicated that 'My client objects to your deliberate and obscene misrepresentation of *Maclean's* journalism and in particular your attribution to *Maclean's* of the phrase "yellow and brown perils"'. It considered the open letter's attribution of this phrase to the magazine as 'objectionable' and 'defamatory'. It culminated with a 'demand that you withdraw the letter immediately and publicly acknowledge that *Maclean's* never made such a statement, and apologize to *Maclean's* for the misquotation and the imputation of racist views suggested by the phrase'. Then, a year later, on 14 December 2011, the Solidarity Committee Against Anti-Asian Racism received a written reply from the Ministry of Canadian Heritage and Official Languages in response to our petition campaign for the federal agency to stop subsidizing the magazine, based on the research by Anna Liu of Asian Canadian Labour Alliance. Minister James Moore stated that:

> Freedom of expression is a concept that is constitutionally enshrined in Canada and one of the cornerstones of our democracy. Our Government supports a free and independent press, and we are committed to making responsible choices in implementing public funds.

In sum, *Maclean's* non-apology response, its legal retribution and the government's invocation of freedom of expression were three solid strikes against the campaign.

However, these strikes did not deter the educational and political work of Asian Canadian activists and allies. In spite of *Maclean's* refusal, organizers continued to lobby politicians to condemn the 'Too Asian?' article and demand a public apology from the magazine. In spite of the legal threat, the Solidarity Committee Against Anti-Asian Racism did not withdraw the open letter, did not apologize to *Maclean's*, and instead used their newly-developed network list of over 100 organizational partners across the country to share information and coordinate actions. In spite of the federal minister's response, activists asserted their support for freedom of expression, but continued to question the government's failure to enforce its own rule regarding withdrawal of public funding from periodicals with offensive content. Moreover, Asian Canadians and allies deployed conventional and new tactics of outreaching, raising awareness and working with racialized minority communities and the general public. They utilized mainstream, ethnic and social media to share critical perspectives, report on events and announce public forums. Organized discussions on race, media and higher education proliferated in many universities and community centers across the country. The Solidarity Committee Against Anti-Asian Racism has convened two 'anniversary' conferences in order to continue the difficult yet necessary conversations on race and anti-racism.[7] When I asked fellow activists about the significance of the 'Too Asian?' controversy, they shared two important positive effects: it produced local and national coalitions for anti-racist, pan-Asian and cross-cultural organizing; and it generated much-needed critical discussions on race and racism, especially in relation to Asians in Canada.

Even though Asians constitute the largest racialized minority population in Canada, their subject position as a racial collective entity has received relatively little theoretical and empirical analysis. I am mindful of the tremendous diversity within this group in relation to ancestral and national backgrounds, migration and generational patterns, socio-economic status, genders, sexual orientations, and religious and spiritual beliefs, among other markers of difference. For instance, the conditions and trajectories of those who came as investor or business immigrants from Hong Kong in the mid-1990s are vastly different from those who arrived from the Philippines as live-in caregivers in the same time period (Coloma, McElhinny, Tungohan, Catungal, & Davidson, 2012). It is also problematic to homogenize the experiences of those from the same ethnic/regional background. For example, Punjabi Sikhs composed the overwhelming majority of South Asian immigration in the early 1900s. Now they are joined by individuals and families from other parts of India, by those of Indian ancestry but are from the Caribbean, Africa and Europe, and by those from other countries in the subcontinent, such as Bangladesh, Pakistan and Sri Lanka (Buchignani et al., 1985). Yet, in spite of such diversity, people of Asian descent are generally construed as Canada's model minority and the main beneficiaries of liberal multiculturalism and immigration policies. They are perceived to be diligent, docile and self-sufficient, traits that are positively regarded and that derive putatively from their cultural traditions and filial obligations (Maclear, 1994; Pon, 2000). These traits were valued by financial elite and industrial capitalists in the past when Canada was establishing itself as a nation-state. They are similarly valued by today's economic, political and educational elite as Canada continues to build its capacity for national prosperity and global competitiveness in the twenty-first century.

In this article, my central objective has been to produce a sharper analytical grammar of race, especially in relation to Asians as a racialized minority group in White-dominant, multicultural nation-states like Canada. Instead of reinforcing the model minority thesis, I consider the racial subject position of Asian Canadians as an un/wanted minority from a broader historical vantage point. The paradoxical subjectivity of Asian Canadians as wanted and unwanted, as desired and undesirable, for inclusion and integration in the nation-state was and continues to be shaped by economic, political and sociocultural conditions locally, nationally and globally. To resolve this paradox, many Asian Canadians claim their affective belonging and assert their juridical citizenship to the nation-state as genuine Canadians. They do so in order to strategically work through and against the violence inflicted on them. These violent acts can range from seemingly mundane micro-aggressions, such as being repeatedly asked 'Where are you from?', to blatant violations of their human rights during times of war in the name of national security.

The discursive tactic of ethno-nationalism, therefore, can be understood as a form of resistance by racialized minorities in general and by Asian Canadians in particular to address and redress racist exclusion and oppression in White-dominant contexts. Ethno-nationalism enables Asian Canadians to identify and associate with the nation-state which desires and disavows them. It facilitates their claim to belonging and citizenship in spite of persistent efforts to reject and marginalize them. In the current moment, Asian Canadians have embraced Canadian ideals of nationalism, infused with social multi-culturalism, economic neo-liberalism and political democracy. Simultaneously, the Canadian nation-state has embraced Asian Canadians for their financial, labor and educational capital. Working alongside Jasbir Puar's (2007) concept of homonationalism, I suggest that ethno-nationalism takes place within contexts of a dual movement in which certain racialized minority groups have embraced White-dominant nationalist agendas and have also been embraced by these nationalist agendas. In the case of Asian Canadians, their ethno-nationalist move occurs in their assertion of Canadian-ness and rejection of Asian-ness. While such a move may seem strategic in order to lay political claim to a White-dominant nation-state, the consequences for pan-Asian solidarity and for community building across racialized minority and diasporic communities are profound.

In particular, foreign-nationals who already have limited juridical and tenuous socio-cultural relationships to the White-dominant nation-state will become disregarded even further. In the end, our task as critical scholars of race and anti-racism is to formulate and enact an educational and political praxis in which the advancement of a racialized minority group does not occur at the expense of another group in the margins.

Notes

1. I employ the categorical term 'Asian' to designate the heterogeneous, dynamic and socio-politically constructed grouping of peoples, cultures, materials and ideas that derive from East Asian, South Asian, Southeast Asian and West Asian backgrounds. It is, admittedly, geographically regional and broadly continental in its articulation. It is attentive to the local and global histories, legacies and continuations of imperialisms, colonialisms, wars and conflicts over sovereignties, nationalisms and territorialities. My use of the term 'Asian', especially in the Canadian context, moves away from the dominant emphasis on East Asia and on the peoples and cultures of Chinese, Japanese, and Korean ancestry. Its conventional use often excludes other Asian ethnic groups, such as Indians and Filipina/os (e.g. Coloma et al., 2012). *Maclean's* reinforces the East Asian emphasis in the article by focusing on 'Asian' individuals and organizations that, in actuality, are primarily of Chinese ancestry. Hence, as a discursive intervention, I mobilize the term 'Asian' to address the broader and more inclusive grouping, and name particular ethnic groups in reference to regulations and events that specifically focus on them.

2. According to Canada's Employment Equity Act (S.C. 1995, c. 44), '"members of visible minorities" means persons, other than aboriginal peoples, who are non-Caucasian in race or non-white in colour' (http://laws-lois.justice.gc.ca/eng/acts/E-5.401/page-1.html). I prefer to use the term 'racialized minority' instead of 'visible minority' since, following Block and Gala-buzi (2011):

   > … the term racialized is used to acknowledge 'race' as a social construct and a way of describing a group of people. Racialization is the process through which groups come to be designated as different and on that basis subjected to differential and unequal treatment. (p. 19)

   Building on my deployment of the term 'Asian' and tracking the racialization of Asians in Canada as an un/wanted minority group, I explicate and expand on an insight made by cultural critic Roy Miki (2000): 'these "undesirables" would translate over time into "Asian Canadians"' (p. 50).

3. I learn from and work alongside anti-racist feminists who refuse to compartmentalize the intellectual and activist, the personal and political, the private and public (e.g. Ng, Staton, & Scane, 1995; Razack, Smith, & Thobani, 2010).

4. Unfortunately, many immigrants experience deprofessionalization, deskilling and downward mobility when they arrive and settle in Canada. Even though the immigration system privileges those with educational, occupational and financial capital, they confront considerable institutionalized barriers, especially in the realm of employment. For instance, their academic and professional credentials are not recognized as on par by Canadian universities and accreditation agencies; they are required to have Canadian work experience; and when employed, they face racial, gendered and linguistic/accent discrimination (e.g. Block & Galabuzi, 2011; Coloma et al., 2012; Razack et al., 2010).

5. At this meeting, educator Maria Yau, who convened a community conference titled 'East Asian Parents: Multiple Pathways to Success' connected the *Maclean's* 'Too Asian?' article to the *Toronto Star* newspaper article on her conference, which were both published at the same time. She indicated that these media outlets practiced sensationalized journalism by stereotyping Asian parents as academically obsessed tyrants who were 'pushing their children into university programs for which many have no real interest or talent and often quit in distress' (Brown, 2010).

6. Other activist and organizing acts included wearing 'Too Asian for Maclean's' buttons; writing letters and postcards to *Maclean's* parent company, Rogers Communications; staging a flash

mob at a Rogers store in a busy Toronto shopping mall, led by the Youth Coalition co-chairs Florence Li and Chase Lo; and creating a satirical YouTube video on multi-racial harmony through a parody of the 'We are the World' song by Tetsuro Shigematsu and his collaborators at the University of British Columbia.

7. The 2012 'anniversary' conference was convened at the Ryerson University in Toronto, spearheaded by professor Gordon Pon and May Lui of CCNC Toronto, in conjunction with a simultaneous gathering at the University of British Columbia, led by Ray Hsu of the Asian Canadian Writers' Workshop. Moreover, Neethan Shan of the Council of Agencies Serving South Asians featured the youth and community organizing on the 'Too Asian?' issue in its Racism Free Ontario campaign, and Estella Muyinda of the National Anti-Racism Council of Canada highlighted the issue at one of its annual events for the International Day for the Elimination of Racial Discrimination.

Acknowledgements

The Solidarity Committee Against Anti-Asian Racism was, and continues to be, pivotal in my political education and organizing in Toronto. To Binish Ahmed, Charlotte Chiba, Ray Hsu, Ken Huynh, Albert Ko, Florence Li, Anna Liu, Chase Lo, May Lui, Estella Muyinda, Ken Noma, Danielle Sandhu, Neethan Shan and Karen Sun: my deepest appreciation for your brilliance and camaraderie. A special thanks to fellow SCAAAR members, Brad Lee and Gordon Pon, for reading and commenting on an earlier draft of this article. My sincere thanks to Kalervo N. Gulson, Zeus Leonardo and David Gillborn for their keen editorial insights and unwavering support. This article is dedicated to Roxana Ng who passed away on 12 January 2013. The first professor of color hired at the OISE University of Toronto, Roxana was an intellectual pioneer in anti-racist, feminist, labor, immigrant and Asian Canadian studies.

References

Adachi, K. (1976). *The enemy that never was: A history of the Japanese Canadians.* Toronto: McClelland and Stewart.

AngusReid. (2010, September 10). *More Canadians are questioning the benefits of immigration.* Retrieved from http://www.visioncritical.com/wp-content/uploads/2010/09/2010.09.09_Immigration_CAN.pdf

Asia/Canada. (n.d.). *Too Asian?* Retrieved from http://asia-canada.ca/new-attitudes/continuing-tensions/too-asian

Asia Pacific Foundation of Canada. (2011). *2011 National opinion poll: Canadian views on Asia.* Vancouver, BC: Author.

Asia Pacific Foundation of Canada. (2012a). *Immigrants by category – all categories.* Retrieved from http://www.asiapacific.ca/statistics/immigration/immigration-arrivals/immigration-category-all-categories

Asia Pacific Foundation of Canada. (2012b). *Immigration by category – economic immigrants.* Retrieved from http://www.asiapacific.ca/statistics/immigration/immigration-arrivals/immigration-category-economic-immigrants

Asia Pacific Foundation of Canada. (2012c). *Immigrants by regional source as percentage of total immigration.* Retrieved from http://www.asiapacific.ca/statistics/immigration/immigration-arrivals/immigrants-regional-source-percentage-total-immigration

Block, S., & Galabuzi, G. (2011). *Canada's colour coded labour market: The gap for racialized workers.* Alberta, ON: Canadian Centre for Policy Alternatives.

Brown, C. (2007). *The illustrated history of Canada.* Toronto: Key Porter.

Brown, L. (2010, November 10). Educators encourage parents of Asian background to let their children study trades and arts. *Toronto Star.* Retrieved from http://www.thestar.com/life/parent/2010/11/10/educators_encourage_parents_of_asian_background_to_let_their_children_study_trades_and_arts.html

Buchignani, N., Indra, D. M., & Srivastava, R. (1985). *Continuous journey: A social history of South Asians in Canada.* Toronto: McClelland and Stewart.

Centre for Immigration Policy Reform. (n.d.). *Aims and objectives.* Retrieved from http://www.immigrationreform.ca/english/View.asp?x=883

Citizenship and Immigration Canada. (2010, June 26). *Government of Canada will welcome more economic immigrants in 2010*. Retrieved from http://www.cic.gc.ca/english/department/media/ releases/2010/2010-06-26.asp

Citizenship and Immigration Canada. (2011, February 13). *Canada welcomes highest number of legal immigrants in 50 years while taking action to maintain the integrity of Canada's immigration system*. Retrieved from http://www.cic.gc.ca/english/department/media/releases/2011/2011-02-13.asp

Coloma, R. S., & Lee, B. (2010, November 23). *Open letter: A call to eliminate anti-Asian racism.* Retrieved from http://asiancanadianstudies.ca/node/31

Coloma, R. S., McElhinny, B., Tungohan, E., Catungal, J. P. C., & Davidson, L. (Eds.). (2012). *Filipinos in Canada: Disturbing invisibility*. Toronto: University of Toronto Press.

Connor, W. (1993). *Ethnonationalism: The quest for understanding*. Princeton, NJ: Princeton University Press.

Findlay, S., & Köhler, N. (2010, November 22). 'Too Asian?' A term used in the US to talk about racial imbalance at Ivy league schools is now being whispered on Canadian campuses–by everyone but the students themselves, who speak out loud and clear. *Maclean's, 123*(45), 76–81.

Foreign Affairs and International Trade Canada. (2012). *International education: A key driver of Canada's future prosperity*. Retrieved March 27, 2013, from http://www.international.gc.ca/ education/assets/pdfs/ies_report_rapport_sei-eng.pdf

Gilmour, R. J., Bhandar, D., Heer, J., & Ma, M. C. K. (Eds.). (2012). *'Too Asian?' Racism, privilege, and post-secondary education*. Toronto: Between the Lines.

Goutor, D. (2007). Constructing the 'Great Menace': Canadian labour's opposition to Asian immigration, 1880–1914. *Canadian Historical Review, 88*(4), 549–576. doi:10.1353/can. 2008.0013

Heer, J. (2010, November 24). Too brazen: Maclean's Margaret Wente, and the Canadian media's inarticulacy about race. *The Walrus*. Retrieved from http://walrusmagazine.com/blogs/2010/11/ 24/too-brazen/

Kymlicka, W. (1996). *Multicultural citizenship: A liberal theory of minority rights*. Oxford and New York: Oxford University Press.

Lai, D. C. (1988). *Chinatowns: Towns within cities in Canada*. Vancouver: University of British Columbia Press.

Li, P. S. (1998). *The Chinese in Canada* (2nd ed.). Toronto: Oxford University Press.

Li, P. S. (2003). *Destination Canada: Immigration debates and issues*. Don Mills, ON: Oxford University Press.

Library and Archives Canada. (2012, March 14). *Driving the nation: The last spike and the faces of CPR*. Retrieved from http://www.youtube.com/watch?v=sQcm4RYrpjw

Maclean's. (2010, November 25). *Merit: The best and only way to decide who gets into university*. Retrieved from http://www2.macleans.ca/2010/11/25/who-gets-into-university/

Maclear, K. (1994). The myth of the 'model minority': Re-thinking the education of Asian Canadians. *Our Schools/Our Selves, 5*(3), 54–76.

Mahtani, M. (2010, November 19). Canadian media: It's time to cover the undercovered. *The Globe and Mail*. Retrieved from http://www.theglobeandmail.com/commentary/canadian-media-its-time-to-cover-the-undercovered/article1314521/

Mallick, H. (2012). Review of the book *'Too Asian?'* by R. J. Gilmour, D. Bhandar, J. Heer, & M. C. K. Ma. Retrieved from http://www.btlbooks.com/othertextinfo.php?index=861

Mar, L. R. (2010). *Brokering belonging: Chinese in Canada's exclusion era, 1885–1945*. Toronto: Oxford University Press.

Mawani, R. (2010). *Colonial proximities: Crossracial encounters and juridical truths in British Columbia, 1871–1921*. Vancouver: University of British Columbia Press.

Miki, R. (2000). Altered states: Global currents, the spectral nation, and the production of 'Asian Canadian'. *Journal of Canadian Studies, 35*(3), 43–72.

Miki, R. (2005). *Redress: Inside the Japanese Canadian call for justice*. Vancouver: Raincoast.

Ng, R., Staton, P., & Scane, J. (Eds.). (1995). *Anti-racism, feminism, and critical approaches to education*. Westport, CT: Praeger.

Noma, K. (2010, November 28). *Letter to Maclean's re: 'Too Asian'*. Retrieved from http://www. najc.ca/human-rights-committee-action/letter-to-mcleans-re-"too-asian"/

Oikawa, M. (2012). *Cartographies of violence: Japanese Canadian women, memory, and the subjects of the internment*. Toronto: University of Toronto Press.

Pon, G. (2000). Importing the Asian 'model minority' discourse into Canada: Implications for social work and education. *Canadian Social Work Review, 17*(2), 277–291. Retrieved from http://www.jstor.org/stable/1602189

Poy, V. (2010, December 16). *Letter to the honourable James Moore*. Retrieved from http://www.viviennepoy.ca/english/speeches/2010Speeches/Moore,J_161210(2).pdf

Preston, V., & Lo, L. (2000). 'Asian theme' malls in suburban Toronto: land use conflict in Richmond Hill. *The Canadian Geographer/Le Géographe Canadien, 44*(2), 182–190. doi:10.1111/j.1541-0064.2000.tb00701.x

Puar, J. (2007). *Terrorist assemblages: Homonationalism in queer times*. Durham, NC: Duke University Press.

Razack, S., Smith, M., & Thobani, S. (Eds.). (2010). *States of race: Critical race feminism for the 21st century*. Toronto: Between the Lines.

Statistics Canada. (2010). *Study: Projections of the diversity of the Canadian population*. Retrieved from http://www.statcan.gc.ca/daily-quotidien/100309/dq100309a-eng.htm

Thobani, S. (2007). *Exalted subjects: Studies in the making of race and nation in Canada*. Toronto: University of Toronto Press.

Toope, S. (2011, January 26). The battle for brains. *The Globe and Mail*. Retrieved from http://www.theglobeandmail.com/commentary/stephen-toope-how-international-students-change-canadian-schools/article602521/?from=4480232

Ward, W. P. (2002). *White Canada forever: Popular attitudes and public policy toward Orientals in British Columbia* (3rd ed.). Montreal, QC and Kingston, ON: McGill-Queen's University Press.

Wildavsky, B. (2010). *The great brain race: How global universities are reshaping the world*. Princeton, NJ: Princeton University Press.

Yu, H. (2010, November 16). Why *Macleans* and racism should no longer define Canada. *Georgia Straight*. Retrieved from http://www.straight.com/news/henry-yu-why-macleans-and-racism-should-no-longer-define-canada

Yu, H. (2010, November 27). *Maclean's* must answer for racial profiling: Asian-Canadians aren't just being too sensitive. There's a history behind their reaction to the magazine's 'Too Asian?' article. *Vancouver Sun*. Retrieved from http://www2.canada.com/vancouversun/news/archives/story.html?id=cbdc0f88-133b-42bb-b0da-88c04168c6e8

The story of schooling: critical race theory and the educational racial contract

Zeus Leonardo

Graduate School of Education, University of California, Berkeley, CA, USA

This article is an engagement of methodology as an ideologico-racial practice through Critical Race Theory's practice of storytelling. It is a conceptual extension of this practice as explained through Charles Mills' use of the 'racial contract (RC) as methodology' in order to explain the Herrenvolk Education – one standard for Whites, another for students of color – that is in place in the USA. At its most general, the article introduces the full offerings of Mills' RC methodology for a study of educational research. Once deployed, the RC as methodology unveils a school system's foundation as deeply racial rather than universal or race-neutral.

If educational research implicates the study of ideology, then conducting it is the realm of methodology. Research on race is an interpretive endeavor concerning the role of schools in a racialized society; it is inherently hermeneutical. However, as understood here, methodology does not represent a 'tool kit' of data-gathering strategies be they qualitative or quantitative. Rather, methodology signifies a set of commitments about the standing of 'reality', and in the end, 'truth' about the matter of race and racism. Although not known as a race scholar, Gadamer (1975) suggests as much in his study of hermeneutics, captured by his book's title, *Truth and Method*. In this influential text, Gadamer lays out a philosophy of methodology and its relationship with truth, thus unveiling the intimate link between them. Before embarking on this discussion, one important issue has to be cleared up: the difference between methodology and methods (Morrow, 1994).

It is not uncommon that scholars use the two concepts interchangeably. Or methodology is associated with conceptual design and methods become the practical implementation of the research. However, there are major theoretical differences between the two concepts. Methodology is a framework for the ideological underpinnings of race research. It is an ontological position on the question of reality, such as whether or not racism is structural in nature or defined as expressions of individual prejudice. In general, the latter is the favored ontology in race studies, relegating the former to the margins. This being the case, mainstream methodological assumptions about race affect knowledge production by setting parameters around legitimate questions that may be posed about it. Furthermore, methodology invokes epistemological assumptions about what constitutes knowledge and how we can apprehend it through research. It implies a relationship between the known and the knower as well who counts as a subject, as opposed to an object, of knowledge. Said's *Orientalism* (1979) is a clear example showcasing cultural imperialism as a knowledge relation when he chronicles the Occidentalist methodology of misrepresenting the Orient through distorted epistemologies. His point, inspired by Foucault's (1980) power/knowledge nexus, is that controlling knowledge about the Orient is a means of exerting control over its institutions and material relations with Europe. Methodology also implicates phenomenological explanations for empirical data, even more, empirical life, or their meaning and social significance. In the USA, there is little debate regarding the significance of race made evident by the complete racialization of President Obama's historic rise. But with the rise of colorblindness, the same event becomes an alibi for postracial orientations to the phenomenon of racism. After all, a Black man in the White House must signal the end of race and racism. Colorblind methodology fails to explain the continuing significance of both in the lives of people of color as well as Whites. Last, methodology's arguably most important function is to justify the purpose and project of social research. In other words, race research comes with a politics of either intervening in racism or becoming spectators of it.

On the other hand, methods comprise a set of field strategies. In their simplest form, methods are techniques for gathering data; they are the practical side of research. Methods are ways of amassing the data required for answering the study's research agenda. Of course, a researcher's ideological commitments influence his decisions for choosing methods in the first place since the mode of data collection recalls his methodological position on reality, knowledge, social phenomena and purpose of research. Although there is no clean way ideologically to separate methodology from methods, they are conceptually distinct. In this special themed issue, my main concern in this article is to understand the realm of methodology as it concerns the study of race.

On methodology

Schoolteachers and students mediate structures, interpret them and create meaning out of them. Understanding this subjective reality is important because 'reality' does not merely come to us in the form of unadulterated experiences, and all we have to do is reflect them, even in an imperfect manner, usually through language. Reality does not make immediate sense to people; it has to be filtered through interpretive frameworks. It does not walk around with a post-it note on its forehead announcing its arrival; it has to be registered, indeed, conceived and then mediated. Reality does not stalk around with a label (Apple, 2004). Objective reality carries different meanings for racialized subjects, depending on their social location without determining those meanings. Thus, research on race is a good venue to observe the dialectical process between objective constraints and the formation of racialized subjectivity. Coming from various racial experiences and histories, subjects live race reality as a relation between their objective and subjective world, much as Althusser (1971) would suggest that ideology is our lived relation to the real relation, his nod to the politics of representation. Seen in this light, race reality appears in flux, never quite clear but fuzzy and ambiguous. It has to be interpreted, which does not make it any less real and gives race its proper force as a social relation.

As Althusser (1971) suggests, we do not have direct access to the real as it exists in its pure state. Yet this does not suggest that the relationship between reality and representation is purely arbitrary, including race. There is some necessity between objective reality and our racial representation of it, albeit loosely coupled, which speaks to the preponderance or patterns of meaning-making between Whites and people of color. From Fanon (1952/1967) to Freire (1970/1993), we appreciate meaning from the position of the oppressed because it does not come with the will to distort that defines meaning from the oppressor. Meaning from the oppressed, or what Sandoval (2000) calls the 'methodology of the oppressed', does not make it right because it comes from the Left, but through education, it becomes a force for liberation. Conversely, meaning from the oppressor, in this case, the master race, is mired in contradictions that a radical methodology or politicization would need to exorcize.

Epistemological assumptions about the production of knowledge are also another critical issue in methodology. As Weedon (1997) reminds us, '[T]he experience of individuals is far from homogeneous. What an event means to an individual depends on the ways of interpreting the world, on the discourses available to her at any particular moment' (pp. 75–76). We only learn from experiences that teach us something, if by learning, we mean an active rather than passive apprehension with respect to *how social processes work*. If this is true, then much of the meaning of our daily experiences escapes us and remains unanalyzed. This appears to be true with respect to White subjects who fail to learn how race relations work despite the fact that they daily experience it. They experience racialization daily, but its significance washes right over them. It is true that they learn the advantages of being White, as the White privilege literature from McIntosh (1992) to McIntyre (1997) informs us, but the truth of its inner workings must remain a mystery in order for Whites to maintain what Mills (1997) calls their 'epistemology of ignorance'. Accurate race knowledge remains cataloged in the deep recesses of their unconscious, made manifest in their race orientation to the actual world, or what King (2004) captures in the phrase 'dysconsious racism'. It was Gramsci (1971), after all, who encouraged us to take stock of a history that has left us no inventory. Anti-racist Whites may have begun this archeological digging, but they are surrounded more by spectators than cultural workers with the proverbial shovel.

The problem of race research does not seem so much an issue of producing 'better' knowledge, but of liberating people from accepting their race knowledge as natural and neutral. Research on race can assist in this political project by challenging the claim that Western-based epistemologies produce objective knowledge about a particular phenomenon when it rules out particular experiences and people from official knowledge production, such as people of color (see Collins, 1991/2000), creating what Harding (1991) calls 'weak objectivity' (see also Apple, 1979/2000). Clearly not rejecting claims to objectivity in the hard and social sciences, Harding argues for a strong form of objectivity, which includes the perspectives of people traditionally left out of knowledge production.

In fact, Linda Tuhiwai Smith (1999) goes so far as to question the practice of colonial methodologies that appropriate the scientific title of 'research'. The victims of the cultural form of colonialism include indigenous people, like the Maori, who are consistently inserted into a history that either distorts their objective reality – because it never meant to 'get it right' – or omits them altogether. Smith's study of Western research's disregard for Maori way of life accomplishes for the context of New Zealand what Said (1979) achieves, two decades earlier, for our understanding of the Orient or the Middle East. The ability to speak back to research interrogates the notion that progress is the production of better, more accurate and reliable knowledge. Instead, research on race justifies its knowledge production in ethical terms, that is, by self-reflecting on the political consequences of the research product and project. What is the knowledge for? How does this knowledge enable people to become more politically responsible subjects? Whom does it benefit or subvert? And how does the research knowledge critically help us to understand schools as sites of change? With these questions in mind, the basic issue of 'how we come to know' becomes problematic.

There is nothing commonsensical about the obvious. Common sense is a long process of naturalizing knowledge that is inherently historical and ideological. Gramsci (1971) has taught us that ideological hegemony is established at the level of common sense in order to persuade people away from questioning certain relations and the social order they produce. Human nature is a myth that mystifies people into accepting as a given that which is social and historical. It turns 'human' into an unquestioned concept, at least racially speaking, and disregards raciology's project of European humanism, which became a modernist burden for everyone who is not White. As Mills (1997) argues, European humanism meant that only Europeans merit the status of 'human'.

Critical race theory (CRT) and education

CRT in education is going strong and gaining momentum, having been a fledgling discourse in education from the mid-1990s. When Ladson-Billings and Tate (1995) wrote their break-out essay in *Teachers College Record*, they may not have predicted such a reception that has now spawned hundreds of paper presentations, panels and preconference workshops at the American Educational Research Association, as well as thousands of articles, books and chapters on the topic. Each year, the Critical Race Studies in Education Association holds its annual conference. It is backed by the journal, *Race Ethnicity & Education*, along with its Chief Editor David Gillborn, as an official sponsor. All of this suggests that CRT has become an intellectual industry. However, by and large the educational scene receives it as mainly a *theory*, a critical one at that. It is perceived as an analytical lens, a racial hermeneutic of sorts. For those outside of CRT's conceptual circles and intellectual production, it appears as a way to interpret school phenomena as inextricably linked with race structures. To its critics, CRT even makes these phenomena racial by describing them as such.

In order to thrive as research paradigms, disciplines from sociology, literary studies to psychology have had to offer their own methodologies. That is to say, these disciplines do not just offer us theories of human behavior and history but a way to capture and represent them through text, metrics or participant-observation. By contrast, education is a borrower discipline, appropriating methodologies from traditional disciplines and having no claims to its own methodology. CRT is not a discipline, yet from its inception as a specialized study within legal studies, CRT has staked a claim on a unique methodology that represents a mixture of existing historiographies, literary and narrative analyses and legal case studies, which is inseparable from its ideological commitments about the reality of race and racism. In other words, CRT offers a way of conducting research that speaks against current objectifications of race, not just a way of interpreting it.

CRT's epistemological claims about race in education is bound up with its methodology and not entirely separate from it, just as Marx's dialectical materialism (his methodology) cannot be divorced from historical materialism (his philosophy). Of course, the marriage between theory and method is not a new idea, but its union within CRT has not been fully worked out despite the fact that using storytelling and counterstorytelling is widespread in the literature using CRT (see Solorzano & Yosso, 2002). Particularly, narrativity is central to CRT methodology, or the way that any research production is bound up with stories and justifications about human behavior and the histories that interpellate it. In this section, I would like to highlight some of these methodological horizons that form the research assumptions behind conducting CRT-inspired work. These developments are not fully worked out and have their detractors from without and critics from within. That said, a perspective that holds promises for a CRT methodology remains untapped. I am talking about Charles Mills' Racial Contract (RC) as methodology, a topic I discuss below.

In CRT, 'stories' are an alternative to calling our work 'research'. The history of social research has been violent to marginalized peoples, such as indigenous groups, who are represented by perspectives that are neither kind to their cultural worldview nor accurate regarding their priorities (see Smith, 1999). In fact, we may go a long way with Said (1979) who suggests that these forms of conceptual violence are not mere misrepresentations since they never meant to represent faithfully places like the Orient, in the first place. Nevertheless, these stories have stuck, like ideology that succeeds at doing its political work, where power is precisely the power to make meanings adhere to an Occidental way of life (see Thompson, 1984). The story that is established between the White or Western self and the Other becomes one based on dependency, hierarchy and binary.[1]

But neither are these consequences accidental for, as Mills (1997) reminds us, they are prescribed by the terms of the RC and maintain the privilege of the looker (sometimes onlooker) over the looked at and the researcher over the object of research. They define the 'nature' of the indigenous, minority or margins through their apprehension of these communities. The dynamics of this relationship are not produced for the benefit of these communities but for the consumption by and self-understanding of the master race. This would have been enough, but these representations do not remain renditions as such, but graduate to policy. From the war on poverty, to the war on drugs, to the war on schools, representations directly impact the lives of people of color through whiteness turned into policy. It produces less a form of rarefied scientific research and more an ideological frame through which educators may understand urban schools, children and their families. Within CRT, these stories are never innocent even if they may be naïve. They are ideological stories and, therefore, create racialized subjects out of normed humans. Said another way, they constitute the known through a narrative structure that the knower, often a representative of the master race, validates through majoritarian storylines replete with assumptions about progress, civilization, sense and self-worth. Its disparaged complementary is the figure of color experienced as a 'problem' (Du Bois, 1904/1989). CRT questions these long-held beliefs in Western methodologies grounded in abstract thought. In their place, CRT offers the methodology of counterstorytelling.[2]

First and foremost, CRT acknowledges the distinction within Western epistemology that there are objective facts on one side and subjective stories on the other. CRT recognizes that minority children suffer higher rates of attrition, study in dilapidated buildings and lack appropriate resources. These are facts, and CRT scholars uphold the evidentiary basis of this research. However, these hard data are narrative in structure for two reasons. One, minority-filled schools evolved the way they have because of the stories surrounding the lives of their student population and what they deserve in terms of resources. The leading and lingering tropes from explanatory frameworks, such as the culture of poverty, deficit thinking and general uneducability of minority students produce material consequences that are now social facts. Two, material differences between underperforming and overperforming schools feed into the same stories and feedback loop that put them there in the first place when the power of narrative is not appreciated. Especially within the current laissez-faire ethos sweeping across the USA, the favored explanation is a 'pull-yourself-up by your own schoolstrap' mentality. This does not vitiate against admitting that many Black and Latino children in particular are falling behind their White and Asian counterparts. Sometimes, the former students even believe the deficit stories that circulate about them. But that they created their own predicament, even as they may help reproduce it, is like saying that the impoverished life of the slave is his own doing.

A counternarrative is arguably another story, so it does not make pretenses about objectivity. It insists on firsthand narratives about racial oppression in schools and society. It values oral traditions within minority groups, wherein unofficial stories may thrive and are evaluated according to different standards, one of which is their ability to illuminate their lived conditions and change a group's status and social standing. To some, this is a reified way to judge stories because they can be false even as they promote a group's interest. This being the case, they are no different from majoritarian stories, which become logical targets of the same critique. *What's good for the major is good for the minor.* The upshot is that in CRT, a different voice is assumed as well as privileged. Indeed, the voice is full of gaps and disjunctures, but it becomes the point of departure for understanding racial dynamics in schools and society.

This is different from saying that a different voice is the end point of dialogue since many contradictions would have to be pulled apart and evaluated for their truth content. In itself, this way of moving forward is not a new insight. Feminists from Carol Gilligan, Nancy Hartsock, Patricia Hill Collins to Sandra Harding have referred to it as 'standpoint epistemology'. Standpoint theorists have insisted on a certain narrative structure to science and its allied disciplines in the social sciences, about who is excluded and the compromised truth gained from incomplete stories. CRT introduces a Black tradition into standpoint tradition, not unlike Hill Collins in sociology and Mills in philosophy, but this time coming into education by way of legal studies. It is not only a conceptual intervention but also a methodological innovation that is hard to place neatly into existing genres and claims about truth.

CRT methodology is arguably made possible by recent intellectual interventions. For example, postmodernism introduced the radical questioning of objectivity as well as deep appreciation for what Hayden White (1986) calls the 'tropics of discourse', or how history is apprehended through the regulatory functionings of language. Complete with plot, protagonists and central dilemmas, 'officialized' history emerges from the figurative use of language. In Derrick Bell's (1992) texts, one senses the weight of history as his fictive characters refer simultaneously to real figures from the past. Yet they retain a literary register, even a poetics, as Bell also embellishes their tale and blurs the line between fact and fiction despite his racial realist orientation.

CRT narratives have an ethnographic, thick descriptive feel to them in spite of the fact that they represent settings that no anthropologist would call 'natural'. Finally, they utilize legal case studies through frequent references to case law and their racial consequences, such as serious attempts by the government to eject Black bodies from the USA, captured by Bell's witty tale about 'space traders', where visitors from outer space would take African Americans to their home star. Like Foucault, who is neither a historian, a sociologist, nor a philosopher but arguably all of these traditions rolled up into one, CRT methodology is neither and all the mentioned research frameworks. These syncretic descriptions escape conventional genres of research and earn suspicions about the apparent need to create stories about which data already exists. In other words, why invent stories about segregation to replace social science research about the matter? Certainly, any self-respecting CRT scholar would have to answer to such an allegation.

One such response could be imagined in terms of the failure of social science research to right the racial ship. There is no paucity of hard data on the effects of racism, yet the jury is still to be convinced about its reality. CRT's counterstories are evocative and do not rely mainly on rational, evidence-based research to prove their point. They are guided by a different ontology. They seek to move their audience to be outraged and to produce appropriate actions. That said, they are based on real trends through composite stories that capture a more complete portrayal of race relations. They combine the existing data from multiple sources and methodologies. Their aggregated appearance dispels notions that racism is happening locally to this or that person or group, but is pervasive and affects an entire society, from micro- to macroaggressions. It is not a methodology to explain the parts but rather the whole much like Lukacs' (1971) Hegelian Marxism accomplished by favoring the concept of 'totality'. In that sense, CRT affirms the community against the preference for individual work; it highlights collective experience as well as group wisdom. It is not guided by the ethos of rugged research and lone writers.

CRT accounts are subjective for two reasons. One, they welcome personal testimonies about the effect of racism. Two, they confirm the ability of research to produce subjectivities, in Foucault's sense. Research is not only a medium for presenting evidence and interpretation but makes its subject matter intelligible as well as positions the subjects it interpellates through repetition. When research is consistently produced in the same manner and produces the same outcomes, CRT disrupts this cycle by challenging and changing the purpose of research on racism from one of reporting to one of testifying.

In education, these composites have been put forth by Bernal and Villalpando (2005), Gillborn (2008), Solorzano and Yosso (2002), Yosso (2006), and others, who expose the debilitating racism that students and faculty of color face in schools and universities. Counterstories are a mixture of evidence and imagination, the combination of which is designed to spur people to act, to strike an emotional chord and to inspire educators to sketch a new society rather than paint themselves into a corner. CRT founders in legal studies urge firsthand stories about racism to counter the positivistic penchant that only validates experience that are verifiable through accepted means and methodologies. But as philosopher of race, Charles Mills (1997) reminds us, these counterhistories are judged by a value system against which they speak, making the situation ripe for a catch-22. When people of color insist on an accurate history of racism, they are deemed irrational by the moral principles (no longer moral or principled) of the RC, which regards them with contempt or amazement. This relationship in turn guides the educational contract, or put simply, the Educational Racial Contract (henceforth, Educational RC). It is in this sense that the RC is the dominant contract in US society and education one of its main racial state apparatuses.

The educational RC as methodology

At this point, I want to turn to the story of schooling within the methodological assumptions of an appropriated Educational RC in order to elucidate the inner workings of racial domination in schools. Within Mills' (1997; see also Mills, 1998, 2003) racial contractarianism, educators find an elegant description of and explanation for an existing race-based hierarchy.[3] In his critique of the social contract theory, Mills (1997) offers the following:

> My claim is that the model of the Racial Contract shows us that we need another alternative, another way of theorizing about and critiquing the state: the *racial*, or white supremacist, state, whose function inter alia is to safeguard the polity *as* a white or white-dominated polity, enforcing the terms of the Racial Contract by the appropriate means and, when necessary, facilitating its rewriting from one form to another. (p. 82; italics in original)

It is not a literal contract that Whites actually signed and, therefore, consensually agreed on, but an actual state of affair that functions statistically *as if* they had entered into a contract with one another. In this political system, all Whites are beneficiaries even if they are not all signatories. The RC does not represent a deviation from otherwise raceless and racially just norms. As history bears out – and empiricism is on Mills' side – the RC *is the norm* and racial equality is the exception.

In other words, the RC is not a *theory* of the US society, but an apprehension of an arrangement that amounts to a lived reality. It is not a *hypothesis* but a *methodology* to unveil what Mills insists on calling a sociopolitical system of 'White supremacy', and not merely 'racism' in general or 'White racism' in particular. Mills privileges the first phrase against the last two, based on the philosophical distinction that the former is an objective, historical system, whereas the latter pair is subjective and based on racial attitudes, beliefs and volitions. The structural system of racial domination may persist despite changing our value system if the accompanying material transformations from wealth to health do not follow.

From the start, Mills' methodology suggests disparate solutions based on this difference in understanding. Historical reparations follow from the story of White supremacy, attitudinal adjustments or consciousness raising for the story of racism. This represents Mills' injunction against traditional social contract theory, which is based on an ideal society or a selective one among Whites, and he promotes an epistemology grounded on the RC, which is based on the society that actually exists.[4] The RC is not cynical or pessimistic but realist and materialist, a willingness to 'look at the facts without flinching, to explain that if you start with *this*, then you will end up with *that*' (1997, p. 102; italics in original). Indeed, it is a philosophy but not in its disciplinary sense and puts it more closely with Marx's philosophy of historical materialism. More to the point, racial materialism indicts, with Michael Peters (2012), 'White philosophy in/of America'.

A central tenet of the RC is the demotion of Blacks to the status of non- or subpersonhood.[5] Mills asserts that European humanism meant precisely that: only Europeans were humans. It shares affinities with Hannah Arendt's (1976) analysis of stateless people, such as Jews between the two World Wars, whose ability to activate their humanity was thwarted by nations that would not recognize their human rights. They could not simply be ejected from the state because they had no home nation, signifying them as *undeportable bodies*. With respect to the RC, Black slaves inside the US nation were defined less by their exclusion and more by their problematic and normed inclusion within the RC's terms. That is, they are not outside the national discourse even if they are not included as humans within American nationalism. They were written into the contract and not as an afterthought. They were central to it.

In the US racial project, Blacks became foils for White personhood, a property solely belonging to the master race (see Harris, 1995). European Enlightenment (and its local, American version) was reserved for those not enveloped in darkness and '[t]he terms of the Racial Contract mean that *nonwhite subpersonhood is enshrined simultaneously with white personhood*' (Mills, 1997, p. 56; italics in original). This makes possible certain logical outcomes, such as:

> [O]ne of the interesting consequences of the Racial Contract is that the *political space* of the polity is not coextensive with its *geographical space*. In entering these [dark] spaces, one is entering a region normatively discontinuous with white political space, where the rules are different in ways ranging from differential funding (school resources, garbage collection, infrastructural repair) to the absence of police protection. (1997, p. 51; italics in original)

Not only does the RC promote the ejection of the Black body from White spaces as evidenced by 100 years of ghettoization but the *rejection of everything Black*, such as ways of knowing and feeling, unless they serve the commodification of blackness within White capitalism.

In the case of African slaves in the USA, Blacks were literally reduced to three-fifth of a White person. Therefore, Mills establishes another fact about the RC, which was not just imagined but actually put in practice, documented in writing, codified in the law (see Lopez, 2006). Its symbolic moment is captured by the 1858 Dred Scott decision that denied Scott of citizenship rights based on the ruling that he was property and, therefore, not human (see Harris, 1995). Although this decision was effectively repealed by the 14th Amendment, there is a prevailing sense that racial minorities cannot count on the law being enforced on their behalf. That laws exist to protect them is not the same as saying that they will be served by them. This is not a statement about preference for a general lawlessness but speaks to the racial inception and interpretation of the law. It also speaks to the moral lawlessness of whiteness when it concerns the livelihood of people of color. For example, the exposition makes clear the referents for the treasured American assumption that, under the constitution, all people are treated equally under the law. As the RC would lay bear, this only applies if you are considered a person or a human, so the edict is not as ironic as it may sound. The ideal world of social contract theory ultimately buckles under the weight of the actual RC.

In education, CRT may get some mileage out of the Mills' RC methodology. Just as the RC stipulates persons and subpersons, we also find that it contains knowers and subknowers. Mills includes an epistemological dimension to the RC, which for Whites means a certain epistemology of ignorance to misinterpret the world they themselves have made. But the epistemological contract comes with a secondary feature that elevates Whites to the status of knowers and demotes people of color to the status of subknowers, usually trading in belief systems at best or superstition at worst, both of which are not considered forms of knowledge (see Scheffler, 1965). As subknowers, people of color are targets of epistemological imposition within the industrial complex of knowledge from K-12 through college.

In schools, many deep-held beliefs about students become less 'natural' if educators keep in mind the referents (or whom they exclude) for such constructions. One, when Ann Ferguson (2001) unearths the layers of punishment that young Black boys experience in schools because they are 'adultified' for the same offenses and infractions committed by White boys, we realize that the fundamental distinction between students (children) and teachers (adults) does not hold for Black children. Thus, just as for Mills, a normed 'human' becomes a loaded signifier, so does the term 'student' become a racially valenced construction in education. On one level, this should not be surprising to the extent that there exist decades of writing about the uneducability of kids of color, casting doubt on their 'student' status. This is not a recent phenomenon. In fact, education was withheld from slave descendants, creating conditions ripe for underground literacy programs for Black kids (Holt, 1990). Similarly, despite the conclusions reached by the *Mendez vs Westminster case*, the USA has cast aspersions on Mexican students' assimilability into American education. Its latest iteration is California's passing of Proposition 227 despite compelling, if not convincing, evidence that bilingualism provides academic and cognitive benefits for children. In its wake, Arizona enacts nativist responses to limit Latino, particularly Mexican, rights in public schools and spaces based on egregious criteria, like linguistic accents. Finally, the racial panopticon included boarding schools for Native Americans, a failed attempt to school the Indian out of indigenous children.

We are tempted to surmise that when educators draft goals that meet the needs of *all* students, this audacity does not include Black, indigenous, or Latino kids. *They may be children but they are not students; they are something else.* From the inception of the common school the story of the student assumes his compliance for purposes of learning. Students are presumed to be teachable, so what happens when they are conceived otherwise, when they fall outside of official ontology? This veritable *law of learning* within the realm of education is fundamental to the racial construction of the student. Without it, there is no educational enterprise of perfectability so dear to Kant and enlightenment philosophers, which does not mean that even White children are not sometimes difficult to teach. But the main difference is that they are *presumed* to have the potential to learn or be taught; after all, they are persons. Like Whites, as the story goes, bear the potentials of rationality so central to the enlightenment definitions of the human, White children are teachable; they can learn. They are knowers.

Minority children lie outside of this learning paradigm because all the dehumanizing machinations of schools have failed to bring them in line. They have not shed their subperson status, thus better to define them as substudents. Within the naturalized RC (not to be confused with the actual RC), minority children are left behind. Like the construct of 'citizen', the student is not a self-evident entity and one has to look behind its history as related to personhood and pronouncements regarding civility in order to arrive at its meanings. Like a body that shares national space with others is not necessarily conceptualized as a citizen, a child sharing a classroom with others is only nominally a student. Within this understanding, minority children are perceived as burdens to the educational system, treated as problems without a solution because *they are the problem.* They are the Educational RC's cursed share (see Bataille, 1988, 1991).

Two, minority children's status as sub- or nonstudents is confirmed through the establishment of a contract that most educators accept by virtue of participating in school structures. Often unbeknownst to them, they become signatories to the Educational RC. In other words, the Educational RC does not require a conspiracy, as Gillborn (2008) notes; it's worse than that. If educators behave according to the stipulations of education as they exist and do not actively change its racial course, the results are predictable, almost as if they resulted from concerted action on educators' part. In a less sinister sense, the Educational RC is the default contract. This does not mean that educators have not been diligent with reforming schools. There are as many reform movements as there are people who have an opinion about education. But like the idealist social contract, the educational social contract fails to capture the basis of an implicit agreement. Until now. CRT, especially when married with Mills' description and explanation of the RC, is a methodological candidate for revealing the real terms of the Educational RC. It makes possible the act of signing off the contract as a gesture toward reconstituting the category of human and, therefore, the student.

Counterstories in critical race pedagogy are mounting (Lynn, 1999). As a subset of the racialized social system, the racial educational apparatus is struggling to resolve its contradictions. There are signs of progress and evidence for success stories of this or that school in this or that city, but the overall story of education for minority children in the USA appears to remain constant. The achievement gap is not being bridged. Like the RC, the terms of the Educational RC have been amended over time due largely to the flexibility of White power. Seen through the lens of the RC, the success of whiteness is found precisely in its ability to rewrite the contract according to the specific and historical needs of whiteness. Understanding this condition necessitates a methodology that looks at the totality of race relations, its awesome determining effects on the creation and continuation of US society, and Americans' daily participation with race structures.

We all create race, and race creates us all. In contract terms, *the Racial Contract constructs its signatories as much as they construct it* (Mills, 1997, p. 78; italics in original). For Whites, this means a silence on the RC signals a near voluntaristic acceptance of its terms. For anti-racist Whites, a deliberate effort to sign off the RC becomes a critical choice. In education, it begins with a methodology that questions commonsensical notions, such as the 'human' and 'student', for their political moorings with respect to who can be saved or in this case, who can be taught. It asks educators to cast down their bucket, to cash a check from a promissory note that remains unfulfilled, a debt still owed.

Notes

1. Of course, this is not the wholesale rejection of Western thought. Just as Said depends on an appropriation of Foucault in Orientalism, Smith also gets much mileage out of French poststructural philosophy applied to the problem of colonialism and schools. Western thought does not merely come from Western thinkers but is a whole way of thinking about social phenomena, from Aristotle's Manichean ethics, to Kant's rationalism and Marx's determinisms. It is a project. Scholars like Said and Smith appropriate Western thinkers against the project of Western thought.
2. Despite these misgivings, I will use research throughout the essay because we do not yet have an appropriate replacement for it.
3. See particularly Mills' Introduction to The Racial Contract (1997) and Chapter 9 from From Class to Race (2003) on the RC as a methodology.
4. There are two senses of 'ideal' worth mentioning. First, ideal represents a Utopia, a projected state of affairs. Second, ideal suggests a philosophical variety of idealism, which – from Plato and then, later, Hegel – gives us a theory of ideal forms from which a society is created. Its opposite is materialism, championed by Feuerbach and Marx. The social contract theory is an instance of both senses of the ideal, a projection and an idea. Mills' favors a materialist RC, one based on an actual relationship, not unlike Marx's treatise on capitalism.
5. Although Mills mentions non-Black minority histories, he was concerned mainly with explicating the Black experience. But his general framework is portable and makes it possible to extend his arguments to include other minorities within their own specific histories.

References

Althusser, L. (1971). *Lenin and philosophy.* (B. Brewster, Trans.). New York, NY: Monthly Review Press.
Apple, M. (1979/2000). *Official knowledge: Democratic education in a conservative age* (2nd ed.). New York, NY: Routledge and Kegan Paul.
Apple, M. (2004). *Ideology and curriculum* (3rd ed.). New York, NY: RoutledgeFalmer.
Arendt, H. (1976). *The origins of totalitarianism.* Orlando, FL: Harcourt.
Bataille, G. (1988). *The accursed share*, Vol. I. (R. Hurley, Trans.). New York, NY: Zone Books.

Bataille, G. (1991). *The accursed share*, Vols. II and III. (R. Hurley, Trans.). New York, NY: Zone Books.

Bell, D. (1992). *Faces at the bottom of the well: The permanence of racism*. New York, NY: Basic Books.

Bernal, D. D., & Villalpando, O. (2005). An apartheid of knowledge in academia: The struggle over the 'legitimate' knowledge of faculty of color. In Z. Leonardo (Ed.), *Critical pedagogy and race* (pp. 185–204). Malden, MA: Blackwell.

Collins, P. H. (1991/2000). *Black feminist thought: Knowledge, consciousness, and the politics of empowerment* (2nd ed.). New York, NY: Routledge.

Du Bois, W. E. B. (1904/1989). *The souls of black folk*. New York, NY: Penguin Books.

Fanon, F. (1952/1967). *Black skin white masks* (C. Markmann, Trans.). New York, NY: Grove Press.

Ferguson, A. (2001). *Bad boys*. Ann Arbor: University of Michigan Press.

Foucault, M. (1980). *Power/knowledge*. In C. Gordon (Ed.). New York, NY: Pantheon Books.

Freire, P. (1970/1993). *Pedagogy of the oppressed*. (M. Ramos, Trans.). New York, NY: Continuum.

Gadamer, H.-G. (1975). *Truth and method*. New York, NY: The Seabury Press.

Gillborn, D. (2008). *Racism and education: Coincidence or conspiracy?* New York, NY: Routledge.

Gramsci, A. (1971). *Selections from prison notebooks*. (Q. Hoare & G. Smith, Eds. and Trans.). New York, NY: International.

Harding, S. (1991). *Whose science? Whose knowledge?* Ithaca, NY: Cornell University Press.

Harris, C. (1995). Whiteness as property. In K. Crenshaw, N. Gotanda, G. Peller, & K. Thomas (Eds.), *Critical race theory* (pp. 276–291). New York, NY: The New Press.

Holt, T. (1990). 'Knowledge is power': The black struggle for literacy. In A. Lunsford, H. Moglen, & J. Slevin (Eds.), *The right to literacy* (pp. 91–102). New York, NY: The Modern Language Association.

King, J. (2004). Dysconscious racism: Ideology, identity, and the miseducation of teachers. In G. Ladson-Billings, & D. Gillborn (Eds.), *The RoutledgeFalmer reader in multicultural education* (pp. 71–83). New York, NY: RoutledgeFalmer.

Ladson-Billings, G., & Tate IV, W. F. (1995). Toward a critical race theory of education. *Teachers College Record, 97*(1), 47–68.

Lopez, I. H. (2006). *White by law*. New York, NY: New York University Press.

Lukacs, G. (1971). *History and class consciousness*. (R. Livingstone, Trans.). Cambridge: The MIT Press.

Lynn, M. (1999). Toward a critical race pedagogy: A research note. *Urban Education, 33*(5), 606–626. doi:10.1177/0042085999335004

McIntosh, P. (1992). White privilege and male privilege: A personal account of coming to see correspondences through work in women's studies. In M. Andersen, & P.H. Collins (Eds.), *Race, class, and gender: An anthology* (pp. 70–81). Belmont: Wadsworth.

McIntyre, A. (1997). *Making meaning of whiteness*. Albany: State University of New York Press.

Mills, C. (1997). *The racial contract*. Ithaca: Cornell University Press.

Mills, C. (1998). *Blackness visible: Essays on philosophy and race*. Ithaca: Cornell University Press.

Mills, C. (2003). *From class to race: Essays in white marxism and black radicalism*. Lanham: Rowman & Littlefield.

Morrow, R. (1994). *Critical theory and methodology*. Thousand Oaks: Sage.

Peters, M. (2012). *Education, philosophy, and politics*. New York: Routledge.

Said, E. (1979). *Orientalism*. New York, NY: Random House.

Sandoval, C. (2000). *Methodology of the oppressed*. Minneapolis: University of Minnesota Press.

Scheffler, I. (1965). *Conditions of knowledge*. Chicago, IL: The University of Chicago Press.

Smith, L. T. (1999). *Decolonizing methodologies*. London: Zed Books.

Solorzano, D., & Yosso, T. (2002). Critical race methodology: Counterstory-telling as an analytical framework for education research. *Qualitative Inquiry, 8*(1), 23–44.

Thompson, J. (1984). *Studies in the theory of ideology*. Berkeley: University of California Press.

Weedon, C. (1997). *Feminist practice & poststructuralist theory* (2nd ed.). Cambridge, MA: Blackwell.

White, H. (1986). *Tropics of discourse*. Baltimore: The Johns Hopkins University Press.

Yosso, T. (2006). *Critical race counterstories along the Chicana/Chicano educational pipeline*. New York, NY: Routledge.

You can't erase race! Using CRT to explain the presence of race and racism in majority white suburban schools

Thandeka K. Chapman

Education Studies Department, University of California, San Diego, USA

Employing a critical race analysis of contemporary suburban schooling in the US, the author challenges the ideology of colorblind racial contexts. The concepts of color-blindness, interest-convergence, racial realism, and white privilege are used to explain how federal mandates and common school policies and practices, such as tracking, traditional curricula, teacher classroom practices, and student surveillance, sustain a racially hostile environment for students of color in majority white suburban schools. Critical multicultural education is offered as a means to openly address issue of race and racism in the curriculum, school policies, and teacher practices.

Introduction

The post-racial era, crafted through discourses of American education by the first election of President Barack Obama, has made it increasingly difficult to discuss the ways in which race and racism continue to create and sustain barriers that limit the social and economic gains of people of color in the United States (Crenshaw, 2011). This post-racial moment is predominantly defined by the concept of colorblindness that is cultivated in public spaces. 'Colorblindness has helped to construe race as an "impolite" or even morally suspect subject "politically correct" whites should avoid' (Tarca, 2005, p. 107). The irony of colorblind policies is the *color-conscious* racism that serves as its foundation. A critical race analysis of schools and schooling counters common sense instantiations of colorblind contexts with examples of how race and racism continue as pervasive barriers to equitable schooling for students of color. Employing a critical race analysis of contemporary schooling in the US, I challenge the ideology of colorblind racial contexts in three ways: first, I interrogate the historical underpinnings of race that continue to impact schools; second, I explore the role(s) of race in current education policies; and third, I present empirical evidence demonstrating how race and racism are manifested in majority White suburban school settings.

To accomplish these three goals, I begin the next section with an articulation of the current research on students of color in majority white suburban schools. The following section is an overview of critical race theory and the tenets of the theory used in the paper. Because of its significant impact on schools, the concept of colorblindness is given a more extensive explanation. Next, I illustrate how desegregation reforms, No Child Left Behind, and existing curricula stand as historical and contemporary policies with racialized instantiations of practice that impact today's schools. I then present data from a study about the experiences of students of color in predominately white suburban schools to discuss how supposedly colorblind school contexts further marginalize students of color. I explore how school practices reinstate race and racism and widen the equity gap between white students who are *privileged by* and students of color who are *oppressed by* white supremacist articulations of schooling (Tarca, 2005; Urrieta, 2006). Lastly, I suggest that schools need to commit to a focus on critical multicultural education for social justice to assist educators in predominately white suburban schools to challenge racist practices, which are supported through a colorblind ideology, and create more equitable schooling experiences for students of color (Grant & Sleeter, 1989/1997; Kincheloe, 1993).

Current research on students of color in majority white suburban schools

As racial demographics continue to shift, many scholars are researching the experiences of students of color in majority white high schools (Carter, 2007, 2008; Chapman, 2007; Diamond, 2006; Diamond, Lewis, & Gordon, 2007; Huidor & Cooper, 2010; O'Connor, Mueller, Lewis, Rivas-Drake, & Rosenberg, 2011). O'Connor et al. interviewed 44 black students, and conducted in-depth research of eight high-achievers, to document the schooling experiences of high-achieving African-American students in racially stratified accelerated courses in predominately white schools. The researchers found that students maintained strong connections with their African-American peers, who were in less rigorous classes, as a means to buffer them from acts of racism. A support system was unavailable to black students in the upper-level Advanced Placement (AP) and advanced courses, causing them to seek alliances with other racial groups such as Asian Americans. O'Connor et al. state that the students' resistance to stereotypes, and their negotiation of the school contexts, interacted with the contexts of the school as an unwelcoming space. The researchers also noted that some students were able to trespass racial boundaries in classes by proving themselves as worthy academic partners. However, many of the high-achieving black students in the study espoused a negative view of black low achievers, and they connected these perceptions with negative stereotypes of race.

Diamond et al. (2007) found comparable results pertaining to issues of racial isolation and negative peer pressure in upper-level courses for black students. Among the black students in regular classes, there was a stronger support system. Diamond et al. also noted that the stress and racism of upper level classes caused black students to doubt their academic abilities. They interviewed 70 black and white high school students with a range of grade point averages. The researchers found that the majority of black students felt that being black would limit their life chances for success, while the white students did not believe that race was a factor in their success. However, the black students' belief in racially stratified success did not impact their academic achievement and desire to be successful. In fact, black students at every level of tracking hoped to attend college.

In her study of high-achieving black students at a majority white suburban elite school, Carter (2007, 2008) noted that black students created homogenous racial enclaves to affirm racial identity and shield them from racism in the school. Carter conducted a series of three interviews with nine African-American 10–12th grade students who accessed the school through a race-based desegregation busing program. Although the students recognized the structural and social inequities embedded in their schools, Carter (2008) found that the students' perceptions of race and racism in school varied across individuals. She also documented how African-American students reinforced their black identities through their forms of dress and informal language styles when socializing in certain areas of the school where black students congregated (2007). The students further supported each other through a formal association, the Black Leadership Advisory Council, which gave them the opportunity to meet and voice their frustrations. Carter asserts that formal and informal spaces for black students help them to maintain positive resistance to racism and a positive sense of self and academic achievement.

Huidor and Cooper (2010) explore how students of color choose to participate or abstain from educational activities based on their levels of comfort and ability to negotiate the different circumstances. In their study of 20 students of color who were bused to a predominately white school, the researchers documented the students' perceptions of their school experiences as significantly more rigorous and engaging than the school experiences in their neighborhood schools. The students recognized the racial segregation in both academic and social components of the school, and mediated these issues by forming close bonds with their same race peers.

Henfield, Moore, and Wood's (2008) themes resonate with Huidor and Cooper (2010) and the previously cited research. Henfield et al. conducted a mixed-methods study of gifted high school students of color to explore how racial identity interacted with their academic identity. As with the previously mentioned researchers, they found that black students maintain strong racial identities despite racism and isolation. Black students also were extremely cognizant of racist practices at the school and classroom levels. Interestingly, the gifted students combated issues of 'acting white' and 'nerd' by joining extracurricular activities where they interacted with black students who were outside of the gifted program.

Although the study in this paper shares many of the conclusions of the previous studies, this paper veers from the trajectory of research to focus on how the institutional climate contradicts the colorblind discourse articulated in white high schools. Similar to critical research on the contexts of integrated schools with histories of desegregation (Chapman, 2007; Diamond, 2006), the author interrogates the structural factors that create racially imbalanced settings and deny students full access to the curriculum. Diamond states, 'One cannot separate the educational experiences, attitudes, and achievement of students from the broader patterns of racial inequality that exist in communities, schools, and classrooms. To do so, distorts the understanding of race and educational achievement' (2006, p. 501). The voices of students of color highlight the hypocrisy of colorblind discourses, and legitimate their 'racially based feelings and viewpoints' (Bonilla-Silva, 2009, p. 11), by articulating the very real ways the students are racialized. The shift from focusing on identity formation to institutional instantiations of racism and oppression is an attempt to move the discourse from a focus on the racial group's reaction to racism to the systems and actions that cause the conflict.

Critical race theory

Critical Race Theory (CRT) is used to interpret the students' perceptions of their experiences in majority white suburban schools. As a theoretical lens, it provides a historical filter for explicating and analyzing past and present contexts that create specific learning environments. Scholars (Ladson-Billings & Tate, 1995; Lynn, 2004; Solorzano & Yosso, 2001) have asserted that one of the goals of CRT in education research is to examine issues of race, class, and gender in educational settings with regard to their historical and local contexts. These applications of CRT address issues in teacher education, educational research paradigms, and the historical and present effects of court-ordered desegregation.

CRT connects the suburban districts' histories of racial oppression to the ongoing unequal system propagated by current reforms. Specifically, interest-convergence, color-blind ideologies, the enduring presence of racism, and white privilege are conceptual tools of CRT that frame the analysis in the paper. CRT is an appropriate theoretical lens for connecting students' everyday experiences of racism with institutional policies and social norms that create and sustain barriers to students' current and future academic success. 'Critical race theory has the benefit of hindsight in drawing on previous critiques of educational inequality to expose and challenge macro and micro forms of racism disguised as traditional school curriculum' (Yosso, 2002, p. 95).

Colorblind racism

Nieto, Bode, Kang, and Raible state that the colorblind discourse is 'tacitly accepted by many educators and evident in classroom practices, including both curriculum and pedagogy ...' (2008, p. 181). Colorblindness 'is a set of understandings—buttressed by law and the courts, and reinforcing racial patterns of white dominance—that define how people comprehend, rationalize, and act on race' (Lopez, 2006, p. 62). The discourse of color blindness allows school adults to disregard the racial identities of students by solely viewing them as individuals who are divorced from the social, economic, and cultural factors that shape their past and present experiences. By denying the 'historical and current contexts of white domination' (Urrieta, 2006, p. 456), colorblind discourses position the perceptions of students of color as irrational and baseless (Lopez, 2003).

Much of the discussion focused on colorblindness in education centers around the classroom environment. In the classroom context, this usually is identified by the teacher's avoidance of topics about race and the exposition of an equal=fair=equity pedagogical stance that influences individual relationships and behavioral consequences. Colorblindness is a false premise because the conscious avoidance of the topic of race, and the unconscious actions based on race, contradicts the notion of racial blindness. However, the context for colorblindness is larger than the individual teacher and impacts the greater school context. The insidious nature of colorblindness designs barriers to student learning and growth, which speaks more to the institutionalization of racism. Bonilla-Silva (2009) explains,

> Much as Jim Crow racism served as the glue for defending a brutal and overt system of racial oppression in the pre-Civil Rights era, color-blind racism serves today as the ideological armor for a covert and institutionalized system in the post-Civil Rights era. And the beauty of this new ideology is that it aids in the maintenance of white privilege without fanfare, without naming those who it subjects and those who it rewards (2009, p. 2).

In white majority high schools, the connections between colorblindness and white privilege, and the maintenance of white supremacy, pose significant challenges for students of color to overcome. Therefore, Bonilla-Silva asserts, a stronger term, such as 'colorblind racism', more aptly captures the damaging effects of colorblindness on students of color and the privileging effects for white students in majority white public schools.

Educational spaces are saturated with 'colorblind racism'. Although the ways in which colorblind racism is enacted vary across different contexts, the outcomes are the same. It constricts the learning and development of students of color and maintains white privilege by further marginalizing students of color in academic settings. In majority white suburban schools, colorblind racism's most blatant expressions can be viewed through the relationships between adults and students of color; more subtle enactments of colorblind racism are documented by curricular and behavior policies. Ironically, the racialized histories and current policy mandates of public schooling, which impact these enclaves of white privilege, highlight racial inequities at the same moment there is a public call to minimize these conversations.

Racial realism and school desegregation: The ghost of past racism

Historically, the legacy of desegregation litigation continues to significantly impact the schooling experiences of all students in US schools. The children in today's schools are the grandchildren and great-grandchildren of *Brown v. Board of Education*, and the descendants of the policy mandates such as cross-town busing, open enrollment, inter-district enrollment, charter schools, voucher schools, comprehensive reform orders, tax levies, and multicultural education, all of which stem from decades of litigation to secure equitable schooling for non-white children. The schooling experiences of children in the US, particularly for urban and suburban children, are the manifestations of political and social acts by stakeholders who have continually pushed for/opposed greater access to an equitable education based on issues of race and racism. Lopez remarks that 'the past is never really past, especially not when one talks about race and the law in the United States' (2006, p. 62). Research has shown that race, consciously or dysconsciously negated, impacts the schooling experiences of students of color (King, 1991; Lewis, 2003; Pollock, 2005). Therefore, notions of a post-race society, situated in contexts constructed and fortified by issues of race and racial privilege, are untenable.

Interest-convergence and present articulations of race in NCLB

Given the intractable nature of racism, Bell (2004) argues that African-Americans only progress in their battles with civil liberties when whites are allowed to benefit as well. Interest-convergence is one lens for explaining how and why urban districts made certain decisions around the implementation of *Brown*. The interpretations or avoidance of *Brown* benefited whites by creating alternate hierarchies of schooling to maintain racially stratified education opportunities. The schools in this study are from a unique subset of inter-district busing programs that were created in the 1960s and 1970s due to court pressures to desegregate schools (Wells et al., 2009). The 1974 *Milliken v. Bradley* had major implications for desegregation across districts if suburban districts were found complicit of de jure segregation. The decision prevented districts from crossing district boundaries to alleviate racial segregation *if* the suburban district had no past culpability for segregation, therefore maintaining segregation in suburban districts. Fearing court-interventions or adhering to court orders, several districts created inter-district busing programs before and after *Milliken* to alleviate segregation in inner-city schools. In some cases, this interest-convergence allowed the suburban districts to avoid more comprehensive desegregation while a small number of urban students escaped their racially segregated schools. In this city, the suburban schools were found complicit in maintaining segregation and forced to fashion a policy to alleviate inner-city segregation (Wells et al., 2009). Since the initial court order in this district, other suburban schools have voluntarily joined the program. The districts in this study continue to maintain these busing programs for various reasons. Some districts welcome the diversity as a means to better reflect society and give white children the opportunity to interact with students outside their race, while other districts value the student monies that accompany inter-district students.

Additionally, due to the housing market and small amount of rental property listings, many of these suburban enclaves are experiencing an increase in families of color moving into the districts (Orfield, 2002). 'Communities experiencing increasing diversity and tension between racial and ethnic groups are on the front lines of the struggle against racism in public institutions of education' (Tarca, 2005, p. 100). Many suburban districts in the area are struggling to respond to families of color who are voting tax-payers in the community. While the number of families moving into these communities remains small, they are making their concerns heard.

A second example of interest-convergence is a result of a No Child Left Behind mandate for schools and districts to disclose student achievement scores using racial demographic data. Before this measure, the majority of white districts with significant achievement gaps between white students and students of color were not concerned with racial disparities. Since these schools, in general, are more highly resourced and rigorous than their urban counterparts, students of color are seen as privileged to acquire the few allotted spots given to them from inter-city busing programs. However, NCLB policy articulations have highlighted current inequities in the schooling experiences of racial minority students in predominately white schools. High-achieving schools with racially mixed populations have a significant gap between the achievement of their students of color and their white students. School/district reputations and funding are now vulnerable to sanctions based on the district's ability to meet the academic needs of all children. This is different from previous years where high-achieving schools, which claimed to be integrated and thriving educational spaces for all children, used aggregated data to obfuscate their achievement gaps. These potential sanctions make administrators take a new interest in the achievement patterns of their racial minority students. Thus, federal mandates foster interest convergence by compelling predominately white districts to better support the education of racial minorities in order to maintain their privileged and elite school status.

White privilege and traditional curriculum

The concept of curriculum as 'intellectual property' (Ladson-Billings & Tate, 1995) is used to explicate reinstantiations of white privilege and supremacy in suburban schools. Curriculum as intellectual property or 'curriculum property' is the means by which the materials, programs, rules, structures, and pedagogies of the school reinstantiate white privilege. The reinstantiation of white privilege is apparent through the absence of racially diverse content and critical stances used to examine power and privilege, regulations targeting racial minority groups, hierarchies of extra-curricular activities in which students of color dominate the lower echelons, and tracking. The school curriculum, in its broadest sense, becomes the tool for further marginalization and maintenance of the status quo, rather than a tool of empowerment and social change. In her examination of school contexts in a dual language program, Palmer (2010) affirms that, 'District and school policies coupled with teachers' unexamined biases continue to systematically undermine black students' access to the highest quality programs' (p. 110). Thus, an examination of colorblind school contexts uncovers the ways in which schools remain complicit in racially stratified educational practices.

A look at majority white schools

When exploring racial stratifications, Teranishi (2002) argues that students' experiences with racism must be understood through their distinct racial contexts. He explains,

> These contexts are predicated by a number of factors such as a school's historical legacy of inclusion or exclusion of various racial/ethnic groups, its structural diversity in terms of the numerical representation of various racial/ethnic groups, the social climate (defined as the racial perceptions and attitudes that different groups have of one another), as well as behavioral climate dimensions characterized by intergroup relations at school (p. 145).

In public schools, the situated nature of race and racism is indelibly bound to the contexts of the schools (Huidor & Cooper, 2010). In predominately white contexts, colorblind discourses become more prominent because issues of equity and equality are framed through the policies and practices that attempt to treat all students the same. White administrators and teachers, who are the majority of adults in suburban schools, create and maintain a facade of colorblind equity by invoking colorblind policies, such as zero tolerance behavior consequences and inflexible tutorial times that students of color who are bused to school cannot attend.

Background to the study

The study was commissioned by a community organization that consists of parents of color from suburban districts, university faculty from multiple universities in the surrounding metropolitan area, and high-ranking school district officials. This organiza-tion was created to address the racial achievement gap between students of color and white students in suburban districts. The purpose of the study was a qualitative exploration of the schooling experiences of students of color in predominately white high schools, with the goal to change various aspects of the school curriculum to increase students' academic achievement. The specific objectives of the larger study were:

- to identify successful and unsuccessful relationships, events, and policies in the schools;
- to identify resources and experiences that support students' academic, social, and emotional growth; and
- to identify policies, events, and school practices that support or create barriers to student learning.

The study took place in four predominantly white suburbs that share borders with a Midwest metropolitan area. These suburban high schools participate in two 30-year-old inter-district busing programs that allow students of color from the urban district to attend suburban schools. White suburban students are allowed to attend urban schools as well, but few suburban families utilize this option. Researchers conducted 22 focus group interviews with 97 high school students of color, from six schools in four districts. The participants' ages ranged from 14 to 19 years. Two thirds of the participants were girls. Students from all racial categories, except white, were solicited for interviews. The racial breakdown of the students included African-American (74), Latino/a (5), and Asian American (4), bi-racial (10), Native American (2), multi-racial (2) students. The students interviewed hailed from across the urban center with a few living in the suburban cities. Depending on the suburban district, these students of color experience various levels of school segregation through tracking and low enrollment of students of color.

Data were collected through single session, 1.5-hours long, audio-taped, focus group interviews with 5–7 high school students and one member of the research team during the school day at each high school site. The focus groups functioned as Freirean 'study circles' with the 'goal for the educator or facilitator within these study circles is to engage with people in their lived realities, producing and transforming them' (Kambrelis & Dimitriadis, 2005, p. 890). The semi-structured interviews focused on three categories: general questions about their high school, adult relationships, and academics. These three areas are aligned with scholarship documenting school capacities that foster student success (Fredricks & Eccles, 2006; Johnson, Crosnoe, & Elder, 2001; Shernoff & Schmidt, 2008) and the *Indiana University Survey of High School Student Engagement* previously given to eighth grade students in the same districts.

Data analysis

The research team consisted of two African-American women, one Latina, one Korean man, and one Hmong woman. The primary researcher, and author of the article, is an African-American woman who is an associate professor at an urban university. The four remaining researchers, each with past lives as educators in K-12 schools, were doctoral students at varying levels of program completion who received instruction in qualitative methods and conducted qualitative pilot studies as part of their doctoral course work. Three research team members are bilingual: two speak Spanish and English, one speaks Hmong and English, and one member purposefully code-switches between academic English and African-American Vernacular English.

Data analysis was conducted using contact summary sheets during data collection to capture the researchers' summaries of the main points of emphasis from the group, significant issues, and recurring themes from previous interviews (Miles & Huberman, 1994). A systematic process articulated by LeCompte (2000) was adapted for a research team analysis. The team: (1) read and marked the interviews with marginal remarks; (2) made external notes on areas of frequency, omission, and declaration; (3) used their individual notes to make initial taxonomies as a team; (4) created a visual matrix of these initial taxonomies; (5) used the matrix to identify sub-categories and patterns as a team; and (6) assembled structures as a team. Concerns for data trustworthiness are addressed through the use of a collective team process in which all five members of the research used identical interview protocols for data collection, conducted the steps to analyze the data, and challenged each other's assumptions and characterizations of the data through the collective analysis process.

The following themes represent multiple concepts of CRT. The concepts of color-blindness, interest-convergence, racial realism, and white privilege are used to explain how common school policies and practices, such as tracking, traditional curricula, teacher classroom practices, and student surveillance, create a racially hostile environment for students of color in majority white suburban schools. These normative school practices inhibit students of color from fully engaging in the school and, therefore, from securing equitable schooling experiences.

Academic tracking

The physical composition of the school challenges notions of colorblind school contexts and reinforces the difference between integrated spaces and desegregated spaces. In these suburban schools, the majority of the students of color remain in the lower tracks of classes. High-achieving students of color noted that they were frequently the only black or brown bodies in their advanced placement or advanced subject classrooms. In speaking with high-achieving students of color, most of them could count the number of students of color in their classes.

> **Student:** In AP Spanish there is only one other black person in there. The rest of mine—no. They are all white.
> **Student:** In my AP classes I have more Asian people.
> **Student:** AP English there is one [Asian].
> **Student:** My regular English classes, I have me, my brother, and two other black people. The others are white. Or my Latin class, there are four black people and the majority are white.
> **Student:** Mostly all my classes are predominantly white. I only have one class with one black person in my entire schedule.
> **Student:** For my first time in high school, I had a class with two other black kids and that was the most I ever had.

Conversely, students, who were in lower tracked courses, could not give the number of students because there were too many to quickly count.

> **Researcher:** So most [students of color] are in regular classes?
> **Student:** Yeah
> **Researcher:** … Are they [students of color] in lower levels?
> **Student 1:** Yes, math especially.
> **Student 2:** Yes, I am in the lower level in every course.
> **Researcher:** What is the representation in those courses?
> **Student 1:** A lot.
> **Researcher:** More than in regular?
> **Student 3:** I have formal geometry, and there is only one white kid in there.

In the case of white majority schools, higher tracks of curriculum serve as the property of white students in which few students of color are able to access the rigorous curricular experiences that lead to greater college access (Ladson-Billings & Brown, 2008; Ladson-Billings & Tate, 1995). These stratifications maintain a desegregated context rather than an integrated one, and reinforce the white supremacist ideology of students of color as intellectually inferior. When asked how students chose their courses, many of them explain that counselors and teachers play major roles in placing them into their current classes. Because most of the students of color have matriculated in these districts since kindergarten, their track positions cannot be dismissed as students of color transferring to suburban high schools from lower status urban middle schools. Instead, the placement of students of color in lower tracks reflects 40-year conversations about how students are tracked into classes based on race and socioeconomic status at an early age and unable to cross into upper tracks later in their schooling careers (Rist, 1970; Oakes, 1985).

The visible racialization of curricular tracking also poses an example of interest convergence. Because even the lower track classes at suburban high schools are considered better than the regular school curricula found in the attached urban district, students of color believe, and the research supports (Goldsmith, 2011), that they receive stronger academic preparation in the suburban schools. In this study and the study of students of color bused into white schools (Huidor & Cooper, 2010), the students felt their suburban schools were more rigorous, safe, and offered more extra-curricular activities than their neighborhood schools. Students in the study explained,

Student: I wouldn't say it is an honor but people say it is a good school. So I feel kind of proud that I go to this school rather than [Urban School 1] or [Urban School 2], [urban district] schools.

Student: Yeah. I think that if you get a 2.5 here that is like 3.5 at [Urban School 1] or [urban school 3] or something.

Student: I feel like our school is a lot tougher than most schools. Whenever I talk to my cousins who go to [urban district] schools, they are—oh yeah—it is real easy here. We never get homework. Like here they kind of get on us. We have a sufficient amount of homework that we have to get done.

Student: This school has a good curriculum school, like to get into better colleges. We are kind of like up here to a point, academically. We are higher than a whole lot of other schools in [metropolitan city].

White students maintain the property of curriculum by being over-represented in higher track classes, while students of color regard their lower track education as valuable. Indeed, even in the Huidor and Cooper (2010) study, the students still thought their education was more rigorous than their neighborhood schools, despite not being enrolled in AP courses. From the perspective of most students of color, the goal is to get into a college – any college. For students in the majority of the high schools in the urban center, meeting the goal of going to college is a great challenge. Even from the lower tracks at the suburban school, students of color are able to meet this goal. However, they are unable to attend the high-ranked colleges and universities where many of their white counterparts apply. Tracking these highly motivated students into lower tracks affects the future possibilities of students of color by limiting their college choices, making them less competitive for jobs, and restricting their exposure to new forms of cultural capital that are present in elite environments (Ladson-Billings & Brown, 2008). Therefore, the economic and social possibilities for these students remain stratified by race.

In addition, broadly defined aspects of the curriculum reflect problematic issues of race. The majority of students segregate themselves by race in the cafeteria and extra-curricular activities. Students of color are over-represented in particular sports activities such as basketball and football and under-represented in other sports, clubs, and leadership activities.

Student 1: Do you guys see a breakup of clubs in who the people in those clubs are, like key club? It is white kids. Multicultural club [is] minority kids. Basketball is all black, like the stereotypical.

Student 2: Most of the people on the soccer team are white. Most of the girls are the rich white girls are on the tennis teams.

Segregation in these social settings is another example of the presence of race in supposedly colorblind settings. When the interactions between students of color and affluent white students are limited to academic settings, students have fewer opportunities to engage in informal interactions where cultural capital and social capital are exchanged. In addition, the stratification of extra-curricular activities by race generates a hierarchy of school activities. Homogenous white activities become more valued, and homogenous black and brown activities become less valued. Once again, curriculum serves as property when academic clubs and student leadership opportunities become the purview of white students who use these activities to support their college applications.

Students as racial authority

When defining curriculum as property as a form of access, Ladson-Billings and Brown (2008) state, 'However, even when students have access to the same curriculum, we know that they have it differentially and that the curriculum can serve to reinforce racial ideology' (p. 155). When issues of race and poverty are introduced in the classroom, students of color experience the curriculum in these high schools differently from their white peers. Rather than feeling empowered by conversations on race and society, students of color feel further marginalized in their classrooms. As a single racial minority in the classroom, students of color become the sole proprietors of knowledge about race and poverty from the perspective of all non-white groups at any point in history.

> **Student:** They have discussions where I will feel a little awkward because we are talking about something like that [race], and because I am the only black person in the class. But I feel like they are all looking at me like, 'is it okay talking about this?'
> **Student:** Like in class, it is not like a burden, but when you are talking about something black like all eyes will swivel to you, like you are the Negro-damus [opinion] or something like that. It is kind of annoying at the same time. Well, I am the only the black person in this class. But just because we are talking about slavery, it doesn't mean you have swivel your eyes over here.
> **Student:** When people ask me about Chinese or China ... it is like we are reading something about the Chinese and [students ask me] like—Does this happen? I say, 'I am Korean'. Some people kind of assume that if you are Asian, you know the whole Asian culture. Like general stereotyping. Not a lot of people know [the difference].
> **Student:** It is kind of awkward sometimes, like in history class, talking about slavery and Black people. It is kind of weird. It is kind of awkward to hear it because I am the only Black person in class and people will look at me.
> **Student:** We were talking about the Civil War and I was the only black person in class. So everyone expects me to know everything about the Civil War. And like, we were reading, and this stocky man said the N word, and everyone said, 'What do you think?' It was like, if we were reading something, I am not going to get all mad.
> **Student:** Like sometimes, like in English class, we will read stuff. That's all we read are books about black people being slaves. And so when my teacher asks me a question pertaining to race, I am just going to say, 'I don't think that is necessary'. Every time we read a book about a black slave, you want to ask me a question about how would it make me feel. How do you think it will make me feel? How would you feel if you were a slave? I would feel the same way, so why would you ask me that question?

Students feel uncomfortable and defensive when issues of race and racism are part of the formal curriculum. When these issues are highlighted in classes, the teacher makes the student the center of attention for all the wrong reasons. Curriculum stands as property in this context, and as a symbol of white privilege, because white students are not asked to speak for their race or made to feel uncomfortable when their group is the focus of the text. When reading Shakespeare, the white students are not asked, 'What is it like to be a suicidal teenager whose boyfriend is a murderer?' In many ways, these events have implications for the pedagogical practices of teachers in these settings. But more significantly, the events demonstrate the color-consciousness of students and teachers in racially diverse environments.

Double standards

During the interviews, students overwhelmingly remark on the unequal behavior standards in their schools. Students describe incidents in which black girls and Latinas were sent home for violating dress codes regarding leggings and 'short shorts', while white girls were not reprimanded. The students were primarily frustrated about the unfair treatment they received in individual classrooms that resulted in students being sent to the office. Once in the office, the teacher's story goes unchallenged, and unquestioned, and discipline is doled out to the student. Students also remark that students of color are disciplined more severely than their white peers. The following quotes explain a few of these numerous incidents.

> **Student:** It is like they were playing a game on a computer one day. He got done with his work so he went to play on the computer. The white kid two feet down from him was playing on the computer, but the teacher called him out and like he got in trouble. He said, 'Well, he is playing too. And she is like, 'well, I am talking to you'. It is like, why don't you talk to him too? Some teachers do that and it makes you think like [they] are racist. 'Well I am not racist' [student mimicking teachers]. Well okay, that is what it seems like. You are pointing me out, but you are not pointing out some of the other ones.
> **Student:** It is a known fact [unequal treatment]. I have turned in stuff late the same day as somebody else did, and we are both late, and I get a lower grade. And [the white] one doesn't even get marked down late. They [teachers] say, 'Oh, it is the quality of it'. So I had the same person write my stuff, but just in a different tone, and the same thing has happened [the paper is still marked down]. So it's just like, I mean I am in a lose-lose situation.
> **Student:** Also just say there is like a double standard. It seems like if a black [kid] it is doing something [talking] … But like white kids are sitting there talking and the black person gets pointed out. Like why are you yelling at him? You know? It is a double standard.
> **Student:** When it comes down to it, teachers are like always calling me out. Sometimes I have to use the bathroom in band a lot and he [the teacher] will let a whole bunch of students go. It is like they are all Caucasian. I always feel like that. Teachers always let them go to the bathroom, but when you ask, 'Oh, you need to hold it'. Like, 'Oh, no, you can't go'. Or they always yell at you when everyone is doing something bad, they just yell at you first.

These incidents speak to the over-surveillance of students of color in majority white schools. Students admit their imperfections, and that they may have been doing something wrong; but because the adults in the school are concentrating more on their behavior, the students of color are more likely to be reprimanded. Thus, the system of colorblindness is perpetuated because the student cannot claim innocence and avoid persecution; they can only point out that white students were also complicit in the negative behavior as part of their defense.

Race as an unsafe space

Students implicitly understand that they are not supposed to discuss race or use it as a form to differentiate themselves from the other students. One student said it best when he said, 'They want you to conform, or don't want you to go and create your own [student] government. They would prefer that you participate in their [student] government. They don't want you to identify yourself kind of'. When students ask adults to address issues of racism in the school, they were ignored or marked as trouble-makers. When students of color defend themselves from verbal attacks, either verbally or physically, they are disproportionately punished for their actions. Although several of the schools have ethnic clubs, the students struggle to maintain them because they cannot find teachers who are willing to advise the clubs or secure spaces for their meetings. The students understand that these clubs are unwelcome additions to the school.

However, the schools' attempts to obscure race do not dissolve the students' performances of race. Students feel the need to perform at higher academic levels than their white peers to combat stereotypes that label them as academically inferior to white students.

Student: I would say that us being minorities here in—We have to be careful because you have to be aware of the way, we kind of are put on a pedestal.

Student: You are a black female and no one is going to take pity on you. No one is going to feel sorry for you. You have to work twice as hard as a white female and that is the way it is. Every time a grade comes in a C, maybe a D, she [pointing to friend] don't like. She is working twice as hard.

Student: Talking as a black male, I would say that you would always have to fight the stereotype. If you make one small mistake, they are going to hold it against you.

Student: Because of [race] you are always fighting against [racism] beside what you are regularly fighting against. And for me personally, I always say, I don't want to be a statistic, someone who has dropped out of school, who has not gotten into college.

The burden of performing race causes the students to want to disappear racially in order to smoothly matriculate through school, not because of low racial identity (Diamond, 2006). However, they realize this is not a rational expectation. Instead, students tried to minimize their presence as much as possible by remaining quiet and unobtrusive, not drawing attention to themselves, and getting good grades. One student rationalizes her behavior:

Student: I know I am black, but if I am going to get through a day, a school year, I kind of have to put that aside, and kind of become colorless, just to get through it.

Unlike previous research that would imply that the student is rejecting a positive black identity (Ogbu, 2003), this student attempts to become invisible in opposition to choosing to become white. Carter (2008) explains, 'It is a resistance for survival in that these black students' psyches are constantly under attack in a learning environment in which their racial group membership is often associated with anti-intellectualism and/or intellectual inferiority' (p. 478). The racialized contexts of the school push the student, and others like her, to bracket their race in order to focus on learning.

Critical multiculturalism

Critical multiculturalism is one strategy for addressing the schooling inequities experienced by students of color in majority white schools. McLaren (1994) suggests that critical multicultural teachers unpack the complexities of meaning and identity constructions and confront the larger societal challenges surrounding social justice. McLaren states 'Critical multiculturalism interrogates the construction of difference and identity in relation to a radical politics' (1994, p. 53). Critical multiculturalism advocates systemic change and contests the ideology of cultural deficiency that serves as a commonsense narrative in majority white schools.

Other scholars support the push to use multicultural education as a change agent (Banks, 2007; Grant & Sleeter, 1989/1997; Nieto & Bode, 2008). Grant and Sleeter suggest that multicultural education, as social reconstruction, offers schools the opportunity to build learning environments and programs that re-envision current traditional policies and practices that marginalize students of color and prevent white students and white adults from empathetically engaging with issues of race, culture, and other differences. Banks (2007) offers a transformative model of multicultural education that challenges all stakeholders to make schools reflect a more socially just and critical multicultural society. Similarly, Nieto (2000) calls for multicultural education for social justice to target systemic inequities through a comprehensive approach to school reform.

> ... Multicultural education permeates the curriculum and instructional strategies used in schools, as well as in the interactions among teachers, students and parents, and the very way that schools conceptualize the nature of teaching and learning. Because it uses critical pedagogy as its underlying philosophy and focuses on knowledge, reflection, and action (praxis) as the basis for social change, multicultural education furthers the democratic principles of social justice. (Nieto, 2000, p. 305)

With a combined history of over 120 years of experience in the field of multicultural education, these scholars implore districts to restructure schools and support teachers to engage with race and other social markers in ways that strengthen, not debilitate, students' academic achievement and personal growth.

Rather than attempting to obscure the racial realities of majority white high school settings, administrators, teachers, and staff must understand how race is consistently and newly constructed in schooling environments.

> School leaders must be prepared to work with individuals who are culturally different and help create learning environments that foster respect, tolerance, and intercultural understanding. They must also have an awareness of the effect of racism and how it intersects with other areas of difference such as gender, sexual orientation, disability, and class oppression. (Lopez, 2003, p. 71)

These constructions of race must be interrogated to acknowledge how institutional policies and practices reinstantiate white supremacy and support inequitable systems. Moreover, Carter (2008) noted that 'schools and educators need to be counter-hegemonic in their practices, challenging traditional dominant discourses and paradigms about what it means to be successful and who is successful' (2008, p. 494).

Only when systemic changes, which include conversations on race and racism, are implemented will schools become more equitable environments for students of color (Banks, 1995). 'To break the interlocking patterns of racial hierarchy, there is no other way but to focus on, talk about, and put into effect constructive policies explicitly engaged with race' (Lopez, 2006, p. 62). But creating policy is an insufficient means of dealing with colorblind racism when the actors, administrators and teachers, implement policy through deficit paradigms of racial groups. As seen in the examples from the study, white privilege is maintained through the structures of the school, the over-surveillance of students of color, and the discussions allowed in the classroom (Yosso, 2002). Critical multicultural education is a solution to minimizing the gap between institutional policy and its practical implementations. The goal of multicultural education is to serve all children; therefore, it can only be achieved when schools embrace all-inclusive school reforms that reflect the racial milieu of public school classrooms.

Conclusions

Students of color remain deeply impacted by racist schooling practices that they are not allowed to name in their schools. Diamond states,

> However, integrated schools (to the extent that they have existed) have failed to create equal opportunity for all students, in part, because racial inequality in the society as a whole or within the schools, in numerous cases, has not been directly confronted (2006, p. 502).

The colorblind discourses in white suburban schools prevent students of color from having meaningful exchanges with adults and maintain the curriculum's role of intellectual property for white students. Lopez explains what happens when color-blindness is allowed free reign in society,

> As a result, the collective frustrations of people of color and/or Black nationalist groups are simply seen as irrational ... This slippage only maintains racism firmly in place by ignoring or downplaying the role of White racism in the larger social order (2003, p. 69).

Students of color are viewed as 'irrational' when they name racism in their schools. 'The trap of colorblindness neither initiates conversations about the influence of race nor empowers those experiencing discrimination to argue their case' (Tarca, 2005, p. 114). Moreover, they are further cast as outsiders and trouble-makers, making it more difficult for them to successfully matriculate through schools.

The irony of the colorblind discourse is evident. Schools in the US cannot erase race. The enforcement of colorblindness serves to exacerbate, not alleviate, issues of race and racism for students of color in predominately white schools. This exploration of colorblind ideology/color-conscious practices in schools serves as an alternate explanation to 'blaming the victim' (Bonilla-Silva, 2009) for under-achievement, racial isolation, and academic disinterest in majority white high schools; and it places the burden of school reform on policy makers and educators to 'dismantle and reconstruct systemic approaches currently in place within the educational system' (Saddler, 2005, p. 53).

References

Banks, J. A. (1995). Multicultural education: Historical development, dimensions, and practice. In C. M. Banks (Ed.), *Handbook of research on multicultural education* (pp. 3–24). New York, NY: MacMillan.

Banks, J. A. (2007). *Educating citizens in a multicultural society*. New York, NY: Teachers College Press.

Bell, D. A. (2004). *Silent covenants: Brown v. board of education and the unfulfilled hopes for racial reform*. Oxford, New York, NY: Oxford University Press.

Bonilla-Silva, E. (2009). *Racism without racists. Colorblind racism and the persistence of racial inequality in America* (3rd ed.). New York, NY: Roman & Littlefield.

Carter, D. J. (2007). Why the Black kids sit together at the stairs: The role of identity-affirming counter-spaces in a predominantly White high school. *Journal of Negro Education, 76*(4), 542–554. Retrieved from http://search.ebscohost.com/login.aspx?direct=true&db=eft&AN=5080079 43&site=ehost-live

Carter, D. J. (2008). Achievement as resistance: The development of a critical race achievement ideology among Black achievers. *Harvard Educational Review, 78*(3), 466–497. Retrieved from http://search.ebscohost.com/login.aspx?direct=true&db=eft&AN=508008080&site=ehost-live

Chapman, T. K. (2007). The power of contexts: Teaching and learning in recently desegregated schools. *Anthropology & Education Quarterly, 38*(3), 297–315. doi:10.1525/aeq.2007.38.3.297

Crenshaw, K. W. (2011). Twenty years of critical race theory: Looking back to move forward. *Connecticut Law Review, 43*(5), 1253–1351. Retrieved from http://archive.connecticutlawreview.org/documents/Crenshaw.pdf

Diamond, J. B. (2006). Still separate and unequal: Examining race, opportunity, and school achievement in 'Integrated' suburbs. *Journal of Negro Education, 75*(3), 495–505. Retrieved from http://search.ebscohost.com/login.aspx?direct=true&db=eft&AN=507901896&site=ehost-live

Diamond, J. B., Lewis, A. E., & Gordon, L. (2007). Race and school achievement in a desegregated suburb: Reconsidering the oppositional culture explanation. *International Journal of Qualitative Studies in Education, 20*(6), 655–679. doi:10.1080/09518390701630791

Fredricks, J. A., & Eccles, J. S. (2006). Is extracurricular participation associated with beneficial outcomes? Concurrent and longitudinal relations. *Developmental Psychology, 42*(4), 698–713. doi:10.1037/0012-1649.42.4.698

Goldsmith, P. R. (2011). Coleman revisited: School segregation, peers, and frog ponds. *American Educational Research Journal, 48*(3), 508–535. doi:10.3102/0002831210392019

Grant, C. A., & Sleeter, C. E. (1989/1997). *Turning on learning: Five approaches for multicultural teaching plans for race, class, gender, and disability*. Columbus: Merrill.

Henfield, M. S., Moore, J. L., & Wood, C. (2008). Inside and outside gifted education programming: Hidden challenges for African American students. *Exceptional Children, 74*(4), 433–450. Retrieved from http://search.ebscohost.com/login.aspx?direct=true&db=eft&AN=508079747&site=ehost-live

Huidor, O., & Cooper, R. (2009). Examining the socio-cultural dimension of schooling in a racially integrated school. *Education and Urban Society, 42*(2), 143–167. doi:10.1177/0013124509350047

Johnson, M. K., Crosnoe, R., & Elder, Jr., G. H. (2001). Students' attachment and academic engagement: The role of race and ethnicity. *Sociology of Education, 74*(4), 318–340. doi:10.2307/2673138

Kambrelis, G., & Dimitriadis, G. (2005). Focus groups: Strategic articulations of pedagogy, politics, and inquiry. In N. Denzin & Y. Lincoln (Eds.), *The Sage handbook of qualitative research* (3rd ed., pp. 887–907). Los Angeles, CA: Sage.

Kincheloe, J. (1993). Representations of identity and difference in education. In L. A. Castenell Jr., & W. F. Pinar (Eds.), *Understanding curriculum as racial text* (pp. 249–262). New York, NY: State University of New York Press.

King, J. E. (1991). Dysconscious racism: Ideology, identity, and the miseducation of teachers. *The Journal of Negro Education, 60*(2), 133–146. doi:10.2307/2295605

Ladson-Billings, G., & Brown, K. (2008). Curriculum and cultural diversity. In F. M. Connelly, F. H. Ming, & J. Phillion (Eds.), *The SAGE handbook of curriculum and instruction* (pp. 153–175). Los Angeles, CA: Sage.

Ladson-Billings, G., & Tate, W. F. (1995). Toward a critical race theory of education. *Teachers College Record, 97*(1), 47–68. Retrieved from http://search.ebscohost.com/login.aspx?direct=true&db=eft&AN=508572449&site=ehost-live

LeCompte, M. D. (2000). Analyzing qualitative data. *Theory into Practice, 39*(3), 146–154. doi:10.1207/s15430421tip3903_5

Lewis, A. E. (2003). *Race in the schoolyard: Negotiating the color line in classrooms and communities*. New Brunswick, NJ: Rutgers University Press.

Lopez, G. R. (2003). The (racially neutral) politics of education: A critical race theory perspective. *Educational Administration Quarterly, 39*(1), 68–94. doi:10.1177/0013161X02239761

Lopez, I. H. (2006). Colorblind to the reality of race in America. *The Chronicle Review, 53*(11), B6.

Lynn, M. (2004). Inserting the race into critical pedagogy: An analysis of race-based epistemologies. *Educational Philosophy & Theory, 36*(2), 153–165. doi:10.1111/j.1469-5812.2004.00058.x

McLaren, P. (1994). White terror and oppositional agency: Towards a critical multiculturalism. In D. T. Goldberg (Ed.), *Multiculturalism: A critical reader* (pp. 33–70). Malden, MA: Blackwell.

Miles, M., & Huberman, A. M. (1994). *Qualitative analysis: An expanded source book* (2nd ed.). Thousand Oaks, CA: Sage.

Milliken v. Bradley. 418 US 717 (1974).

Nieto, S. (2000). *Affirming diversity: The sociopolitical context of multicultural education* (3rd ed.). New York, NY: Allyn & Bacon.

Nieto, S., & Bode, P. (2008). *Affirming diversity: The socio-political context of multicultural education* (4th ed.). New York, NY: Addison Wesley Longman.

Nieto, S., Bode, P., Kang, E., & Raible, J. (2008). Identity, community, and diversity: Retheorizing multicultural curriculum for the postmodern era. In F. M. Connelly, M. F. He, & J. Phillion (Eds.), *Handbook of curriculum and instruction* (pp. 176–197). Los Angeles, CA: Sage.

Oakes, J. (1985). *Keeping track: How schools structure inequality*. Princeton, NJ: Yale Press.

O'Connor, C., Mueller, J., Lewis, R., Rivas-Drake, D., & Rosenberg, S. (2011). 'Being' black and strategizing for excellence in a racially stratified academic hierarchy. *American Educational Research Journal, 48*(6), 1232–1257. doi:10.3102/0002831211410303

Ogbu, J. U. (2003). *Black American students in an affluent suburb: A study of academic disengagement*. Mahway, NJ: Lawrence Erlbaum.

Orfield, M. (2002). *American metro politics: The new suburban reality.* Washington, DC: Brookings Institute.

Palmer, D. (2010). Race, power, and equity in a multiethnic urban elementary school with a dual-language 'Strand' program. *Anthropology & Education Quarterly, 41*(1), 94–114. doi:10.1111/j.1548-1492.2010.01069

Pollock, M. (2005). *Colormute: Race talk dilemmas in an American school.* Princeton, NJ: Princeton University Press.

Rist, R. (1970). Student social class and teacher expectations: The self-fulfilling prophecy in ghetto education. *Harvard Educational Review, 40*(3), 411–451. Retrieved from http://search.ebscohost.com/login.aspx?direct=true&db=eft&AN=507726591&site=ehost-live

Saddler, C. A. (2005). The impact of Brown on African American students: A critical race theoretical perspective. *Educational Studies: American Educational Studies Association, 37*(1), 41–55. doi:10.1207/s15326993es3701_5

Shernoff, D. J., & Schmidt, J. A. (2008). Further evidence of an engagement-achievement paradox among US high school students. *Journal of Youth and Adolescence, 37*(5), 564–580. doi:10.1007/s10964-007-9241-z

Solorzano, D., & Yosso, T. (2001). From racial stereotyping and deficit discourse toward a Critical Race Theory. *Multicultural Education, 9*(1), 2–8. Retrieved from http://search.ebscohost.com/login.aspx?direct=true&db=eft&AN=507717093&site=ehost-live

Tarca, K. (2005). Colorblind in control: The risks of resisting difference amid demographic change. *Educational Studies: Journal of the American Educational Studies Association, 38*(2), 99–120. doi:10.1207/s15326993es3802_3

Teranishi, R. T. (2002). Asian Pacific Americans and critical race theory: An examination of school racial climate. *Equity & Excellence in Education, 35*(2), 144–154. doi:10.1080/713845281

Urrieta, L. (2006). Community identity discourse and the Heritage Academy: Colorblind educational policy and White supremacy. *International Journal of Qualitative Studies in Education (QSE), 19*(4), 455–476. doi:10.1080/09518390600773197

Wells, A. S., Baldridge, B. J., Duran, J., Grzesikowski, C., Lofton, R., Roda, A., Warner, M., & White, T. (2009). *Boundary crossing for diversity: Equity and achievement. Inter-district school desegregation and educational opportunity.* Cambridge, MA: Charles Hamilton Houston Institute for Race and Justice. Harvard University.

Yosso, T. J. (2002). Toward a critical race curriculum. *Equity & Excellence in Education, 35*(2), 93–107. doi:10.1080/713845283

'We had to hide we're Muslim': ambient fear, Islamic schools and the geographies of race and religion

Kalervo N. Gulson[a] and P. Taylor Webb[b]

[a]School of Education, Faculty of Arts and Social Sciences, University of New South Wales, Sydney, NSW, Australia; [b]Department of Educational Studies, University of British Columbia, Vancouver, BC, Canada

Over the past 30 years, there has been virulent urban politics surrounding the provision of government-funded Islamic K-12 schooling in suburban south-western Sydney, Australia. In this paper, drawing on examples of local government opposition to Islamic schools, we argue that race and religion constitute contestations of urban space around the establishment of government-funded Islamic schools. We argue that these particular contestations arise from the changing nature of, and historical continuities between, urban politics, education, Islamophobia and racialisation, in pre-9/11 and post-9/11 Australia. The politics surrounding Islamic schools reveals a coded urban politics that can be understood by paying attention to the ambiance of racialised-religious fears produced – in part – by the policies of government-funding of non-secular education.

One of the biggest Islamic schools in Australia will be built in south-western Sydney after Bankstown City Council lost an appeal in the Land and Environment Court.

The decision will allow construction of a 1200-student primary and secondary school in Bass Hill, which has been fought by residents since the land was bought in 2006.

It is one of several applications for Islamic schools that have divided communities in NSW, leading to allegations that residents are using town-planning arguments such as traffic to cloak racist sentiment. (*The Sydney Morning Herald*, May 15, 2009; Murray, 2009)

The majority of objections have been on planning considerations. I don't think that we had that campaign of race that took place [against another Islamic school]. [Bankstown Mayor, Tania Mihailuk, 2008] (AAP, 2008)

Over the past 30 years, there has been a virulent urban politics surrounding the provision of government-funded religious schooling in suburban south-western Sydney. Our concern in this paper is to emphasise how race and religion constitute contestations of urban space around the establishment of government-funded Islamic schools. We argue these particular contestations are unique, and fail to emerge when other types of government-funded religious schools, such as Christian schools, are proposed and established in Sydney. The politics surrounding Islamic schools reveals a coded urban politics pertaining to Islamophobia and racialisation, that can be understood by paying attention to the ambiance of racialised-religious fears produced – in part – through the policies of government-funding of non-secular education.

To begin, we outline our conceptual framework premised on the relational geographies of race and religion, with a focus on links between race and Islamophobia. Second, we provide detail on Muslim residents and Islamic schools in the local government area of Bankstown in south-western Sydney. We then examine the role of religion in the management of urban space, illustrated through local government decisions concerning the rejection of Islamic schools. The penultimate section draws on the idea of 'ambient fear', a concept developed by Papastergiadis (2012), to demonstrate how local urban and educational politics may be connected to various forms of Islamophobia, racialisation and everyday disorientations associated with encountering difference. We conclude that in south-western Sydney, the opposition to Islamic schools indicates new socio-spatialities of edu-urban politics, in which local planning is playing a role in constituting a racialised religious politics in education.

The relational geographies of religion and race

This paper works with the idea of space and race as relational. We are interested in how race and racism are located in the city, how racial meaning is constituted in and through spatial effects and policy affects (Webb & Gulson, 2012), and the power relations that make both space and race-contingent accomplishments (Nayak, 2004, 2006). We are, thus, concerned with the performative constitution of race, in which designations of race and ethnicity, such as 'Black', 'White' and 'Lebanese', are more than descriptions of a priori categories and identities. These designations 'are part of on-going processes that create or *discursively constitute* these categories and the people allocated to them' (Gillborn & Youdell, 2009, p. 181, original emphasis). The performative aspect of race and ethnicity is only made meaningful when these categorisations are mobilised through discourses that are intelligible in reference to 'enduring relations of discursive, productive power' (Gillborn & Youdell, 2009, p. 181).

We are interested in how the phenomenon of Islamophobia interacts, rather than being conflated, with race and racism (Dunn, Klocker, & Salabay, 2007; Dwyer, 1993). This interaction occurs when religion moves between attachment to ethnicity – and thus to different cultural and geographical notions of belonging – to racialisation of the 'Other'. Islamophobia is based on assumptions and reductive characterisations, on stereotypes, about Islam and Muslim people; notably Islam is both Other as civilisation and Other as religion. Islamophobia, arguably, remains separate from racism as it is not a biological or somatic premise for pernicious action, and Muslim is not constituted as a genetic disposition (Miles & Brown, 2003). What is argued to make Islamophobia unique, however, is the combining of nationality, religion and politics, that is 'frequently produced in Orientalist, Islamophobic and racist discourses. In contrast, most religions are not represented in an amalgam with terrorism, or even ethnic and national distinctiveness' (Miles & Brown, 2003, p. 164). The turn to race is made when a religion, and subsequently a religious group and/or individual, is 'seen as representing a racialised Other' (p. 165).

The racialisation of Islam in Australia has rested on assumptions of Muslim homogeneity connected to geographical regions, such as the 'Middle East', and ethnicities, such as 'Arab' (Dunn et al., 2007). As Keith (2005) suggests:

> ...race making sits between historically complex demographic trajectories and highly spurious systems of categorisation. Temporalities and spatialities are consequently not just the context of these processes, they are instead a constitutive feature of them. (p. 9)

In this, we can see that race and space are contested, dynamic and temporal (Neely & Samura, 2011), unfolding in reference to contestation over religious space in particular areas of cities, and in reference to particular bodies, and as we will discuss, constituted through a localisation of transnational racisms. This racial-spatial biopolitics entails the ways:

> ...[b]odily traits and 'ethnic' cultures are becoming the basis upon which peoples are allocated rights, identities, a place in the world ..., at the expense of other modes of marking community and negotiating difference. (Amin, 2010, p. 10)

The somatic aspect is, therefore, important for accessories and clothing become more than merely accoutrements but threats. And it is Muslim women wearing head-scarves, Burqas and Hijab, who bear the brunt of responses perceived threats, for '[t]he contemporary racialization of Muslims in Australia draws heavily upon observable elements of culture' (Dunn et al., 2007, p. 567). While men's beards may be markers that conflate Lebanese Christian men with Lebanese Muslim men, both captured by the notion of the 'Arab' other, a woman's headscarf is simultaneously performative of Islam and interpreted as incontrovertible evidence of unassimilable difference. This performing materiality maintains disproportionate schooling, for many Islamic schools require female students to wear school uniforms with long sleeve pants and shirts, and Hijab. Bodies are the geographical markers of the distinctiveness of the Islamic school and bearers of a school's distinctiveness while coding disproportionate gendered significations within and outside of schools.

Muslim people and the south-western suburbs of Sydney

The south-western suburban areas of Sydney, approximately 25 km from the Central Business District, has been the 'receiving' area for multiple generations of migrants (Collins & Poynting, 2000). This area has been characterised 'as the "other side" of a social boundary, one which contains several groups of society's "others"' (Powell, 1993, p. xviii), and an area demonised in public discourses that conflate crime, poverty and ethnicity (Poynting, 2000).

The south-west, including the local government area of Bankstown, has historically high proportions of Muslim people – from a variety of geographical and ethnic backgrounds, with the largest proportion being Australian-born residents – relative to national population and other local government areas (Saeed, 2003; Wise & Ali, 2008). In Bankstown in 1986, 10.3% (5958 residents) of the population was Muslim. In 2001, 11.8% (19,499) was Muslim, with a significant jump to 19.1% (34,796 residents) in 2011 (Bankstown City Council, 2012). Key cultural institutions like mosques have been established in Bankstown, along with government-funded private Islamic elementary and secondary schools. In Australia, parental choice of schools is the paramount policy framework in both federal and state government sectors, and Australia has one of the highest rates of government funding for private schools in the OECD (Musset, 2012).[1] Of these choice schools, 94% are religious and over the past 10 years, Islamic schools, along with small Christian schools, non-Anglican or Catholic, are among the fastest growing (Buckingham, 2010). Nonetheless, there are not many Islamic schools in Australia, 41 in total, out of over 2000 government-funded private schools. Islamic schools educate approximately 20% of all Muslim students in Australia, with the majority of schools located in western and south-western Sydney: 23 in all, with 6 in Bankstown.

Some of these proposed and established schools have been opposed at the local government level (Al-Natour, 2010). Government-funded private schools, in addition to being accredited by educational authorities, must gain development approval at a local government level. This is the only role for local government in the process of educational provision in Australia – aspects such as curriculum policy, overall accreditation, funding, and so forth are within the purview of other levels of government. All religious schools can receive state and federal government funding if they fulfil the requirements set down by state curriculum boards, and meet the requirements of local government through land-use approvals (Bugg & Gurran, 2011).

There is, however, no educational policy framework that advises local government on how to deal with development applications for private schools within the broader provision of education (Bugg & Gurran, 2011). In the absence of articulated frameworks for the establishment of schools in local government areas, urban policy becomes de facto and ad hoc education policy. The contestation over, and decision-making about, urban space, thus, becomes significant for the provision of education and Islamic schools, for 'culture is not simply contested within particular territories but is spatially as well as socially constituted' (Dwyer, 1993, p. 143).

Methods and methodology

The following sections are based on data generated by a qualitative case study, carried out during the course of 2011 and early 2012, on opposition to Islamic schools in Sydney. The interview-based design of the study was influenced by the theoretical considerations discussed above. It focused on Bankstown as home to some of the more controversial establishments of Islamic schools – Al Noori Islamic School opened in 1983 and was one of the first Islamic schools in Australia, and Al Amanah School was proposed in 2007. Data were generated from extensive archival work, using local government and Land and Environment documents, including meeting minutes, and newspaper articles. This paper also draws on two semi-structured interviews with Adeeba (pseudonym), a Muslim female who helped found Al Noori Islamic school, and Joe (pseudonym), a White, male, long-term politician in Bankstown local government.

The management of religious, educational (suburban) space

The political configuration of the city allows certain kinds of individual and group identity to become visible. The technological arrangements through which patterns of identification emerge and transform . . . (the planning of its urban form) become likewise implicated in the political constitution of urban cultures. (Keith, 2005, p. 42)

Planning decisions are not deterministic, but as Keith (2005) contends, they may well be 'inescapable': 'There is not world untouched by the multiple regimes of power that structure the regulation of domesticity, labour, public and private life and the rights of the citizen' (p. 40). It is the very mundaneness of this power that leads to the 'banality of government' (p. 40). Urban policy constitutes space as part of governing activities that manage space. As such, governmental intervention requires that 'its spaces of intervention are not merely the sites of this governmental practice, but, first and foremost, its outcomes' (Dikeç, 2007, p. 280). Part of these outcomes concern the ordering and policing of spaces of race (Mitchell, 2000), in the case of the rejection of Islamic school applications, a governmental intervention at the convergence of race and religion.

Opposition to mosques and Islamic schools has intensified in Sydney's west over the past 10 years or so (Dunn, 2001). This opposition, however, has a lineage back to the 1980s in Bankstown. The first Islamic school established in Sydney was Al Noori Muslim Primary School, founded by a small group of mothers, including a Muslim convert from a white, middle class Christian background. The school was opened in the backyard of a house, moving to a hall on a main road, and private homes. In the 1980s, like now, to be accredited and registered as a school required land use approval from a local government (council). As Adeeba, a Muslim female involved in founding the school, states, the school's application to open was repeatedly rejected by councils in south-western Sydney:

> Now the difficulty we had was we couldn't get any council to give us approval for any property . . . Every council we would go to would say 'not here' . . . and we couldn't get funding, any sort of funding until we got council approval . . . We just had to keep on moving and fighting to get approval, and we didn't have much [*sic*] funds. We were a group of mothers, a voluntary association . . . . (Adeeba, Islamic school co-founder)

A local government level can only reject development applications on the grounds of amenity, such as land use, suitability of dwelling, traffic and parking concerns – the last especially significant for schools. In the case of Al Noori, the founders kept the school open without council approval and, thus, without registration. The school was moved nine times before finally being approved.

> To prepare an application was extensive . . . we asked the council. They always rejected you on traffic grounds initially, that was usually the way they would knock you out. (Adeeba, Islamic school founder)

Twenty years after Al Noori, in June 2007, an application proposed the establishment of the Al Amanah School, a 1200 student Islamic school, to be built next to an existing public secondary school. Bankstown council rejected this development application and an appeal was made to have this decision reviewed. Rejected planning applications can be appealed and are heard in the Land and Environment Court, a court of appeal for planning issues in New South Wales. In the hearing over the Al Amanah School, Bankstown council provided a variety of reasons for rejecting the application including:

Traffic and parking; Noise; Ecology; Character, scale and design; The site is too small; Social impact; Excessive impervious areas; Excessive cut and fill. (*Mohamad el Dana vs Bankstown City Council*, 2008, Point 10)

For both Al Noori and Al Amanah – 20 years apart – the rejection of development applications, on grounds of urban amenity, elides other contestations of urban space, especially regarding race and religion (Bugg & Gurran, 2011; Hackworth & Stein, 2012). In the case of Bankstown, what perhaps is being managed through local government is multiculturalism – that is, even issues of traffic, in reference to the proposed schools, are concerns tied up with cultural relations in suburbia. While government-funded, private religious schools are common in Australia, controversy about the establishment of new religious schools has focused only on Islamic schools, despite many other religious schools such as Greek Orthodox and Anglican schools being proposed and established in western Sydney over the past 30 years. In the case of the rejection of Al Amanah School by Bankstown council, the magistrate in the Land and Environment Court noted:

Throughout the hearing there was an unacknowledged presence in the courtroom: a topic of which, I suspect, everyone was aware, but which was not discussed because the discussion would have been too uncomfortable. That topic was whether the council would have raised quite so many contentions as it did if the application had been for an Anglican school? Would, for example, a social impact statement have been required? (*Mohamad el Dana vs Bankstown City Council*, 2008, Point 46)

This absence of controversy concerning the opening of non-Islamic schools seems to be a broader issue than merely the case of Al Amanah. In relation to a general question about how decisions are made on schools and planning decisions by council, and why it seems that there has not been similar attention paid to non-Islamic schools, Joe, the local politician, identified the possible role of religion in decision-making.

Joe: Most of the other schools, that have been [approved] in the past everybody [on council], falls over backwards to make sure it happens . . . anything they want approved it will just go through . . . they sign off on it.

Interviewer: Why is that the case?

Joe: I think predominantly because . . . [local politicians are] Christians, you know what I mean. When you've got an [Islamic] organisation that preaches to their people that we're all infidels and we've got be got rid of . . . That puts a bit of a blank in your mind.

Schools intensify cultural relations, for it is schools in and through which people come into close and sustained contact with difference – even if schools, such as religious schools, are seen as homogenous; they are encounters, or at the least the forced proximity, with the other. Proposals over Islamic schools, while dealt with by councils as neutral planning issues – in process and as ostensive outcome – are planning issues imbued with remnant and future encounters with difference (Bugg & Gurran, 2011). Joe (of the Bankstown Council) notes that issues of race and religion were not discussed directly in local government meetings over planning decisions about Islamic schools:

> [But] there's a ...perception that ...the Muslim's are, they're different, but there's a
> perception ...with some people that they're not good for our community, but I don't
> find that ...I mean ...they're no different to anyone else, you know. It's just the attitude –
> [Muslim people] get this attitude from their bloody clerics, and I think that's where a lot
> of the problems ...But you know, we've got a couple of, a few Muslims running for
> council, and they're some characters, even the women, they're really good, they're funny
> bastards, they don't take a backward step, they're on the attack right from the start. And
> that's what worries people, they're on ...they attack. But once you sit down and have a
> talk with them ...they're not bad people. (Joe, Bankstown Council)

Joe both repudiates and reinforces the racialisation and racism regarding the status
of Muslim people in Australia, and exhibits precisely how lapses and contradictions
challenge any claims to neutrality of planning.[2] Islamic schools can, therefore, be
opposed through council planning decisions on the basis of difference, while these
decisions are occluded by claims that opposition is on neutral grounds of increased
traffic flow or disputes over appropriate land use, and zoning concerns. What we
suggest is that this ostensibly neutral management of space runs the risk of both
simplifying and misrepresenting the complexity of race and religion in the practices
of opposition to Islamic schools, or at worst, perpetuates a colour-blind or naive
diversity discourse in spatial-educational policy and politics.

Islamic schools and the geographies of ambient fear

The management of urban and, in turn, religious educational space can be re-
articulated through reference to what Papastergiadis (2012) calls 'ambient fear', a
fear generated in a post-9/11 world of new forms of terrorism and associated state
violence. In the modern state, migrants are constituted as a 'problem' that has
'always been cast in terms of the challenge to either convert them into national
citizens, or keep them out' (Papastergiadis, 2012, p. 41). This 'problem' is a psycho-
geographic fear permeating and pervading contemporary life post-9/11 in countries
like the US, Australia and England, and is a fear connected to the 'the invisibility of
the intimate enemy' (p. 24). This '[a]mbient fear is a kind of dread that has become so
widespread that its sources appear to be both unlocatable and ubiquitous' (p. 24).
This shifts the discussion of fear from the notion of an entity located in individual
subjectivity to a social function, or we suggest in the case of managing space, a socio-
spatial function.

Elsewhere, we have discussed fear as a policy prolepsis, a circulation of ubiquitous
affect that in effect becomes a technology to mobilise education policy-making and
policy enactments in particular ways – the affective manipulation of manufactured
crises (Webb & Gulson, 2012). In this case, conversely, Islamic schools in Sydney are
not afforded the status of crisis – as the Mayor of Bankstown noted in the epigraph
above: Decisions to oppose Islamic schools were not about race but about planning.
This refusal to acknowledge the role of race and the racialisation of religion in
planning decisions reinforces the mythology of the neutral decision, while fear
continues to circulate about the Muslim other. Ambient fear does not simply happen;
it is built, even as it is simultaneously naturalised.[3] Ambient fear, then, produces urban
policy decisions and politics concerned with movement, mobility and direction. This
ambient fear is, furthermore, premised on unstated and prior (White, Christian)
boundaries, as part of managing difference. This management will, like other racial

spatial orderings such as apartheid (Mitchell, 2000), aim to contain, and ideally purify, any racial and cultural 'contagions' that may be inadvertently, or by design, brought to bear on an otherwise undefiled, imaginary space of homogeneity. This notion of ordering space is only the purview of governmental practices of the state, and practised by disorienting others. It occurs, furthermore, in mundane and micro-geographic ways. In the Land and Environment case on the rejected Al Amanah School, the presiding magistrate referred to submissions by residents of Bankstown. These submissions included references to violence, 'exclusive' and 'inclusive' spaces, and the need for 'buffers' between cultural groups – namely the Islamic school and the public high school, nominally between homogeneity and heterogeneity, as discussed below.

> [A female resident involved with the Bass Hill High School's Parents and Citizens Associated]... foresaw conflict between the two schools and believes there should be a buffer between them... (*Mohamad el Dana vs Bankstown City Council*, 2008, Point 12)

> The social impact of building an '*exclusive*' school next to an '*inclusive*' one has not been assessed... [A] retired teacher... said he is concerned about the safety of the Bass Hill pupils. Both sets of children are likely to congregate at Bass Hill Plaza, will fight each other making the shopping centre a battleground. (*Mohamad el Dana vs Bankstown City Council*, 2008, Point 13, original emphasis)

Planning regulations reinscribe representations. In describing opposition to things like mosques and temples in the UK, Westwood and Williams (1997) suggest the politics of these sites is connected to the disruption of belonging, and the disorientations associated with becoming:

> Invariably, extant, usually white residents complain about noise and traffic, about people and the 'alien' presence constituting a politics of space which has nothing to say about faith and religion but is organised around discourses of the nation, culture and belonging. Those who complain run against time and to an imagined homogeneity of the neighbourhood. (Westwood & Williams, 1997, p. 10)

This notion of homogeneity, and the threat and promise of heterogeneity in the idea of the public (inclusive) versus the Islamic (exclusive) Al Amanah school, relates to the framing of culture as attachment to place. This is a residentialist argument that frames mobility as a problem if there are competing claims to cultural authority in the same place (e.g., Freidman, 1999; for critique Papastergiadis, 2012). A key assumption in the residentialist position is that 'original' culture is connected to a place. This implies the disqualification of most national identities for 'loss of certain boundaries has not meant the disappearance of cultural differences, but rather the appearance of new forms of mixture and more complex patterns of differentiation' (Papastergiadis, 2012, p. 134). The residentialist position, nonetheless, perhaps suggests that place is fixed and bounded, a type of abstract space that bounds social relations and identity formation. This invokes a nostalgic notion of place as boundaries (re)inscribe identities, a territorializing politics that reterritorializes against the perceived threats of deterritorializing efforts (Deleuze & Guattari, 1987).

This notion of residentialism is, further, connected to ambivalence and fear of migrants, what Papastergiadis (2012) calls 'kinetophobia' – or fear of mobility. This takes a variety of forms, from racist scapegoating to the notion that there is a political and social body that will be defiled by newcomers, unless they are adequately integrated or ideally assimilated. Adeeba notes how in Australia in the 1980s:

> [T]here was this whole feeling amongst a lot of educated White Australians that Muslims were not deserving of recognition and support in any area, and they represented a foreign race that needed to be assimilated into Australian...So there was just this attitude, 'you have to be like us, you have to do things the way we do it here. Your way of doing things is not what we want here'. So...it was a...conglomeration of foreign culture, foreign look, and foreign religion that [was to be rejected]. (Adeeba, Islamic school founder)

Assimilation as the necessary technology of the 'White Australia' immigration policy is a discourse that has been revived, in the early 2000s, by commentators and politicians, who have made reference to Muslim people who have not assimilated into 'Australian ways', and who are just one step away from being radicalised into terrorists (Dunn et al., 2007; Humphrey, 2005). In talking about Australia and Sydney in the 1980s, Adeeba suggests:

> All the time Muslims have been seen as being not Australian, and a threat because of the religion, because of the culture, because of the dress and the whole concept of having schools that are not 'like us' was un-Australian. So, for example with [one school site]...the lady who's now passed away and who had the house directly adjoining it and who was most affected because it was in, it was the battle axe block, went around the back of her property. She went on media saying...that 'they're like cockroaches, sweep them off our back step and go back to the bush where they came from'...It was very, very hard, very irrational, always. Very, very emotional and...there were allegations that, that you know if our school went ahead you know Australia, that we were going to convert the whole of Australia, we're going to try and make all of Australia Muslim and, and why couldn't we learn how to be Australian in Australian schools...that was, that's been...the, the current all the way through. (Adeeba, Islamic school founder)

These references to Muslim people as 'cockroaches', and this dehumanising discourse, exemplifies the link between race and Islamophobia and the complex connections between nation, religion and politics, along with the assumptions of cultural inferiority that parallel that of biological racism (Dunn et al., 2007; Miles & Brown, 2003). As Dwyer (1993) has argued, following Said (1978), this further resonates with a construction of Islam as the other of the white Christian nation. This is to apportion these schools with the marker of fundamentalism, which is mobilised as explanation and description. The construction of fundamentalism builds upon 'a long legacy of Orientalist discourse which relies upon the oppositions of West and East, rationality versus irrationality, modernity and liberal tolerance versus fundamentalism' (Dwyer, 1993, p. 155).

The ambient fear produced through Islamic schools, we suggest, reflects not only post-9/11 but also are remnants of pre-9/11 fears about Islam, often located in reference to Iran and Ayatollahs, the Palestinian Liberation Organisation and general unease about Muslim people. There is historical continuity embedded in shifting yet resilient geographies of xenophobia, racism and Islamophobia that are global and transnational in scope. As Papastergiadis notes:

> This process of connecting disparate entities in the imagination gives rise to a much more intimate sense of threat. Each new formulation of fear proves to be highly unstable

and quickly overlaps with the residual sediments of archaic fears, as well as inserting itself into the as yet undefined fears of the future. (Papastergiadis, 2012, p. 25)

In reference to contestation over establishing the Al Noori Islamic School, Adeeba reflects on how fears of difference were tied to flippant yet pathologising ideas linking the school to the terrorist organisation of the day.

> There were allegations by . . . locals, [who] would say, 'oh they're probably manufacturing bombs for the PLO [Palestinian Liberation Organisation] in their back yards' kind of thing. So there was a lot of hysteria, we're always in the news . . . And then we managed to stay [in one place] . . . for one year in relative peace but then they wouldn't renew the lease. So then we approached a Syrian church, we didn't tell them who we were, *we had to hide that we're Muslim all the time.* (Adeeba, Islamic school founder, our emphasis)

Eventually, after moving nine times in five years, the school received approval as an Earth Integrated school; it was landscaped so that it could not be seen. Not only was it necessary to pass as non-Muslim, as the school founder noted, 'eventually with this Earth Integrated School . . . they couldn't see us and they couldn't hear us' (Adeeba). The school gained recognition, finally, but only by becoming invisible, this was recognition through obscurity.

Islamic schools as the 'enemy within'

Ambient fear takes shape, or is embodied, provisionally, in the form of 'sleepers' who lie amongst 'us', awaiting activation from an overseas controller, always the spectre of the other. 'Sleepers' evoke fears that migrants and 'foreign cultures' will transgress borders and 'destroy all forms of social control' (Papastergiadis, 2012, p. 71).

> It was very, very apparent that . . . the biggest opposition [was from] . . . people who thought we were bringing in something which was going to be unstoppable . . . and was going to change their way of life. (Adeeba, Islamic school founder)

Opponents of Islamic schools mobilise a politics that simultaneously refuses and reifies ambient fear. Islamic schools are locatable and definable, if essentialised – Islamic schools as the 'face' of the other. Ambient fear, concomitantly, pervades this politics as these schools become the mark of the 'enemy within' – the unassimilable 'other' taking over suburbs and cities, one school at a time (Al-Natour, 2010; Al-Natour & Morgan, 2012).

> It's a factor . . . and when they get funded to build these schools, they get funded by the Sunnis and stuff like that . . . you think 'oh shit what the?' they're not funding it with they're own community, they're being funded by outside. So that gives . . . some people . . . a bit of a blank . . . you know they think what the hell, this is not growing out of their own people that are here, its growing from something that's an external . . . I think they're a bit worried . . . And then you've got the enemy from within, you know, they get that sort of picture that 'can we trust them', . . . because they're being funded by other organisations, where do their [loyalties] really lie? (Joe, Bankstown Council)

The reactions to Islamic schools posit that these schools will ostensibly operate as insertion points for Muslim people to proselytise and convert non-Muslims, to take over suburbs and undermine social stability (Al-Natour, 2010). This is despite the very small numbers of Islamic schools compared to other forms of schooling. As noted, there are only 41 schools in Australia, and while the majority are in south-western Sydney, we suggest the reaction to Islamic schools is redolent of what Appadurai (2006) calls 'fear of small numbers'. This is a disproportionate reaction of majority populations towards minority populations, that are reminders and remainders of the 'anxiety of incompleteness'; 'Minorities, in a word, are metaphors and reminders of the betrayal of the classical national project' (2006, p. 43) in a globalised world. This has been evident in opposition to Islamic schools in other parts of Sydney that are characterised as 'non-Muslim' – a maintenance of the residentalist myth of homogeneity that is invoked to counter the possibility of encountering difference. In this way, difference is inscribed as irreducible and separate, even in places like Bankstown where the majority of Muslim residents are Australian born.

> It's a fear, its an unknown, basically...But it's not entrenched...It's not something people openly bloody go on about...they don't have debates about it or anything...its just something in the back...of their minds. (Joe, Bankstown Council)

Ambient fear, in relation to Islamic schools, requires a materiality to be encountered – ambient fear is unknown and unlocatable but becomes manifest through proximity, in the possibility of being made concrete through mosques and schools. The result then is that '[u]nder such a biopolitics, the taming of the errant body—in this case the Muslim body [and school]—is urged as a necessity, a matter of everyday vigilance from the responsible citizen, wronged for thinking and doing otherwise' (Amin, 2010, p. 10). The marking out and then blurring of migrant and *assumed* migrant – the Muslim other – distinction is what is perhaps prominent in these psycho-social geographies of fear; the monstrousness of all of this comes from realising that despite elaborate denial, 'the enemy is more similar than we could bear to consider' (Papastergiadis, 2012, p. 31).

Conclusion

In this paper, we posited that urban politics around the establishment of Islamic schooling could be understood through geographies of race and religion. This spatial aspect allows us to conceptualise the development of Islamic schools and the connected role that urban policy-making has with educational policy and politics. It is these local and transnational spatial-educational politics, furthermore, that repudiate the supposed neutrality of market mechanisms in education that support the establishment of government-funded religious schools. The controversy over Islamic schools – and the lack of controversy over non-Islamic schools such as Christian schools – reinforces a need to focus on the racialisation and geographies of religion, to provide insight into what would otherwise be seen as a set of both techno-rational urban policy problems and a set of neutral educational policy initiatives around the provision of religious schools within choice frameworks (Gulson & Webb, 2012). We suggest, therefore, that contestations of urban and religious educational space have been heightened through a confluence of market policies in education, leading to the increased establishment of ethno-cultural schools like Islamic schools, and global shifts that are mediated in local instances and places. Market mechanisms like choice schools provide impetus for commodifying difference – a quasi-market of neo-pantheonism – while surreptitiously eroding a secular-humanistic educational discourse (Gulson & Webb, 2013).

We argued that to understand these geographies of Islamic schools, and the contestation over urban space, it is necessary to identify the way that these schools are part of the management of space and the future of urban multiculture. As Murdoch (2006) posits, 'spaces are made of complex sets of relations so that any spatial "solidity" must be seen as an accomplishment, something to be achieved in the face of flux and instability' (p. 23). The (provisional) accomplishments of space through urban planning are part of the managing of race and religion that are emptied of complexity. The management of urban space is necessarily crude, and claims amenity as its primary foci, but is inexorably caught in the negotiations and accommodations over space in reference to the racialisation of Islam, and the mobilising of the ensemble of nation, religion and politics to constitute the racialised religious Other. This mobilisation is imbued with what we have, following Papastergiadis (2012), identified as ambient fear, in which Islamic schools are the material manifestation of ubiquitous and unlocatable fears about others connected to difference. And this is where schooling is significant in what we might see as new edges of race and fear that have shifted the emphasis of concentrated fear of the other from the very visceral notions of close contact in the inner city – the notion of proximity as a proxy for dealing or not dealing with difference – to the suburb. These are the new geographies of suburbia, connected to race and global Islamophobia, in which local planning is playing a role in constituting a racialised religious politics in education.

Notes

1. In Australia, the federal and state governments fund 'private' schooling. In OECD terms, these schools would be classified as government-dependent private schools (Musset, 2012).
2. Our thanks to one of the anonymous reviewers for alerting us to this idea of lapses and contradictions.
3. Our thanks to one of the anonymous reviewers of this paper for suggesting this idea about the built and naturalisation aspects of ambient fear.

References

Australian Associated Press (AAP). (2008, December 11, 2012). Court approves Islamic school in south-west Sydney. *The Sydney Morning Herald*. Retrieved from http://www.smh. com.au/news/national/court-approves-islamic-school/2008/12/11/1228585030997.html

Al-Natour, R. (2010). 'The mouse that dared to roar': Youths and the Camden controversy. *Youth Studies Australia, 29*(2), 42–50.

Al-Natour, R., & Morgan, G. (2012). Local Islamophobia: The Islamic school controversy in Camden, New South Wales. In G. Morgan & S. Poynting (Eds.), *Global Islamophobia: Muslims and moral panic in the West* (pp. 101–118). Farnham: Ashgate.

Amin, A. (2010). The remainders of race. *Theory, Culture and Society, 27*(1), 1–23. doi:10.1177/0263276409350361

Appadurai, A. (2006). *Fear of small numbers: An essay on the geography of anger*. Durham: Duke University Press.

Bankstown City Council. (2012). *Community Profile*. Retrieved from http://profile.id.com.au/ Default.aspx?id=101

Buckingham, J. (2010). *The rise of religious schools.* Sydney: Centre for Independent Studies.

Bugg, L., & Gurran, N. (2011). Urban planning process and discourses in the refusal of Islamic Schools in Sydney, Australia. *Australian Planner, 48*(4), 281–291. doi:10.1080/07293682.2011.593531

Collins, J., & Poynting, S. (2000). Introduction: Communities, identities and inequalities in Western Sydney. In J. Collins & S. Poynting (Eds.), *The other Sydney: Communities, identities and inequalities in Western Sydney* (pp. 19–33). Melbourne: Common Ground.

Deleuze, G., & Guattari, F. (1987). *A thousand plateaus: Capitalism and schizophrenia.* Minneapolis: University of Minnesota Press.

Dikeç, M. (2007). Space, governmentality, and the geographies of French urban policy. *European Urban and Regional Studies, 14*(4), 277–289. doi:10.1177/0969776407081162

Dunn, K. M. (2001). Representations of Islam in the politics of mosque development in Sydney. *Tijdschrift voor economische en sociale geografie, 92*(3), 291–308. doi:10.1111/1467-9663.00158

Dunn, K. M., Klocker, N., & Salabay, T. (2007). Contemporary racism and Islamaphobia in Australia: Racializing religion. *Ethnicities, 7*(4), 564–589. doi:10.1177/1468796807084017

Dwyer, C. (1993). Constructions of Muslim identity and the contesting of power: The debate over Muslim schools in the United Kingdom. In P. Jackson & J. Penrose (Eds.), *Constructions of race, place and nation* (pp. 143–159). London: UCL Press.

Freidman, J. (1999). The hybridization of roots and the absence of the bush. In M. Featherstone & S. Lash (Eds.), *Spaces of culture: City-nation-world.* London: Sage.

Gillborn, D., & Youdell, D. (2009). Critical perspectives on race and schooling. In J. A. Banks (Ed.), *The Routledge international companion to multicultural education.* New York, NY: Routledge.

Gulson, K. N., & Webb, P. T. (2012). Education policy racialisations: Afrocentric schools, Islamic schools and the new enunciations of equity. *Journal of Education Policy, 27*(6), 697–709. doi:10.1080/02680939.2012.672655

Gulson, K. N., & Webb, P. T. (2013). 'A raw, emotional thing': School choice, commodification and the racialised branding of Afrocentricity in Toronto, Canada. *Education Inquiry, 4*(1), 805–825.

Hackworth, J., & Stein, K. (2012). The collision of faith and economic development in Toronto's inner suburban industrial districts. *Urban Affairs Review, 48*(1), 37–63. doi:10.1177/1078087411420374

Humphrey, M. (2005). Australian Islam, the new global terrorism and the limits of citizenship. In S. Akbarzadeh & S. Yasmeen (Eds.), *Islam and the West: Reflections from Australia* (pp. 132–148). Sydney: UNSW Press.

Keith, M. (2005). *After the cosmopolitan? Multicultural cities and the future of racism.* London: Routledge.

Miles, R., & Brown, M. (2003). *Racism* (2nd ed.). New York, NY: Routledge.

Mitchell, D. (2000). *Cultural geography: A critical introduction.* Oxford: Blackwell.

Mohamad el Dana vs Bankstown City Council. (2008). NSW Land and Environment Court.

Murdoch, J. (2006). *Post-structuralist geography: A guide to relational space.* London: Sage.

Murray, E. (2009, May 15). Court allows Islamic school. *The Sydney Morning Herald.* Retrieved from http://www.smh.com.au/national/court-allows-islamic-school-20090514-b4t8.html

Musset, P. (2012). *School choice and equity: Policies in OECD countries and a literature review.* OECD Education Working Papers No 66, OECD Publishing. http://dx.doi.org/10.1787/5k9fq23507vc-en

Nayak, A. (2004). White lives. In K. Murji & J. Solomos (Eds.), *Racialization: Studies in theories and practice* (pp. 141–162). Oxford: Oxford University Press.

Nayak, A. (2006). After race: Ethnography, race and post-race theory. *Ethnic and Racial Studies, 29*(3), 411–430. doi:10.1080/01419870600597818

Neely, B., & Samura, M. (2011). Social geographies of race: Connecting race and space. *Ethnic and Racial Studies, 34*(11), 1933–1952. doi:10.1080/01419870.2011.559262

Papastergiadis, N. (2012). *Cosmopolitanism and culture.* Cambridge: Polity Press.

Powell, D. (1993). *Out west: Perceptions of Sydney's western suburbs.* Sydney: Allen & Unwin.

Poynting, S. (2000). Ethnicising criminality and criminalising ethnicity. In J. Collins & S. Poynting (Eds.), *The other Sydney: Communities, identities and inequalities in Western Sydney* (pp. 63–78). Melbourne: Common Ground.

Saeed, A. (2003). *Islam in Australia*. Sydney: Allen & Unwin.

Said, E. (1978). *Orientalism*. London: Penguin.

Webb, P. T., & Gulson, K. N. (2012). Policy prolepsis in education: Encounters, becomings and phantasms. *Discourse: Studies in the Cultural Politics of Education, 33*(1), 87–99. doi:10.1080/01596306.2012.632169

Westwood, S., & Williams, J. (1997). Imagining cities. In S. Westwood & J. Williams (Eds.), *Imagining cities: Scripts, signs, memory* (pp. 1–16). London: Routledge.

Wise, A., & Ali, J. (2008). *Muslim-Australians and local government: Grassroots strategies to improve relations between Muslim and non-Muslim-Australians*. Sydney: Centre for Research on Social Inclusion, Macquarie University.

Index

academic spaces, race inequities, 18–33
academy schools, 9–10, 14
achievement gaps, 8–13
Advanced Placement (AP) courses, 138, 145
advisory local school councils (ALSC), 99–100
Afghan students/communities, 78–85
Al Amanah School, 158–159, 161
ambient fear, 2, 155, 160–165
antiracisms, 58–61
Arizona, 6, 134
Asian Americans, 70–71, 75–84, 138
Asian Canadians, 105–122
Asiatic Exclusion League, 111
assessment, English Baccalaureate, 10–13
assimilationism, 81, 161–162
Australia, Islamic schools in, 154–165
authenticity discourses, 74–75, 81–85
authority, anger and resentment toward, 3–4, 14

Bad Black Mother stereotype, 67–69
Baldwin, James, 59, 65
benevolent liberal race talk, 38–39, 41–42, 49–53
Black academics, 18–33
Black Caribbean families, 20–21, 23
Black culture, 66–67
Black female scholars, positioning of, 18–33
Black feminism, 18
Black identity, 29–31
Black middle class, educational strategies of, 20–33
blackness, 28–29
Black representation: in protest novels, 59; in *Waiting for Superman*, 57–72
Blacks: economic downturns and, 7, 13; stereotypes of, 10–11, 67–69; unemployment rates for, 7, 14
Black students: academy schools and, 9–10; English Baccalaureate and, 10–13; high-achieving, 138–139, 145; measures of educational attainment and, 72–73; negative impact of reforms on, 4–14; racial contract and, 133–134; special education and, 49–52; in white suburban schools, 137–151

born again racism, 71–72
Brown vs Board of Education, 5, 43, 84, 141
busing programs, 141–142

Canada: Asian Canadians, 105–122; ethno-nationalism in, 105–122; higher education in, 107–109, 112, 114, 117; multiculturalism in, 106, 111–112; nativism in, 113
capitalism, 59, 92–93, 133
Centre for Immigration Policy Reform, 113
Chicago 21 Plan, 92
Chicago Public Schools (CPS), 88–103
Chinese Americans, 75
Chinese communities/students, 76–77, 81–82
Chinese migrants, 110–111
civil rights, legal decisions on, 5, 43
class, 24–25, 52, 53, 76–77, 80–81, 88, 89
college towns, 39–40
colonialism, 6, 127
colorblind hate speech, 45–48
colorblindness, 137–142, 144–145, 150–151
colorblind racism, 45–48, 52, 140–142
common sense, 128
communities of color, marginalization of, 88–103
Conservative/Liberal Democrat Coalition, 8, 9
Continuous Journey Regulation (Canada), 110
counterstories, 90–91, 129–131
critical multiculturalism, 149–150
critical race praxis, 91
Critical Race Theory, 1, 3, 4, 89–91, 102–103; education and, 128–135, 137–151; interest-convergence in, 4–5, 7, 13, 78, 84–85, 141–142; interest-divergence in, 5–7, 8, 13–14; methods/methodology, 128–129; model minority discourse and, 74–79, 84–85; racial discourses and, 42–43; stories/counterstories in, 90–91, 129–131
cultural deficiency, 50
cultural imperialism, 125–126
cultural politics, 58
culture of pathology, 66–67